CLIENT
WHISPERERS

By Jim Lyon

with
Judith L. Lyon, Ph.D.

ISBN: 0615494587
ISBN-13: 9780615494586

TABLE OF CURIOUS CONTENTS

THIS BOOK IS DEDICATED TO
CLIENT WHISPERERS EVERYWHERE,
AND TO OUR CHILDREN AND GRANDCHILDREN

PREFACE

"A Personal Board of Directors,"…is that what he said? During a sales meeting many years ago, a motivational speaker introduced me to this concept, and subsequently explained the idea of having a group of people to whom one is ultimately responsible. Intrigued by the concept, I mentally formed my Personal Board of Directors, searching for both past and present individuals from whom I would want to seek counsel and to whom I would feel personally accountable. My resulting Personal Board includes the following influential roles: parents, brother, spouse, children, grandchildren, coaches, teammates, and close friends. These board members have personified a values-based life, set examples to guide my actions, and/or given me pure enjoyment. Although some of my board members have since passed away, they posthumously remain on my board, and I cherish these associations. I will never forget the important influence that they have had or currently have on my life, both personally and professionally.

I extend a special thanks to one of my Personal Board Members, Dr. Judie Lyon. She is a multitalented person, whose contributions during the past twenty years as a business partner, executive, and senior management consultant for our more creative client engagements were nothing less than world-class. As the chief information officer of a large research university told me recently, "Judie is the smartest, prettiest, and nicest person I have ever worked with." Her review of and contributions to this book add a special flavor reflective of her experience and expertise. And a special thanks to G. Michael Bridge, J.D., for his feedback and suggestions.

The success story that will shortly unfold was made possible not only by the influence of my Personal Board of Directors, but also by the many contributions of other highly valued colleagues. Working together to achieve success, they accommodated my shortcomings and advanced my personal development. Their dedication to the success of our clients resulted in an insightful cadre of consultants whose unique nature will be explained in this book. Most importantly, a big thank you to all of our highly valued clients of the past three decades who made this refreshing success story possible.

1. Introduction

Overview

The twelve-year time period from which this story emerged was a dynamic and erratic period in United States history, which included the economic slowdown triggered by the 9/11 catastrophe. Despite the economic challenges of that period our business successfully competed against companies many times our size with annual revenues approaching $100 billion.

During this time, we created and sustained a differentiation strategy that was more art than science. In the process, we reviewed popular business management concepts and strategies, psychological research and insights, and personal philosophies and principles. From this unconventional combination of sources, we "borrowed wisdom" to formulate our uniquely blended differentiation strategy. For our purposes, the most useful borrowed wisdom was developed by people of high integrity, supported by research, gleaned from experience, and/or based on values that we shared. I came to believe that true wisdom has applicability and general utility across multiple domains.

In every stage of our growth, we attempted to not be limited by the past, but to be informed by it. Our success was a combination of great people, trusting relationships, intense competition, effective strategy, and artful execution. Although the primary focus of this story is market share growth during a specific twelve-year period, the story reflects forty years of personal development and professional experience in providing services to a specialized industry. That experience included much trial and error, which eventually resulted in the guiding principles and strategies that formed the foundation for our journey to a market share leadership position.

What is Client Whispering?

In the summer of 2003, Judie and I traveled to Sweden for a much anticipated vacation to visit sites of our ancestors. It was June 21st, a major holiday in Sweden when many urban dwellers exited the cities to visit the rural village festivities. As we checked out of our hotel in Uppsala, a bold thief grabbed my briefcase and dashed off with it. He fled out the side door, where there were no security personnel. We were shocked! The worst part was that my briefcase contained not only my laptop computer, but also our passports, airline tickets, Judie's jewelry, and our traveler's checks. We were devastated! We also were in need of help from a variety of American, Swedish, Finnish, and English service providers. After much frustration, and even anger, we did manage to get new passports, obtain some cash and traveler's checks, and replace our airline tickets. The jewelry? Well, that's another story...and it didn't have a happy ending.

On the long flight home, we discussed the many people who were both helpful and unhelpful in our Swedish nightmare experience. Based on this discussion, Judie and I developed a service provider matrix in which we put each of the people we encountered in one of four service quadrants based on our guiding business principle of "relationships and results" that we had adopted from the work of Stephen R. Covey.

Quadrant One – "Facilitator" (High on Relationships, Low on Results). The America West agent in Phoenix who convinced her boss to arrange for the British Airlines Executive to reimburse us for the $14,000 that we had to pay for our British Airlines ticket home was a *facilitator*. She had no authority and could not solve our problem, but she took the initiative to find someone who could.

Quadrant Two – "Place-holder" (Low on Relationships, Low on Results). The "can't do" Finnair agent who insisted that this was not her problem because she was just a subcontractor for British Airways and was not authorized to make any decisions, was a mere *place-holder*.

Quadrant Three – "Service Provider" (Low on Relationships, High on Results). The American Express agent who listened to a short version of our story without showing any emotion, and then quickly gave us cash to replace our stolen traveler's checks, was a *service provider*. In response to a question about our lost passports, he responded, "Sorry, I can't help you with that."

Quadrant Four – "Client Whisperer" (High on Relationships, High on Results). The American Consulate staff who listened empathetically to our entire story, and told us how sorry she was about all of the hassles that we were experiencing was a *whisperer*. She quickly issued new passports for us. Although we were very relieved to have new passports, we also benefitted emotionally from the empathetic and caring way in which she dealt with our problems.

Upon our return to the States, Judie and I shared our Swedish nightmare experience with our extended leadership team. We presented the matrix of service providers that we created on our flight home and described how each had impacted our experience...for better or worse. Following the presentation, several of our team members told us that they were near tears during the presentation, which wasn't surprising. After all, these people were caring, empathetic people. We realized that they were "client" whisperers;' we just hadn't referred to them as such. They clearly had traits in common with horse-whisperer Monty Roberts, dog-whisperer Cesar Millan, and lion-whisperer Kevin Richardson. One of those common traits is that they are all self-taught. To my knowledge, there are no client whispering classes; but, like these other whisperers, our team of consulting professionals became client whisperers *extraordinaire*. They were able to unobtrusively discover client "pains," credibly build solid relationships, and collaboratively achieve the desired results for their clients. And, like their whispering counterparts, they didn't necessarily follow rules—rather, they were driven by their values, principles, and instincts.

This book is based on the underlying strategy of a *client whisperer* approach to business—an approach that clearly differentiated us from most of our competition and achieved client successes that ultimately resulted in our market leadership position. In telling our story, I organized this book into four parts: The Client Whisperers' Wild Ride, in which I describe our business journey; FCB, which is our faster, cheaper, better approach to delivering solutions; The Client Whisperers' World, where I delve into the culture of client whispering; and the client whisperers' Legacy, the concluding part of the book, which discusses leadership and the perpetuation of client whispering. If the end does justify the means, then this surely is a compelling story.

Our Name...over Time

The seven mergers and acquisitions that occurred during our story included the following:

Year One:	Our management buy-out of USA Group Information Solutions to become InfoSolutions. edu (ISEDU)
Year Three:	Acquisition of ISEDU by The Hunter Group, which was owned by Renaissance Worldwide
Year Five:	Acquisition of The Hunter Group by Cedar Group, a British software company
Year Six:	Acquisition of The Cedar Group by Alchemy Partners, a British equity firm
Year Eight:	Acquisition of Software Armada by The Cedar Group
Year Nine:	Merger of Crestone International and The Cedar Group to become CedarCrestone, Inc.
Year Twelve:	Acquisition of E2E by CedarCrestone

For readability purposes, I refer to our company as CedarCrestone when describing events that occurred after Year Five.

A Personal Touch

At the outset, I acknowledge my penchant for the sports domain, based primarily upon my lifetime passion for basketball. Many of the lessons I initially learned on the basketball court were applicable to my subsequent business career. Not surprisingly then, I occasionally use a sports metaphor to share my sports experiences in the context of this business story. These experiences are presented under the header of "Lyon's Pride," accompanied by a picture of a lion. These metaphors are not about winning games at all cost, but rather are about the long-term focus on values, relationships, teamwork, strategies, leadership, and mastery of the fundamentals of success. Perhaps my comfort with incorporating this metaphorical approach is best explained by Pulitzer Prize winner James A. Michener, "The masters in the art of living make little distinction between their work and their play, their labor and their leisure, their minds and their bodies, their information, their recreation, their love and their religion. They hardly know which is which; they simply pursue their vision of excellence at whatever they do, leaving others to decide whether they are working or playing."[1]

PART I: THE CLIENT WHISPERERS' WILD RIDE

2. WHY WAS IT A WILD RIDE?

BORROWED WISDOM

> "Sweet are the uses of adversity."[2]
>
> **Shakespeare**

GUIDING PRINCIPLE

> Do the unexpected...no one will expect it.

INTRODUCTION

It was the mid-1990s. The Robinson Group (TRG) was a company on the verge of becoming a successful, entrepreneurial software business using innovative technology. The founder was well known in the market place, having previously started Information Associates (IA), a company that at one time was recognized as the leading provider of administrative software in the higher education market. Well into the TRG software development process, however, newer technology with potentially broader market acceptance became available. Both management and technical staff became engaged in intense discussions regarding technical direction. But this uncertainty was not all that was contributing to a sense of anxiety. The scope of development had changed, as TRG responded to the needs and wants of its initial clients. A software development effort originally envisioned to include only a student information system, expanded to encompass a full suite of administrative software. To accomplish this, TRG required considerable additional funding from its parent company, USA Group. Questionable technology...too broad a scope...modest revenue...all were contributing to management uneasiness. USA Group, who had no prior experience with software development operations of this scope, faced the difficult business decision of whether to continue funding this large development and potentially re-development effort or de-fund TRG software development. The decision? De-fund TRG software development.

The result of this de-funding was the formation of a much smaller services company called USA Group Information Solutions. The executive
team of USA Group, of which I was a member, asked me to head-up this
new entity. Charged with transitioning the organization from a software
development operation to a viable consulting services business, I began this very trying process of transformation. But something even better – and unanticipated -- emerged from the process. In less than a year,
our small USA Group Information Solutions management team decided
to make an offer to acquire this new business from our parent company.
Our timing was fortuitous. Working in collaboration with the USA Group
executive team, I created an agreement for a new private company.

I contemplated what name we should use to convey the nature of our
business and competitively position our new brand. In discussions with
our small management team, we came to agreement on InfoSolutions.
edu, known in the market by its acronym, ISEDU. We thought the name
would be a good transition from USA Group Information Solutions, and
we liked the idea of using the ".edu" extension as part of our name
to reflect both a technology and an education orientation. No market
research here...just a good afternoon discussion among people experienced in the higher education market.

I expected that our business initially would be to service the residual
TRG/USA Group clients that were on maintenance for TRG's previously developed higher education products. Additionally, I thought we
could immediately provide management consulting services related to
information technology in higher education. Strategically, I hoped that
we also could begin a consulting practice to implement software developed by the emerging market leader, PeopleSoft, Inc., later to be acquired by Oracle Corporation. PeopleSoft was using a business model
new to the higher education market that relied on third parties to implement its software. Word among the higher education community was
that PeopleSoft was coming on strong. I wanted our new company to
be in the PeopleSoft wake – even if the ride would be wild.

Shortly before our management buy-out, one of PeopleSoft's key executives, who was focused on growing their higher education market share,
contacted me. We agreed to meet to discuss our future in the PeopleSoft
world. We collaboratively formed an agreement that PeopleSoft would
assume ownership of TRG's advancement (fund raising) software–a

product that would complete PeopleSoft's higher education suite of software offerings. In exchange for this software, we would become an official PeopleSoft partner and our consultants would be able to participate in PeopleSoft's training programs to gain product expertise and certification. The arrangement was a win-win. PeopleSoft now had a foundation for another higher education product offering; and by having PeopleSoft partner status, we gained a competitive advantage atypical of a small start-up company. We were in for a ride!

Was It Wild?

Carol Roth, author of *The Entrepreneur Equation*, said in an article entitled, *Start-ups Take Extra Effort; Making Millions is Tough*, "Too many people think they can successfully run their own business when the reality is that 90 percent of businesses fail in the first five years."[3] With this in mind, we quickly identified the three big challenges ahead of us: getting a client, hiring qualified staff, and scaling-up. To overcome our first big challenge of getting a client, we used Bosworth's solution selling methods and a bold prime contractor strategy. To our delight—even surprise—we won *three* software implementation contracts during the first eight months of our new PeopleSoft venture. Each of these contracts represented more than one million dollars of total revenue over an eighteen to twenty-four month period. Two of these early clients had enough faith in us to pay a "start-up fee" upon contract signing, which allowed us to immediately begin recruiting additional staff.

As we had essentially no investment capital, our second big challenge was to hire enough qualified staff to meet our contractual commitments for on-site consulting services. This opportunity came at a time when the demand for experienced PeopleSoft consultants exceeded supply, especially in higher education. Because we knew that our small company, ISEDU, could not successfully compete for high-priced PeopleSoft talent, we had to think differently. We developed a two-pronged strategy of hiring higher education professionals who had little or no PeopleSoft-specific experience and subcontracting some of our non-mission critical implementation work to one of our competitors.

Our higher education professionals with no PeopleSoft experience proved almost immediately to be of high value to our clients and, therefore, to us. The subcontracting arrangement worked well for a while;

however, we came to realize that if we really wanted to become a market-share leader for enterprise resource planning (ERP) services in higher education, we had to develop our own comprehensive capability. This was closely related to our third big challenge of scaling up.

We decided that our best course of action was to merge with another company that had complementary and additional capabilities in the PeopleSoft implementation business. After considering six offers from reputable firms, we selected The Hunter Group, a company founded in 1981 that was an early and successful PeopleSoft partner in the implementation of the human resources and financial management systems. Unlike some mergers, this one accomplished the desired results for both of us. They acquired a company who knew higher education, a market in which they were positioning themselves to become a player. We gained the capability to offer implementation services not only for a student information system but also a human resource and financial management system in our higher education market. The Hunter Group also brought the additional benefits of a well developed and documented method of implementing software and marketing and sales capabilities.

Despite some difficult economic conditions, our revenue continued to grow after the merger. We weathered a general post-9/11 market decline that eventually affected the funding base of colleges and universities. We also survived a plateau in the upward-buying trend for ERP systems in higher education resulting from the announcement that Oracle was pursuing an acquisition of its rival PeopleSoft. Even with these complicating influences, our revenue increased faster than the growth rate of the higher education PeopleSoft services market. We continued to grow throughout the extended difficult economic times, and even through a few subsequent corporate mergers and acquisitions.

To what can we attribute this growth during such a depressed market and uncertainty in the ERP market? Certainly our good people and supportive clients made it possible, but I also borrowed and applied wisdom from those who had researched and/or created and executed successful business strategies. I illustrate in **Figure A** below when I infused the wisdom of three of our sources into our business model. In subsequent chapters, I describe in more detail how we adapted the wisdom of all our sources to our business. It is interesting to note that the positive impact of this borrowed wisdom on our revenue growth occurred approximately twelve to twenty-four months after we introduced such wisdom to our consultancy. We painfully learned patience as we nurtured internal buy-in.

Figure A: Higher Education Service Revenue

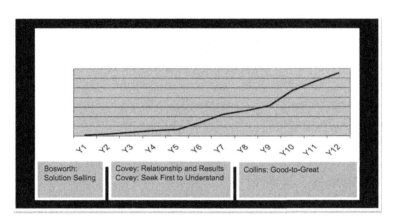

The significant revenue growth that began during our fifth year of operation was primarily due to an improbable sales success with the California State University System (CSU), which is comprised of twenty-three somewhat independent universities with a combined enrollment of more than four hundred thousand students. In 2000, CSU issued a request for proposal (RFP) calling for professional services to configure a baseline version of the PeopleSoft software that would meet CSU's mission-critical business needs and to implement it at two pilot institutions. The CSU goal was to eventually have the baseline software implemented at all twenty-three campuses. The RFP was sent to all companies that had experience implementing the PeopleSoft software, including ours.

Prior to the release of the RFP, virtually all of our competitors, including some of the largest consulting companies in the world, had invested heavily in CSU sales and marketing efforts, particularly at the centralized, CSU System executive level. In contrast, a few of our principals and our lone salesperson for the Western region quietly made visits to the campuses. We talked to people about their issues, vision, and the challenges that they anticipated would impact their campus as part of being involved in this large, highly complex CSU system-wide project. Because of our size and lack of name recognition, the other bidding firms surely did not consider us a threat—if they even knew that we existed.

During this pre-RFP period, one of these large consulting companies, which was aware of our small business, invited us to an interview for consideration as a potential subcontractor for their CSU proposal. Our warm handshakes were met with cool ones, even though we were ac-quainted with some of them. Through their formality and lack of inter-action when we responded to their questions, a condescending aura pervaded the interview. After the interview, they told us that we were too small and inexperienced a company to be considered as a part-ner for such a large, complex project. I thought of Eleanor Roosevelt's comment, "No one can make you feel inferior without your consent."[4] Despite the risk of this bold move, all of our management team agreed that we should go it alone and prepare our own CSU proposal. And that we did. We emphasized our higher education experience, explained how we had recently implemented the PeopleSoft student information system, and featured the highly positive client testimonials from those projects.

Incredibly, we were chosen as one of four finalists. Each of the other finalists consisted of a partnership of two or more of our big competitors, including Coopers & Lybrand; IBM; Peat, Marwick & Mitchell; PeopleSoft Consulting and a number of smaller firms. All of the other finalists had spent much more time and money, particularly with the executives in the CSU Central Administration, in pursuit of this CSU opportunity than we had. Little did our competitors know that I was well acquainted with some of the campus people because they were former clients of mine when I worked at IA, the company whose legacy software they were using.

The CSU selection committee was structured to include representatives from both the Central Administration Office and the individual campuses. When our competitors appeared before the selection committee, they focused on their own credentials, rather than on the CSU campuses. We took a much different approach. During our finalist presentation, we talked about how we could respond to campus needs, issues, and the political dynamics associated with a system-wide implementation. We discussed the challenges in achieving the vision of the Collaborative Management

Lyon's Pride

Our CSU win affected me much like my first big win as a high school basketball player. The last regular season game of my junior year was against our undefeated archrival that had beaten us soundly earlier that same year. We were heavy underdogs and outmanned at most every position. Our only competitive advantage was our depth of talent as compared to our opponent's reserve players who were used sparingly. I had a high energy level as I attempted to pump-up my teammates during warm-ups prior to tip-off. I loved this opportunity to compete against such an accomplished team! From the opening tip-off, we played a very active pressure defense and deployed our fast-break offense at every opportunity. It was a real team effort as we substituted freely to leverage our lone competitive advantage. I remember how much I enjoyed the keen competition and how thrilled I was when we won the game 75 to 73. There was no doubt about my intense passion for the game of basketball after this huge upset – I was hooked on basketball, winning, and doing whatever was asked of me by my inspirational and strong willed coach. I relate the dynamics and outcome of this game to our CSU achievement: both were about big challenges, tough competition, huge upsets, gratifying wins, and terrific teammates.

System (CMS). In particular, we emphasized that the success of the University's system-wide implementation would be determined by the success of each individual campus. We drew in examples from our higher education background, explaining how we had worked in other similar institutions, as faculty, staff and administrators as well as in consulting roles.

The outcome? CSU selected us! For me, this was the emotional equivalent of winning a post-season basketball championship. We—a small, relatively unknown company—had been chosen as the partner for one of the largest and most complex PeopleSoft implementation projects in the higher education industry. Amazing! There was shock in the marketplace. When the CSU Selection Committee presented our name to their executives as their preferred implementation partner for the student information system, the executives reacted unbelievingly, asking, "Who are these people?"

The response that the Selection Committee gave to their executives was, as paraphrased: these are experienced higher education professionals. They demonstrated a thorough understanding of the issues confronting our campus stakeholders and presented a point-by-point solution to address each of those issues. Based upon our reference checks, their track record is impeccable.

Our proposal and presentation must have been in sharp juxtaposition to those of our competitors, many of which consisted of various combinations of large teams of consultants, high hourly rates, high-powered corporate capabilities, sophisticated corporate videos and myriad executive promises. The selection committee members pointed out that we could give specific examples of issues that we had heard about from the campus personnel and understood how important it was to get campus buy-in for the project to be successful. They did not hear that kind of insight from our competitors.

Our competitors openly expressed skepticism regarding the risk that CSU was taking in selecting this small, untested company to complete a project of this size and complexity. After all, no one had done an implementation project that entailed designing a common baseline version of the PeopleSoft student information system while concurrently piloting the software at two campuses. I did receive a call from the company that previously rejected us as a subcontractor for their CSU proposal…they asked if we might consider using them as a subcontractor. Smile…

The outcome: we were able to complete the initial twenty-month project *on time* and *under budget*, doing so with a minimal number of subcontractors. Compared to the bids from our competitors, we saved CSU more than ten million dollars. This was a client success story of the best kind! By taking the time to discover campus needs and issues, we were able to develop a sufficient level of trust to allow CSU to make this high-risk decision of hiring us as their implementation partner. The further development of that trust in our relationship became the foundation for the delivery of a faster, cheaper, and better solution—one many said could not be accomplished. In response to the question, "Was it wild?" I answer, "Yes, it was—but we loved every minute of it—well, almost every minute of it."

Sun Tzu said, "Opportunities multiply as they are seized."[5] Our CSU success was a harbinger of things to come. As we began our market leadership journey, word of our success spread throughout the college and university industry. We had established our company as a significant player in the large institution market segment. In our first four years, we had no clients that produced annual revenue of one million dollars. After this success, we began to see some of those million-dollar per year clients. In **Figure B,** below, I show the number of individual projects that produced more than one million dollars in revenue in a given year for each of the last eight years of our journey. For most of this period we were forced to turn away business, due to our inability to hire enough experienced higher education professionals to keep up with market demand. Although passing up new business was frustrating, we never changed our hiring model or lowered our hiring standards.

Figure B: Number of Million Dollar Clients: Years 5–12

PROOF OF PERFORMANCE

"Feedback from the CedarCrestone workshops has been extremely positive. This collaborative approach has gone far beyond producing key planning documents. The activities have solidified our team, given them voice in the project and exposed us to excellent facilitation approaches. Our consultants are maximizing our ability to succeed from the very beginning."

Assistant Vice President Enrollment Services
Large, Masters University in the California State University System

LESSONS LEARNED

- When you anticipate that the end may be coming, consider that it might turn out to be the beginning.

- The trust-building process begins with your very first contact.

- Most people buy from people who understand and care about their problems, not from companies.

- Superiority is not dependent upon size.

- When risk runs high, run faster.

3. WHERE IN THE WORLD ARE WHISPERERS?

BORROWED WISDOM

> "Get the right people on the bus...before you figure out where to drive it."[6]
>
> Jim Collins,
> Distinguished Teacher and Author

GUIDING PRINCIPLE

> The right people create an Energy Bus...and it can pass all the other buses.

The TRG software business had attracted a very talented team of higher education professionals and expert software developers. Unfortunately, when this software development business lost its funding, there was not enough remaining service revenue to retain all of the great people who had been employed by the now defunct company. Thus, my first task had been to determine who of the more than 100 people should depart and who should stay. I pondered at length which people would be best for our transition from a software to a services business. Unfortunately, we were only able to retain 30 of these highly skilled people. Not surprisingly, many of the people who departed went to work for our competitors including PeopleSoft. What a lost opportunity!

Those very difficult early personnel decisions had been my first attempt at following Jim Collins's advice. In his book *Good to Great*, (Copyright © 2001 by Jim Collins. Reprinted with permission from Jim Collins) Collins's five-year research project revealed that a common strategy of the eleven most successful companies was getting "the right people on the bus."[7] Collins called it "first who...then what."[8] My adaptation of Collins's concepts included the following basic personnel principles: create an effective team before crafting a long-term business plan, get the right people in the right roles, and reward the people who produce the best results.

Winning baseball teams can be assembled by recruiting the best player for each position (i.e., "all-star team"). If all nine players perform well, the team will perform well, even if most of those nine all-stars are primarily focused on their individual performance. Basketball is a much more interactive sport than baseball. The interaction among teammates and with the opposing players is dynamic, fast paced and unpredictable. The coach has much less time to influence the action during a game than do baseball managers. Successful basketball teams require high trust relationships that enable all five players to know intuitively how their teammates will perform under pressure. I had to consider how each individual would work as a member of our team. Optimizing team performance requires a fragile balance between individual performance and team performance. This balance is true in sports and business as well.

THE STARTING LINE-UP

I kept eight from USA Group Information Solutions, all of whom had higher education experience. Fortunately, because each of us had very different but complementary skill sets, it was relatively easy to get our people in the right seats on our bus. Most of us occupied multiple seats depending on the needs of our initial – and very short--list of clients. Five of our eight founding partners made the entire twelve-year journey; without them, there would not have been a success story. They all possessed knowledge of higher education, worked well as a team, had a shared set of values, and focused on our guiding principle of building trusting relationships and achieving client results. They also were extraordinarily talented and dedicated professionals, who did whatever was needed to be successful—independent of title, compensation, corporate structure, and ownership.

Judie, one of the three founders of TRG, joined us after brief tenures with Coopers & Lybrand's higher education practice and PeopleSoft's public sector practice. She headed up our marketing and management consulting services. Judie was well acquainted with the higher education community because of her service as president and member of the board of EDUCAUSE (formerly CAUSE). Working for IA as the executive responsible for business development of professional services, she was acquainted with many of IA's higher education clients. She also brought her higher education experience as a faculty member, administrator, and executive. Her Ph.D. credential helped us to establish credibility with our higher education audiences, especially if faculty were present.

One of our founding partners, and later a member of our four-person management team, was Chris. Judie had first known him when he was the Chief Information Officer at the University of Northern Colorado. Among other innovative accomplishments at his institution, he had created one of the earliest and most creative approaches to providing services to students through his "one-card" solution in which students had a single card that they could use with multiple vendors who supplied products and services to university students. Not surprisingly, MCI recruited innovative Chris away from the university environment to head up their commercial one-card solution. Chris had just the experience that we needed: a technical background in a higher education institution, client service, and marketing experience in the corporate environment. He also met periodically with Bill Gates. Chris possessed that highly valued ability to establish all important one-on-one trusting relationships. Have a problem with a client that no one else could solve? Call Chris!

Todd, a key designer of the financial aid module of the student information system at TRG, was a critical player in the formation of our new company. He possessed a combination of technical experience with an understanding of student business processes because he previously worked in a university for thirteen years. Todd had that unusual ability to synthesize client requirements into what was most important to meet our clients' critical needs. He achieved the distinction of leading the first full implementation in the country of the newly released PeopleSoft student information system. Working with Palomar College, a community college of approximately 30,000 students in California, Todd and his small team not only implemented the student information system but they also implemented the human resource and financial management system—all within18 months--record time in the PeopleSoft world and ahead of the year 2000 deadline imperative. This success and the resulting client testimonials were the beginning of our positive reputation in the PeopleSoft world.

In the early days of TRG, Judie hired Shawn right after his graduation from the University of Arizona, not knowing at the time that he would continue on with her as a founding partner at ISEDU. A brilliant person, Shawn was critical to our success during the transition when we had to support our clients whose residual service contracts were our initial business. While at the outset he did not possess any PeopleSoft expertise, he came to be known by us and our clients as one of the most, if not the most, creative and talented PeopleSoft technical consultant. He also brought his experience working with TRG partner institutions and had that unusual ability to explain highly technical concepts in words that non-technical people could understand. Most of all, Shawn could figure out solutions to complex technical challenges that others tried in vain to solve. Shawn became "the" mentor for the other technical people that we hired. His combined understanding of higher education, his technical brilliance, and his creativity were absolutely critical to the success of our CSU project. And Shawn surely understood the wisdom in the 1977 Apple Computer tag line: "Simplicity is the ultimate sophistication."

Gene had also worked at TRG, heading up the development team for information access technical solutions. He managed the TRG residual contracts, so necessary to the ISEDU cash flow. His experience working with partner institutions and development staff at TRG was an asset as he helped us to also build our PeopleSoft client base. With a degree in electrical engineering from the University Michigan, Gene had been a network and communications specialist and manager of technical support in the technology industry. As we launched our PeopleSoft implementation business, Gene developed risk management and other project tools that became integral to our methodology. He had that inventive kind of mind that we came to refer to as "the wizard." He left for a short period to start his own business, then later rejoined us as a key senior project manager.

Cynthia, one of our original eight, was a colleague of ours for many years prior to the formation of ISEDU. Having worked in fund raising in a university environment, she had been a natural to lead a design team for a fund raising system for colleges and universities. Her quick-start instincts and her willingness to do whatever it took to get new projects off the ground helped us succeed with some of those early software implementation projects. When it came to projects, Cynthia really knew how to organize and manage them. We knew that our PeopleSoft implementation business would require her much needed project management expertise. Her direct, friendly style enabled her to quickly develop relationships and build trust with our early clients. If something needed to be done, Cynthia wholehcartedly accomplished it. Cynthia left to pursue a career in real estate, but always stayed in touch.

Then there was Moe, so essential to our daily operations. He had been responsible for operations at TRG and knew every asset that TRG possessed. He was critical to our transition as we first downsized from TRG to our small operation and then quickly grew as ISEDU. In addition to his operational experience, Moe also had extensive expertise in telecommunications that we drew upon for an early client who needed someone to help them plan and set up a new telecommunications system. Ever reliable, always dependable, Moe took every detail into account. Moe turned out to be our biggest team player. When we decided to sell ISEDU, he knew that any likely buyer would not need his services, and that he would be part of the cost-reduction that every acquirer uses to help justify the cost of a strategic acquisition. However, he was steadfast in his support of our decision to sell the company, and made a big contribution to our transition from ISEDU to The Hunter Group.

RECRUITING TIME

Our next challenge in this start-up phase was to identify whom we should recruit to fill the other empty seats on our bus. We had very little cash, and knew we could only hire people when we had sufficient revenue under contract to meet our payroll. Hiring a new employee was a very big decision, and a couple of bad decisions could have been disastrous. As it turned out, most of these early hires were based more on intuition than on the content of the applicants' resumes.

We established a hiring model that served us well, both initially and throughout our twelve years of steady revenue growth. For our functional consulting needs, we recruited people with experience as college and/or university administrators, staff, and faculty members, who understood the business of higher education. Unlike most of our competitors, we were convinced that it would be easier for people experienced in higher education to learn new software, than it would be for non-higher education people who knew the software to learn the unique business of higher education.

Our hiring model for technical consultants was much different. We pursued the most talented PeopleSoft technical consultants we could find, independent of industry experience. The combination of our experienced higher education functional consultants with our very talented technical consultants allowed us to deliver the highest level of service to our clients. Because we were able to address some very complex technical implementation challenges, our reputation grew as a leading PeopleSoft service provider.

Another essential aspect of our CSU success was project management. Our approach to management of this large, complex project was a little different than the project management services offered by some of our larger competitors. Because the CSU project was all about people, politics, and processes, we assigned Todd, one of our original partners, as the project manager. I knew that his many years of higher education experience and skills in conflict resolution and team building would be essential for the successful completion of this project. However, our project management evolved as we experienced both success and new challenges at CSU. In support of our CSU project manager, Chris, another one of our original partners, and I provided executive sponsorship to assist with conflict resolution and negotiations on an as-needed basis, which was weekly during the first year of the project and less frequently as the project neared completion. Throughout the project Chris worked very closely with CSU's highly skilled and experienced Project Director.

We also provided a substantial amount of professional project management support to build and manage the project plans and to conduct periodic quality assurance reviews. This critical support allowed Todd to stay focused on people, politics and task completion. Our professional project management support was provided by Vickie, an experienced professional project manager who was certified by the Project Management Institute (PMI). She was outstanding! The combination of Todd and Vickie made a very effective project management team. The project management approach that evolved during the CSU project became our approach for all subsequent large, complex projects and dictated our hiring model for project managers. We recruited experienced higher education project managers and used our project management office, led by Vickie, as support to ensure an appropriate level of risk identification and mitigation and quality assurance.

The next personnel challenge was to figure out where to find these rare client whisperers. The most promising source of potential whisperers was from the more than four thousand American colleges and universities. Thus, our first new hire, Shannon, was an experienced student services administrator from Arizona State University who had been through a major business process redesign project, but had no experience with the PeopleSoft software. After his first week shadowing Todd on the student information system implementation project at Palomar College, we received positive feedback from the client regarding the value that Shannon was bringing to the project, which reinforced our approach of hiring people with higher education experience.

This initial recruiting success sent us searching for more experienced higher education professionals, especially those from institutions that had recently implemented the PeopleSoft software. However, we soon encountered some significant challenges with this strategy. Many of the best candidates that we identified were very concerned about making the transition from the safe haven of higher education to the unknowns of the corporate world. This concern was exacerbated by our heavy travel requirement that represented a very significant life style change for many of our new recruits. During our twelve-year journey, I traveled more than one million miles, as did many of our consultants. In most cases, we could offer higher compensation, but we quickly realized that company culture was a much more important factor than compensation for most of these people. Since the majority of us were former college administrators, we understood this issue well. We quickly changed our recruiting approach from "you can earn more money" to "you can be part of an exciting company with a higher education culture—and also earn more money." This appeal became our most important recruitment and retention approach.

One of our most gratifying personnel success stories involved the recruitment of a professor from Southern Methodist University (SMU). With his Ph.D. in religious history from Vanderbilt University, O.T. had a distinguished thirty-year career in academe as a faculty member, administrator and student adviser. Pursuant to SMU's decision to become one of the first institutions to implement the PeopleSoft software, O.T. immersed himself in the SMU implementation project. He soon became known as the "father of PeopleSoft Academic Advising." When

I first called O.T., I was not optimistic about his interest in our company. However, the more we conversed the more interested he sounded. After talking with some of our client whisperers, he agreed to join our team as our lead senior consultant for all things related to academic advising. We were elated! More importantly, as our clients got to know him, they realized how much he understood about the philosophy and practice of effective academic advising and how to use the PeopleSoft software to strengthen the academic advising process for faculty members, staff and students.

Collins's research provided some additional insights into the efficacy of our hiring strategies. He concluded that although compensation was important, the primary objective was to get the right people on the bus and keep them there. Unexpectedly, our approach also became an important sales strategy that made us an attractive alternative when prospects compared our people to those of many of our competitors.

Our success in recruiting higher education professionals created a new challenge: most of them had little or no consulting experience or knowledge of the PeopleSoft software. If they were to be successful client whisperers, they would need both. To accelerate this evolutionary, professional development process, our approach was on-the-job mentoring. We placed our new consultants on a team of experienced client whisperers. In some cases, we assigned a specific practicing client whisperer as a mentor to a new consultant. This approach had an additional benefit beyond satisfying the primary objective of new hire training. As characterized by management guru, Peter Drucker, "Knowledge workers and service workers learn most when they teach."[9]

Our second source of potential client whisperers was our competitors. At that time, many of them had consultants who were potential client whisperers. The good news was that some of these people once worked with us at IA during the 1980s, and we had already established personal and professional relationships with them. Although we realized that they may have slipped into the non-whispering methods typical of big companies, we felt sure that once they were back in a higher education culture like ours, they would revert to client whispering behavior. We knew these individuals would bring three important qualifications: higher education experience, student system experience, *and* consulting experience.

Another source of talent was the higher education software vendors. Many of their employees had experience working with the higher education community and, in most cases, had consulting experience. However, only people working for PeopleSoft would have knowledge of the PeopleSoft software, and our partnership arrangement with PeopleSoft precluded hiring their employees. Our recourse was to seek out client whisperers from other higher education software vendors, even though there were only two such companies that we could target. With our initial hires from these companies, we discovered that they tended to be seasoned professionals with acceptable levels of higher education experience. Some of these individuals did become very effective client whisperers.

We also found client whisperers in unexpected places. For example, one of our early hires was Mary who was teaching elementary school in northern California. This type of hire wasn't as unusual as you might think. Mary also had been a former university administrator holding the positions of controller and budget director. Fortunately, she also had consulting experience. An open and caring person, she evolved into an excellent client whisperer who was resolute about her commitment to client success—and her clients knew it.

In his book *Winners Never Cheat* (Copyright 2009. By permission of Wharton School Publishing), businessman Jon M. Huntsman Sr. explains, "There are, basically, three kinds of people: the unsuccessful, the temporarily successful, and those who become and remain successful. The difference, I am convinced, is character."[10] As suggested in one of the Good-to-Great findings by Collins, high character begets high character which facilitates teamwork.

Throughout our growth period, the demand for experienced PeopleSoft consultants continued to exceed supply. Many consulting companies experienced high consultant turnover. Our consistently low consultant turnover rate indicated that we had a clear focus on employee retention. I attribute this low turnover rate at least partially to our success in creating a comfortable working environment for the type of people we were recruiting and our understanding that, as Collins observed, "...the right people don't need to be tightly managed or fired up."[11]

Many of our best client success stories resulted from some of our most challenging projects, to which we assigned an experienced consulting team led by some of our best client whisperers. Although there were always people whom we considered to be our most accomplished consultants, we didn't put labels on people or in any explicit or implicit way indicate that some people were less capable than others. We left that evaluation up to our clients. We called everyone a senior consultant... and they earned that title.

A consulting company's staffing decisions reflect their values, strategies and priorities. Companies that use bait and switch tactics and low ball pricing are focused primarily on company success. Companies that focus on client success treat these less than honorable tactics with disdain. However, even high integrity companies must evaluate many options and make difficult decisions regarding the staffing of a large number of concurrent projects. Assembling a project team for a new long-term project was time consuming and required consideration of many factors, including the following primary considerations, listed in priority order:

- Guiding principles
- Teamwork optimization
- Client preferences and priorities
- Consultant preferences and priorities
- Availability of consultants relative to start dates for new projects
- Assignment of our best people to the biggest opportunities
- Experience working on similar projects for similar institutions
- Risk mitigation

Each staffing situation was different and required much insight into all aspects of the above considerations. It was easy to be intoxicated by the next big project at the expense of the successful completion of existing projects. The two most important aspects of these staffing decisions were to be true to our guiding principles and strategies and optimize team performance.

Gallup Global Practice Leader, Tom Rath, and renowned Gallup consultant, Barry Conchie, share the results of a landmark thirty-year research project in their book, *Strengths-Based Leadership: Great Leaders, Team, and Why People Follow.* Our use of their strengths based leadership concepts produced dramatic results in all aspects of our business as we attempted to deploy and support the right people in the right roles at the right time. Their work also provided useful insight into the relationship between leaders and followers. We quickly discovered that when our consultants were assigned to project roles that played to their individual strengths, they produced great results, and they enjoyed doing their work. Rath and Conchie suggest that, "Once you have the right people on your team, it's relatively easy to tell you're headed in the right direction."[12]

We also used consultants from within our company who reported to non-higher education business units on an as-needed basis. Most of these people were either highly skilled technical consultants or very experienced project managers. These non-higher education consultants played critical project roles for us on many of our large projects. Interestingly, we found that these cross-industry consultants enjoyed working with higher education clients and requested more assignments in higher education.

Most of our competitors approach to staffing was similar to staffing baseball teams. They treated consultants as interchangeable parts based on their software expertise. However, as project complexity increases, so does the interaction among the consulting teams and the client's project participants. A change in players can dramatically change team performance, which in turn, can change the level of both client and company success. Our additional strategy of basketball-style team staffing was an important part of our success with some of our most complex PeopleSoft projects, and helped differentiate us from many of our competitors

Some companies refer to their consultants as "resources." We always referred to our consultants as individuals, which was much more consistent with our guiding principles and strategies. We walked away from a couple of projects, for which we were not the prime contractor, because the prime contractor was not treating our consultants well. Those were difficult decisions, but they were consistent with our strategy to attract and retain the best consultants in the industry and to provide a positive working environment.

In hindsight, our hiring strategy was aligned with Malcolm Gladwell's observations and research as described in his book. Outliers: The Story of Success (Copyright 2008. By permission of Little, Brown, and Company.). He includes a story about a small isolated town in Pennsylvania where the existence of heart disease was almost non-existent. He says this is what the medical profession calls an "outlier." A doctor named Stewart Wolf and a sociologist named John Bruhn conducted some intensive research to determine the source of this medical outlier; and, according to Gladwell, "Wolf and Bruhn had to convince the medical establishment to think about health and heart attacks in an entirely new way: they had to get them to realize that they wouldn't be able to understand why someone was healthy if all they did was think about an individual's personal choices or actions in isolation. They had to look beyond the individual. They had to understand the culture he or she was part of, and who their friends and families were, and what town their families came from. They had to appreciate the idea that the values of the world we inhabit and the people we surround ourselves with have a profound effect on who we are."[13]

PROOF OF PERFORMACE

"Several years ago, I asked if there was some sort of 'human qualities' test that you folks had to pass before you were hired. Speaking from a client standpoint, the depth at CedarCrestone to provide true expertise for just about every nuance of PeopleSoft really sets you apart from other firms."

Functional Lead
Large Community College

LESSONS LEARNED

- Reach beyond traditional sources for new talent. You'll likely find just the right person for your bus

- When recruiting players for your team, make sure you understand the game.

- Peer mentoring yields benefits to both.

- Give full rein to your employees. They will show you how far and fast they can ride.

- Building a team is like building a culture: look for shared values at the outset.

4. WHAT'S THE WHAT?

BORROWED WISDOM

> "The main thing is to keep the main thing the main thing."[14]
>
> Stephen R. Covey
> Leadership Authority and Author

GUIDING PRINCIPLE

Stay focused—just like a hedgehog!

Once we had the right people on our bus, we had to determine "what" business we were going to be in and how we were going to pursue it. We turned to Collins's *good-to-great* business strategy, in which he uses the metaphor of a hedgehog. Regarding these hedgehog leaders, he explains, "They took a complex world and simplified it."[15] According to Collins, "The essential strategic difference between the good-to-great and comparison companies lay in two fundamental distinctions. First, the good-to-great companies founded their strategies on deep understanding along three key dimensions…Second, the good-to-great companies translated that understanding into a simple, crystalline concept that guided all their efforts—hence the term 'hedgehog concept.'"[16]

Our adaptation of Collins's three dimensions was as follows:

- Emotion: What was our passion?
- Excellence: What could we do potentially better than anyone else the world?
- Economic: What business would produce sustainable profit margins?

To define our adaptation of the hedgehog concept, we assembled thirty of our best "right people" for a two-day meeting in Phoenix. The combined higher education experience of this group was more than five hundred years. This extensive amount of experience was both an asset and a challenge for our discussions, deliberations, and negotiations. On the one hand, we had an extraordinary breadth of understanding of the higher education market; but on the other hand, we all had our favorite aspects of the market that we wanted to include within our scope. As the late Steve Jobs once said, "…among other practices, it's 'saying no to a thousand things' so as to concentrate on the 'really important' creations."[17]

We first addressed the easiest dimension for us, the emotional dimension. What was our passion? We then spent considerable time identifying and reaching consensus on the second dimension of excellence: what we could potentially do better than anyone else? Finally, we addressed our economic dimension. What business would produce sustainable profit margins? The outcome of our meetings was agreement on our three primary dimensions as I describe below.

WHAT WAS OUR PASSION?

In the very early stages of our company's evolution, Judie, along with a small team of her former TRG colleagues, met personally with the late Steve Jobs at NeXT Computer Inc.'s headquarters. With briefcases in tote and "suited up" for a business meeting, they walked into the naturally lit conference room whose walls were either windows or white boards. Steve burst open the door, carrying his bottle of juice, wearing faded jeans, a tee-shirt, and sandals. He plopped down on the table in front of them…with one leg off to the side. Then he leaned over and said to them, as paraphrased, "I hear you want to develop software for personal computers that could get management information from a mainframe student information system."

The small team quickly started to explain their plans of how they could develop such tools, Steve moved over to the white board and sketched out a visual schematic, commenting that the circle in the upper left hand corner represented "mainframe stuff." Then he completed the diagram in the lower right corner—illustrating what a student, faculty or staff member might see using a personal computer on his or her desktop. The remainder of the conversation was about how he could help make this vision happen. Then he said, "Would some NeXT computers help with your development?" The reply: "Absolutely!" The team of aspiring entrepreneurs left the room elated about having met Steve Jobs and highly motivated about the prospect of creating innovative software for college and university decision makers that would be available on personal computers...on the latest and greatest personal computers at that. And while TRG's vision was not realized, the invigorating experience of meeting with Steve Jobs who was passionate about what he was doing carried forward.

Some eight years later, in our management team meeting in which we were formulating our hedgehog concept, Judie recalled the excitement that Steve Jobs had conveyed about his business during her meeting with him. She asked the other management team members, "Are you really *passionate* about higher education?" After all, at the outset of our professional careers, we had self-selected into higher education. We worked in roles such as faculty member, academic administrator, counselor, bursar, financial aid director, and enrollment manager, to name just a few. We had experienced the intrinsic rewards of helping students learn, navigate university processes, and achieve their educational goals. When we transitioned into the corporate environment and worked in companies that offered products and services to colleges and universities, we were well-received because we had previously worked in higher education. That made us feel good—which made us perform well—which in turn made us feel passionate about higher education.

However, as Judie began circling the words "higher education" with the red felt pen on the flip chart positioned in the front of the room, Art piped in with something like, "But maybe we need to consider also offering professional services to non-profit fund raising organizations and the public sector market. After all, we have experience with PeopleSoft's fund raising software, and some of us know what it's like to work in non-profit organizations." Art was one of those highly creative, articulate individuals who preferred a broad arena; after all, he had formerly worked in Washington D.C. as a lobbyist and activist. However, Art had been tempered by having worked as assistant registrar at Georgetown University. In response to that suggestion, we discussed the pros and cons of moving into such a market. After some bantering back and forth, we came to agreement that those markets were outside of our hedgehog concept primarily because we would not be the best in the world at it since there already were a number of firms who excelled at implementing fund raising systems.

Lyon's Pride

In high school, I played soccer, basketball, and baseball. However, my will to win was much greater on the basketball court than on the soccer and baseball fields. I attributed this emotion to my intense passion for basketball. In the summer months, I played in two basketball leagues and virtually played basketball every night of the week. My year-round commitment to basketball was inspired by my new coach who was ahead of his time. In those days, most high school basketball players only played basketball in the winter months. Although encouraged by several teachers and advisors "not to put all of my eggs in one basket," my decision to take a different approach was based on three factors: my love of the game, my belief that I could be the best player in our county, and my hope that I could eventually earn a college scholarship based on my basketball achievements.

Thus, long before Jim Collins developed his hedgehog concept, I was betting my future on my own personal hedgehog concept that was based on the same three dimensions used by Collins. Perhaps that is why Collins' innovative concept was attractive to me for use in planning and growing our business.

By the end of our highly energized discussion, we concluded that we wanted to become "The trusted advisor to higher education for all things related to information systems." Art? Well, he was a team player: he agreed with the outcome of our discussion. I suspected that he was thinking of something very creative that he could do within the higher education market...and he did go on to do so...with passion. In the words of Steve Jobs, "The only way to do great work is to love what you do. If you haven't found it yet, keep looking. Don't settle. As with all matters of the heart, you'll know when you find it."[18]

WHAT DID OUR WHISPERERS DO BEST?

When I first encountered Collins's good-to-great concepts, I immediately thought about a poem that my favorite elementary school principal, Mr. Miller, wrote on our blackboard. To this day, I am not sure why that little poem has stuck with me, but I suspect it has to do with my respect and affection for that special principal. He wrote: "Good, better, best, never let it rest; till the good gets better and the better best."

Collins stated, "The good-to-great companies understood that doing what you are good at will only make you good; focusing solely on what you can potentially do better than any other organization is the only path to greatness."[19] Collins also observed that the comparison companies in his study, those that never made it to greatness, "...set their goals and strategies more from bravado than from understanding."[20]

The student information system, in particular, is what makes the higher education market unique when compared to other markets. The system is highly complex because higher education has diverse but interrelated business requirements. The scope of the system is broad because it impacts all constituencies in the institution. Business processes are non-standard, based upon differing interpretations of both approved and implied policies throughout the institution. A rules-based system is difficult to set up in higher education because exceptions to policy are the norm. Although the system is expected to provide timely information for decision-making, many institutions have difficulty determining common definitions of and agreement regarding key performance indicators.

There are serious negative consequences of an ineffective student information system or a system failure. Having the system go down during registration is an administrator's worst nightmare! You do not want to have an article in the student newspaper about how slow the registration system is. At least the president surely doesn't.

It was common for key stakeholders to feel that their jobs were on the line when they were involved with a student information system implementation project. Hiring consultants who didn't understand the criticality of a student information system was very risky. This risk was especially true if the consultants were working with an early release of a student information system. That was the case with the PeopleSoft student information system when we began our PeopleSoft consulting business.

Software and service vendors who had served other markets assumed that their consultants, who had implemented back-office financial and human resource systems, could quickly learn how to implement a student information system. Most service providers consistently underestimated the amount of functionality that was needed to support student administration business processes. They further underestimated the flexibility that was required to accommodate the diverse ways in which these business processes are structured, within an institution and from institution to institution. It was this complexity and diversity, however, that we best understood. We were confident that our initial specialization in implementing student information systems was at the core of what we did best—and potentially could do better than any of our competitors.

Limiting our scope to student information systems, however, created a dilemma, due to the conflict between our hedgehog concept of focusing on what we potentially could do best, i.e., student information systems, and our broader vision of becoming the trusted advisor to higher education for all things related to information systems. In the end, we chose to include all ERP software services for higher education, including finance, human resources, grants, and fund raising.

Our decision was based upon a number of factors. First, many of the large higher education institutions were in need of a fully integrated ERP solution. Some had suffered the negative staffing and cost consequences of maintaining non-integrated systems. Furthermore, each of the ERP software applications had some aspects that were considered mission-critical by most institutions. Given the complexity of a student information system, many institutions thought it best to implement it last. We recognized that if we were not positioned to implement the other systems, we would diminish our chances for winning the student information system implementation because of an incumbent vendor. Offering full implementation services also was consistent with our desire to be the prime contractor. We quickly came to realize that PeopleSoft wanted partners who could offer a full set of implementation services, not just services to implement the student information system. And a very important factor was that we needed to offer a full PeopleSoft ERP service solution to optimize our economic dimension.

It was difficult reaching an agreement regarding whether to extend our consulting services beyond PeopleSoft into multi-vendor service support. However, we were able to agree that our ability to generate revenue was tied most closely to implementing PeopleSoft software. Confining our focus to just PeopleSoft services was a difficult decision, but PeopleSoft was the only higher education software vendor that encouraged the use of third-party implementation firms. We also recognized PeopleSoft's rapidly growing market share and the attractive price umbrella created by the much larger consulting companies that were the PeopleSoft market share leaders in other markets.

Plus, we had our perceived initial competitive advantage in implementing the PeopleSoft student information system. We resolved any hesitation that we had about limiting ourselves to a PeopleSoft-only strategy by concluding that our focus could be expanded down the road if the dynamics of the market and our economic engine changed.

Once we determined that we had to develop the capability to offer full PeopleSoft ERP services to higher education, we felt that the best and quickest way to accomplish this was through a merger or acquisition. Acting as our own broker, we pursued a merger with several of the established, cross-industry PeopleSoft companies that were trying to penetrate the higher education market. We decided to merge with The Hunter Group.

Although The Hunter Group was not the highest bidder, they met all three of our merger criteria. First, they had a solid reputation as a PeopleSoft consulting firm. They were an early and successful PeopleSoft partner in the implementation of human resource and financial management systems. Second, they had a commitment to the higher education market. To launch their higher education practice, they had recently hired John, who previously had been a senior manager in the higher education practice with American Management Systems (AMS). He also had been the Bursar at the University of Maryland Baltimore. John was a perfect fit for our higher education management team. Third, we had a shared vision of market leadership. Over time, The Hunter Group became a significant player in higher education. Together, we took a giant step forward in our quest for market leadership in the higher education industry.

Later in our journey we expanded our excellence dimension as we targeted outsourcing of the operation and support of the PeopleSoft software. This solution area encompasses several types of service offerings, including software hosting in our data center, application management, and business process outsourcing. Establishing a leadership position in this arena required expertise that we did not possess. After several false starts with partnership ventures, our equity partner acquired Crestone International, which was founded in 1995 and was one of our big competitors. Crestone had already developed a hosting solution, and was emerging as a viable player in this domain. The timing of our corporate merger with Crestone was fortuitous, because the combination of our higher education leadership position, our newly acquired outsourcing expertise, and expanded client base was an instant winner. It expanded our hedgehog concept because we had a new and highly competitive offering at which we could and did excel.

CAN WHISPERING BE PROFITABLE?

Upon completion of the internal roll-out of our new hedgehog concept of PeopleSoft ERP Services for Higher Education, we had a much more focused approach to our business. This new focus helped us to eliminate most of the tangential services that were outside of our hedgehog concept, and mostly unprofitable.

A key question that we had to answer regarding our economic dimension was, what was our "denominator"? This aspect of Collins's research was described as follows: "...we did notice one particularly provocative form of economic insight that every good-to-great company attained, the notion of a single 'economic denominator.' If you could pick one and only one ratio—profit per x—to systematically increase over time, what x would have the greatest and most sustainable impact on your economic engine?"[21]

We had some interesting debates while determining our "x." First, we decided the "x" for most of our competition was either "contract" (profit per contract) or "project" (profit per project). We thought that using such an x-factor was too shortsighted for our market leadership goal. We also did not think either of these two denominators would fit our view of client retention. Once we contracted with a new name client, we wanted that client to be our client for a long time. If we provided high value to each client, they should want to continue to do business with us as new needs surfaced. We decided that, because our clients would continually need to upgrade and expand their ERP capabilities, our "x" denominator would be "client"—profit per client. If we could keep client satisfaction high by focusing on client success and increase our profit per client, that would have the greatest and most sustainable impact on our economic dimension. During our twelve-year journey, profit per client did actually increase steadily as we maintained a very high level of client retention. I summarize our hedgehog concept in **Figure C** below using the three dimensions of emotion, excellence, and economic.

Figure C: Our Hedgehog Concept

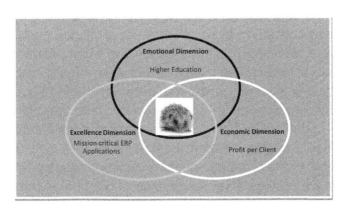

The development of our hedgehog concept left us with a list of management consulting services that were outside of our hedgehog concept. For example, we had provided management consulting services to develop a marketing and communication plan for Thunderbird Global Council, a group comprised of leading corporate executives from throughout the country, who were advisory to the Thunderbird School of Global Management. We provided services to Regis University, a private Jesuit University, to rebrand their image and restructure and redesign their website (by the way, Art got that one going). For the Maricopa Community Colleges, one of the largest community colleges in the country, we conducted a cost analysis of the SCT and PeopleSoft implementation costs. We were able to call on colleagues in institutions who had implemented these systems and provided costs based on their implementation experiences, not what the vendors had told them it would cost. For a time, we even provided short-term services related to The Balanced Scorecard approach to institutional effectiveness. We conducted organizational assessments and IT restructuring at Washtenaw Community College and California State Polytechnic University Pomona. For Cornell University, we provided management consulting services to examine their business processes in information technology and make recommendations to streamline their operations and management systems.

We debated considerably about whether to continue to offer such services. We came to the conclusion that we either could not potentially be the best in the world at providing them and/or that they diluted our economic dimension. Typically, these stand-alone management consulting engagements were projects of less than four months, and required skills sets that were scarce in our organization. Often, these management consulting projects were not profitable due primarily to the lack of a dedicated full-time consulting team. With consultants working partial weeks, with gaps in between on-site activities, our travel costs per hour of consulting were very high. Typically, there was a significant opportunity cost associated with these projects, because we could not assign our management consultants to larger, more profitable implementation projects while they had outstanding commitments to their management consulting engagements. If it was critical that we provide a service outside of our primary range for any strategic sales opportunity, we would usually pursue that work. The service could open an opportunity to become that client's implementation partner when the time came.

The CSU opportunity opened up many short term management consulting engagements related to the PeopleSoft implementation. With the assistance of a professional services firm, CSU had created a set of "readiness guidelines" that each campus had to meet before they could receive the baseline PeopleSoft software. Our management consultants who conducted these assessments usually were Judie and Tim, another Ph.D. with a faculty background who very successfully headed up our proposal team. Jan, who had been vice president for student registration and financial services at the University of Toledo, joined them for a number of the readiness assessments. He also was a former IA executive responsible for designing a student information system and had worked with Judie at the Maricopa Community Colleges. This highly experienced team conducted interviews with campus presidents and other executives, project managers, supervisors of various organizational units, and the CIO. In response to a question about project success that Judie asked one executive, he answered, "We won't even notice when the consultants are gone." That response became the basis for our knowledge transfer strategy of continuously transferring knowledge throughout the project so that when our consultants left the client team was fully prepared to maintain the system.

Our management consultants also conducted focus groups with students, faculty, and staff. In faculty focus groups, we found that participants usually regarded a software implementation project as having more administrative benefit that would take dollars away from faculty salaries and classroom equipment. One faculty member said in a focus group, "I came here to teach music, not to use computers." This was in 2001....wonder what he's doing now? At one institution, the readiness assessment revealed a negative attitude on the part of a highly influential faculty member who was in a faculty leadership role. When we discussed the implication of her negativity on the project, the client project manager and executive sponsor decided to invite her to join the project team. To the delight-- and relief-- of everyone, she became one of the strongest advocates for the project.

Students were typically unaware that such a project was about to begin and wanted to know more about the self-service capabilities that would be available to them. Once they heard examples of its capabilities, they said it couldn't happen fast enough. The project leaders at one CSU campus took action on student focus group feedback regarding automated voice response registration. The campus was going to discontinue using automated voice response registration once the PeopleSoft system was in place because the new system would offer web access to conduct registration. The students explained that they really needed both because they could be in a location where they didn't have access to a computer (this was 2001) but would always have access to a phone. The decision makers listened and changed their registration strategy. They decided that students should be able to continue to use the automated voice registration system; and once the new system was implemented, they also could register for classes on the web. We liked to share that story with other campuses as an excellent example of obtaining student feedback – and then doing something about it.

The focus groups with staff consistently yielded a great deal of uncertainty and anxiety, as illustrated in the following comments: "Promises for the project are built up so high that it may not measure up...We feel as though we're not getting the whole story, both positive and negative...Outside leaders' perceptions are both good and bad. They're excited that we're doing this, but have also heard some bad stories." In most cases, the staff were uninformed and/or misinformed. One of the most common follow-ups to the readiness assessments was for the client to plan and launch a communication plan that informed staff about the capabilities, timelines, and expected outcomes of the project.

The findings resulting from these readiness assessments were presented to the president of the institution and submitted to the CSU central administration. If a campus met the criteria or had in place a plan to meet the criteria by their targeted implementation start date, the information technology staff in the CSU central administration sent the baseline software to the campus. These readiness assessments were a pre-requisite that the campuses had to complete before they--and we—could begin a PeopleSoft implementation.

We did not want our competitors to conduct these readiness assessments because of all the "foreknowledge" that could be gleaned from the process. I share a few examples of foreknowledge that helped us understand the strengths that one of our CSU clients would bring to the project. The first one pertains to the campus culture: "The campus employees have a strong work ethic. Even though staffing is limited in some areas and the staff know that participating in the PeopleSoft project will increase their workloads, they have a 'can do' attitude and will do 'whatever it takes' to be sure that they have a successful implementation." For another campus, we found that their preparatory activities were helping to create a vision of what would be possible with the new system: "The project management staff is working with the user departments to map current business processes in preparation for the implementation. They are identifying areas that could be streamlined through information technology, and there is an increase in receptivity to change." At a third campus, we were relieved to find out that the perceptions of the campus information technology organization were highly positive: "We received numerous commendations in our interviews regarding the level of service, the discipline, the accomplishments, and capabilities of IT leadership and staff. They have strong relationships with their respective user communities. They are eagerly looking forward to the PeopleSoft project and have a commitment to be successful." We knew that the project had a head start with this kind of client strength.

We also gained foreknowledge about critical areas that needed attention and if not corrected would increase the risk to the project. The most common issue pertained to staffing: "Those who will be backfilled are concerned about not having sufficient time to document their processes and train their backfills. They feel that they may not meet expectations for the same level of on-going service while participating in the project." Not surprisingly, the budget was of considerable concern: "The project budget for the first year of the project has been planned and resources have been committed. However, given the likely reductions in budgets, the funding for subsequent years is perceived to be in jeopardy." The decision making process was one that could make or break our planned timeline. An example of our foreknowledge on this issue was: "The decision making process is very well structured and thoughtfully defined. However, the execution to date has not been timely due to lack of appropriate information, consensus building, and sufficient input from others."

These and other insights and information resulting from the campus readiness assessment were an important beginning for our project teams regarding the strengths of the campus and areas that needed improvement for an implementation to be successful. And while management consulting was not within our hedgehog concept, if a client needed some external assistance prior to the beginning of an implementation project, we had to be prepared to help.

Whether in or out of our hedgehog concept, we attempted to address any critical needs that surfaced during a large implementation project. This approach was consistent with our first priority of staying focused on the success of our clients. If we did not possess the right skills to address the client's need, we would find a third party to help, either as an independent contractor or as our subcontractor. Sometimes the best third party was a competitor, but that was acceptable if we could adequately address the client's need and ensure successful completion of our implementation project.

One of those subcontractors was Bill, a retired Brigadier General who was the former Superintendent of the United States Air Force Academy. Prior to assuming the role of Superintendent, he was the dean of the faculty at the Academy having earned a doctorate in applied mathematics from Brown University. A Vietnam veteran, he was an outstanding person of the highest character. As our subcontractor, he agreed to help us assess our client's computer operations and make some recommendations for improvements as a critical aspect of our implementation of their new ERP software. After a few months on the job, the general reviewed his preliminary findings and informed me that I probably was not going to like his recommendations because they might not be in our best interest. I asked him if his recommendations were in the best interest of the client, and he assured me that was in fact the case. I then told him to move forward with his recommendations and that we would be supportive because what is good for the client will be good for us. Although a bit surprised, he seemed relieved and appreciative of our approach to client service.

During our many years of providing software and services to higher education, our client list included some very interesting international institutions in such places as Australia, France, the Netherlands, Newfoundland, Puerto Rico, Saudi Arabia, South Africa, United Arab Emirates, and the United Kingdom. Although each of these projects was exciting, none was very profitable: we lacked local support and insight into the cultural differences of each of these countries. Based on this experience, we were certain that the international higher education market should be excluded from our hedgehog concept.

THE LONGEVITY OF A HEDGEHOG

Reflecting back on our hedgehog deliberations, I realized that I'd been a hedgehog most of my life. First surfacing when I was thirteen, I deliberately decided to focus on my passion--basketball. My hedgehog orientation continued during my business career as I attempted to make the most of my higher education experience and leadership skills rather than trying to compete with the many technical wizards that I encountered at IBM and IA. As an entrepreneur, I quickly determined that profit per client would serve both me and my investors well over the long haul, somewhat independent of corporate structure and job title. For example, let's take my involvement over time with the University System of Maryland (USM). In the mid 1980s while I was the senior vice president of IA, we won a hard-fought competition for a very large software and services opportunity with five of the USM campuses. About two decades later when I was in the PeopleSoft business, we once again competed for the opportunity to be the implementation partner for those same five USM campuses. They had just acquired the PeopleSoft software to replace what had then become their twenty-year old IA software.

Due primarily to our familiarity with their legacy systems and our recent PeopleSoft successes, we were selected as one of three finalists for this new USM business. At that time, John was our lead executive for all USM opportunities. Just prior to our orals presentation, John and I met with one of the key USM stakeholders. He immediately recognized me from our encounter twenty years ago. His first words to me were something like, "I remember you! You're the guy who negotiated our IA contract back in the 1980s. We still talk about the time you got up and walked to the back of the room and stared out the window immediately after our lawyer told you that IA would have to provide a performance bond as part of your software contract. We really wanted your software, and we began to panic when you went silent for fear that our performance bond requirement might be a deal killer." Although I clearly recalled the tension in the air at that point in our USM contract negotiations, I was surprised to learn about their near panic reaction to my several moments of silence as I walked over to the window. During our preparation for this negotiation session, we decided that we would provide a performance bond, but only if we believed that not doing so would kill the deal for us. Greg then went on to say how pleased they had been when I returned to the negotiation table and we resolved all contract issues, including no performance bond. He also expressed his appreciation for our support during the subsequent and very successful implementation of the IA software.

The presentation of our PeopleSoft implementation services at USM went quite well, especially during the questions and answers at the end of the three-hour session. They asked tough questions and we responded candidly. Several weeks later, they notified us that we were USM's preferred implementation partner. Once again, we began contract negotiations. This time, however, there was no performance bond requirement and no corresponding long moments of silence. Contracts were executed, and we began the multi-campus USM implementation project. During the next seven years, we entered into more than twenty additional contracts with USM institutions. During my thirty-three-year software and software services career, total profitable revenue from USM contracts exceeded $60,000,000. This surely is a testament to our focus on profit per client as our primary economic driver.

As you might imagine, we targeted all of the institutions that were still using the aging IA software, but so were most of our competitors—fiercely so! Although we won more than our share of the IA legacy system replacement work, we also experienced some very painful losses. Two that were particularly painful were Texas A&M University (TAMU) and Washington State University (WSU). While at IA, I was heavily involved with both the sales and delivery aspects of these two strong IA clients. I also took the lead on our PeopleSoft sales effort for both institutions, each of which conducted parallel procurement processes for software and implementation services.

TAMU selected us as a finalist and expressed optimism to us about our chances. We received positive feedback from our presentation to their selection committee and we felt certain that they were leaning our way. However, we also knew that at least one of the key players at TAMU was partial to the SCT software, Oracle's biggest competitor. In the end, they contracted with SCT for both the software and implementation services. I was crushed!

About five years later, WSU issued an RFP for PeopleSoft implementation services and hosting. Unfortunately, we had no foreknowledge that the RFP was going to be issued, and we had not spent time getting reacquainted with the client or its new leadership team. We prepared an extensive proposal that we thought would be very competitive, particularly because we could offer hosting services. We were very pleased when WSU selected us as a finalist. We began intense preparations for our two-day final orals presentation to their selection committee. Unfortunately, we had little insight into the needs and politics of this current situation and almost no remaining relationships from the IA days. The WSU selection team was very large and the selection process was difficult to understand. At the end of our presentation, I was exhausted. However, we felt that we were generally well received based on audience questions and even the informal comments they made to us during breaks at the vending machines. We did remain concerned, though, about certain aspects of the procurement process that were still unclear to us. When we were notified that our proposal was no longer under consideration, it came as a surprise and a big disappointment. I recalled the following Sun TZU quote: "What enables the wise sovereign and the good general to strike and conquer, and achieve things beyond the reach of ordinary men, is foreknowledge."[22] As we debriefed from the loss, we realized that we had not obtained sufficient foreknowledge and re-established relationships so that we could have better understood their issues and processes. Big, painful lesson!

WHAT WAS ON THE HORIZON?

With a high level of motivation, a good understanding of market opportunities, and a focused business strategy, we established the following aggressive long-term goals:

- Achieve steady profitability
- Grow revenue
- Grow market share
- Create the highest client satisfaction in the industry
- Create the highest employee satisfaction in the industry
- Be recognized as a market leader in our hedgehog concept
- Become the "trusted advisor" forever for each new name client

Our goals remained virtually unchanged throughout our twelve years of steady growth. We did in fact become a market-share leader for PeopleSoft implementation, hosting, and upgrade services for colleges and universities. During this same period, our growing business produced steady profitability, even as many of our competitors were forced to lower their consulting rates when the market began to view their services more as a commodity than as a specialty service.

PROOF OF PERFORMANCE

"Based on the experience we had with similar services from another provider, we had a clear set of criteria for the selection of our new provider. We were looking for a financially and legally stable vendor that had a proven methodology, a deep understanding of and experience with the applications, a strong track record of credentials and references for the same services, and is a proven Oracle partner. CedarCrestone successfully met all of these criteria."

Chief Information Officer
Multi-campus Public Research University

LESSONS LEARNED

- It's difficult to develop a hedgehog concept with a team attitude of "we can do everything."

- Begin with your passion; everything else will follow.

- You must be brutally honest to identify what you can potentially do better than anyone else.

- Keep client success the focus when you craft your hedgehog concept.

- Mergers and acquisitions aren't easy; but when blended just right, the result can be rewarding.

5. WHO'S IN THE WHISPERING FIEFDOM?

BORROWED WISDOM

> "If you know your enemy and know yourself, you need not fear the result of a hundred battles. If you know yourself but not the enemy, for every victory gained you will also suffer a defeat. If you know neither the enemy nor yourself, you will succumb in every battle."[23]
>
> Sun Tzu,
> Chinese Philosopher

GUIDING PRINCIPLE

> Do what is right. You can't go wrong.

At this early stage of our journey, we were determined to craft both short-term differentiation that would get us into the market and long-term protection to build market share. Warren Buffet's wisdom is particularly relevant to the approach that we used: "In business, I look for economic castles protected by unbreachable moats."[24] To create and monitor what I now refer to as our moat, we conducted the following three-step process (1) adapt to the uniqueness of the market, the fiefdom in which we would build and maintain our economic castle; (2) analyze the competition, and thereby know how best to defend our castle; and (3) determine our high value competitive advantages that would expand our protective moat. Armed with information, analysis, and insights, we synergistically developed a business plan to continuously expand our moat.

Our approach to understanding the higher education market was based upon our having worked in higher education institutions, and our continuous involvement in higher education through professional associations and events. Not unlike a faculty member's approach to staying current with his/her profession, we researched the higher education field through surveys, reviewed higher education publications, had contact with professional peers, and interacted with the higher education community with on-site visits and participation at professional conferences. We frequently made joint presentations and collaboratively wrote publications with our higher education clients. One of the key conferences that we always attended was EDUCAUSE. The concluding session of the conference was a "Current Issues Panel" comprised of the leading chief information officers of colleges and universities. They spoke to the current issues in information technology specifically within the higher education domain…we listened very carefully…for these represented the people in our fiefdom. Keynote speakers at this industry conference included notable individuals such as Bill Gates, whom Judie recalled as habitually adjusting his glasses on his nose throughout his presentation, and Steve Jobs, whom Judie accompanied when he did a dress rehearsal for his keynote address that entailed running down the aisle and enthusiastically jumping up on the stage…as if he were jumping over a moat. Gate's and Job's visions were an inspirational harbinger of the potential of technology to improve higher education.

Lyon's Pride

WHO TRIED TO BREACH OUR MOAT?

A number of companies that had been successful in other markets with their ERP services decided to enter the higher education market as the ERP bandwagon showed signs of gaining momentum within colleges and universities, largely triggered by the approaching year 2000 issue and aging legacy systems. We suspected these companies naively assumed there were universals across markets that would easily translate their success in one market to the higher education market. However, as described above, higher education regards itself as unique—and it is.

The basis for our differentiation strategy was our understanding of how higher education is distinct from other industries, and how we and our competition positioned our companies relative to the idiosyncrasies of the market. We knew that if the comparison of these two perspectives revealed gaps, there would be an opportunity for a differentiated market approach.

To craft our strategy, we had to "think like a client." Fortunately, we had a good basis for doing so. We routinely engaged in conversations with our clients, especially those who were also clients of at least one of our competitors. We also had conversations with former higher education colleagues. Our competitors' proposals and other marketing materials were useful sources, and conversations with our competitors, one of whom was our business partner, usually revealed some important insights.

Much information and dogma were gathered quickly from all these sources. We then compiled our findings into a competitor profile that could be compared to a profile of our market to indicate our differentiation opportunities. After that analysis, everything we did was influenced by those differentiation opportunities. Although this process was completed for each major competitor, our competitive advantages evolved over time as we expanded our moat by enlarging our capabilities and responding to changes in our competitive landscape.

Over the past thirty years, we had seen a variety of competitors in the higher education services industry. Most of these competitors could be categorized as either large, cross-industry companies, or small higher education boutique firms. Other than size, the primary differences in these two types of companies were in their corporate cultures and the percentage of their revenue that was attributable to higher education. This latter difference tended to correlate highly with the company's long-term commitment to higher education. We had seen several large companies come and go in higher education as industry economic conditions changed. Many of the boutique firms were acquired by larger companies. Often, they gave way to the pressure to conform to the parent company's cross-industry business practices and rules-based operating standards. As a result, their level of personal commitment to meet the specialized needs of colleges and universities became diluted by corporate compensation and recognition programs that were aligned with other, larger markets.

I have been involved with three higher education software companies that were acquired by large cross-industry corporations. All were pursuing a bigger share of the higher education market. In each of these, the acquiring company divested their acquired higher education business within three years of making the acquisition. For the large companies that entered our market without making an acquisition, the typical approach consisted of hiring a few respected figures in the industry to be the company's face and voice to higher education, winning a big contract in the upper end of the market, and bringing in the cross-industry consultants and recent college graduates to develop the contractual deliverables. The outcome? They failed to meet client expectations and quickly departed our market. About three years later new management would be in place, and the cycle would repeat.

The following graph in **Figure D** depicts the changes in the number of competitors by competitor type that we encountered during our journey. Tier A consisted of the large consulting companies, such as the Big 6, IBM, and PeopleSoft/Oracle Consulting. We were in Tier B along with other companies that focused primarily on software implementation. All of the niche players were in Tier C. Of course, over time the Big 6 consolidated into the Big 4 and many of the smaller Tier C companies were acquired by Tier A and Tier B companies.

Figure D: Changing Competitive Landscape
(Number of Competitors by Tier)

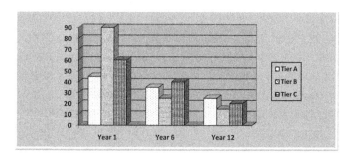

This graph could be titled "Only the Strong Survive." When we entered the PeopleSoft services market, profit margins were high and competition was keen. Although the number of competitors decreased over time as margins fell, one thing remained constant during our journey: at each stage of our growth, we encountered very strong competitors who always provided our prospects with solid alternatives to doing business with us. In retrospect, our strong will to win was a formidable defense against this constant and intense competition.

Was Our Moat Unbreachable?

To answer whether our moat was unassailable, I turn to four sources of borrowed wisdom that provide insight into our competitive advantages and disadvantages. The first is Buffet, whose metaphor of a castle and moat was particularly relevant to our competitive advantages. According to Buffet, the wider a business' moat, the more likely it is to stand the test of time.

To Buffet, the castle is the business and the moat is defined by the company's competitive advantages. He suggests that his managers continually increase the size of the moats around their castles. Buffet's rationale is that high profit margins attract companies to a new market opportunity. This in turn causes margins to fall due to increased competition. To counteract this phenomenon, Buffet buys companies with large moats, i.e., those that have durable competitive advantages.

My second source of relevant borrowed wisdom is Gladwell's book, Outliers: The Story of Success. Gladwell shares some thought-provoking observations on opportunity, timing, and preparedness that relate to our competitive advantages. On his website, Gladwell defines "outlier" as "…a scientific term to describe things or phenomena that lie outside normal experience."[25] In support of the notion that timing is critical to an outlier's success, Gladwell makes an interesting observation about highly successful people in the computer field. "If January 1975 was the dawn of the personal computer age, then who would be in the best position to take advantage of it?…note the birth dates of Bill Gates (1955) and Paul Allen (1953) at Microsoft, Steve Ballmer (1956) and Steve Jobs at Apple (1955), Eric Schmidt at Novell (1955), and Scott McNealy at Sun Microsystems (1954)."[26] According to Gladwell, "Barnsley argues that these kinds of skewed age distributions exist whenever three things happen: selection, streaming, and differentiated experience. If you make a decision about who is good and who is not good at an early age, if you provide the 'talented' with a superior experience, then you're going to end up giving a huge advantage to that small group of people born closest to the cutoff date."[27]

Like the ultra-successful outliers discussed by Gladwell, our natural selection occurred because most of us were born at the right time to take advantage of the market opportunity that surfaced in the late 1990s. Our streaming resulted from the coaching, mentoring, and practical experience that resulted from being involved with the pioneers of the higher education software business in the 1970s and early 1980s. The mission-ary work in which we were intensely involved paved the way for the pack-aged software market. More than twenty former staff from IA founded or co-founded new software service companies following the acquisition of IA in 1980 by Westinghouse. Our differentiated IA experience helped make our start-up, ISEDU, well-positioned to take advantage of a big market opportunity and eventually establish ourselves as a market leader.

My third source of borrowed wisdom is Daniel Levitin, a neurologist, who has conducted many studies related to opportunity preparedness. Levitin says, "The emerging picture from such studies is that ten thou-sand hours of practice is required to achieve the level of mastery asso-ciated with being a world-class expert—in anything in study after study of composers, basketball players, fiction writers, ice skaters, master criminals, and what have you, this number comes up again and again. Ten thousand hours is the equivalent to roughly three hours per day, or twenty hours per week, of practice over ten years. Of course, this doesn't address why some people don't seem to get anywhere when they practice, and why some people get more out of their practice than others. But no one has yet found a case in which true world-class ex-pertise was accomplished in less time. It seems it takes the brain this long to assimilate all that it needs to know to achieve true mastery."[28] Certainly this amount of practice requires great passion.

Most of our client whisperers invested much more than ten thousand hours developing their expertise prior to pursuing our market oppor-tunity. At the start of our journey, our typical consultant had at least fifteen years of experience in or related to higher education. Using an average annual investment of two thousand hours, ten years equates to twenty thousand hours. We felt that most of our competitors had not yet invested the obligatory ten thousand hours in the higher education software services market.

My fourth source of borrowed wisdom is Ron Zemke. In 1989, my last year as senior vice president of IA, Zemke published a book entitled, *The Service Edge: 101 Companies that Profit from Customer Care* (Copyright 1989. By permission of The Penguin Group). Zemke was a noted business consultant, who had established the concept of cus-tomer service as a high priority for leading companies. In his book, the first client service book that I had ever read, he tells the "definitive inside story of how America's top service companies and organizations create, manage, and maintain their edge."[29] At that time, he was one of the first people to introduce the concept that improving service quality could translate into a better bottom line. "The obvious conclusion is that those organizations willing to commit to superior customer service profit on the bottom line."[30]

My thirteen years with IA was an important learning experience; but after reading Zemke's book, I realized that there was still much to learn about client service, especially about the difference between a product company and a service company. His research points out that, "To manage service effectively, especially if you are coming to the task from a product background, you must first understand the unique characteristics of a service, the things that distinguish it from a product."[31]

One of Zemke's 101 top service companies in 1989 was American Management Systems (AMS), about which he said, "Through the 1970s they evolved from a strictly consulting-oriented firm into a service-oriented provider of custom software systems and the expert integration of those systems into an organization's day-to-day business."[32] AMS focused on "five carefully targeted industries,"[33] including higher education. The AMS story was inspirational for those of us who were also focused on client service.

Early on, we were fortunate to have several talented, experienced players come to us from AMS. Two of them, John and Elizabeth, were members of our leadership team. Their superior understanding of the service methods and techniques that helped AMS succeed in the higher education market were valuable assets as we crafted our strategies and differentiated our company from most of our competition. They also provided important leadership in sales and delivery of our services and in the development of our concept of client whispering.

THE MAKE-UP OF OUR MOAT

Based upon the analysis of our competition—from a higher education market perspective—we narrowed our competitive advantages into seven that we deemed would most differentiate us from our competition.

Advantage 1: Student Information Systems Experience. Many of us were involved with the emergence of packaged higher education software in the 1970s and 1980s. During those years, the term "packaged" was a misnomer. In the 1970s, "packaged" meant reusable tools to develop customized solutions for each individual client. In the 1980s, our software actually became much more packaged. However, we had to learn how to design, document, and deliver generalized software that was flexible enough to meet the majority of each client's needs without extensive customization. Our software maturation process was painful as we learned how to deliver "packaged software" that met client expectations.

When we entered the PeopleSoft business, we knew that the initial software releases would lack maturity, and there would be many software deficiencies to address during implementation. Our painful experiences in the 1970s and 1980s made us better prepared than many of our competitors, who just kept throwing more people at their myriad implementation problems. In many cases their approach exacerbated the problem, and added considerable cost to the implementation.

In the beginning, our student system experience was our most significant competitive advantage. We leveraged it for all it was worth. Our approach to implementing a student system was to begin by reviewing our client's unique processes. We quickly understood these because of our contextual knowledge of student administration business processes. From the outset, we involved their business process experts in designing and configuring "their system," as we jointly made a multitude of decisions that would give them both structure and flexibility to accommodate their decentralized/centralized governance structure.

The majority of our competitors had little understanding of the significant differences between student information systems and the back-office systems that support finance and human resources. Our competitors typically began the implementation process by setting up tables, determining values, configuring the system, all without much user input. Then, when they trained the users and handed the system over to them, they expected the client to be successful, even though the users hadn't been an integral part of the design and configuration process.

Advantage 2: Higher Education Experience. Our team spoke the "parlance" of higher education, didn't refer to their titles, and had first-hand experience working in colleges and universities as faculty members, staff, and administrators. We also used sales support personnel who had significant experience in similar institutions. We always shunned "boilerplate" language and tailored our proposals to each prospect's perception of their unique issues and needs. We used client testimonials and references from similar institutions and projects. On several occasions, we were able to "write our way" into a new opportunity by demonstrating our higher education insight with the content, style and vocabulary of our proposals.

We recognized the dynamics of decentralized governance, the reality of representational decision-making processes, and the influence of a functionally driven ERP decision-making process. We used a stakeholder-centered, issues/discovery approach that revealed issues such as the political dynamics, financial constraints, and staffing concerns. Once we identified and confirmed these issues with the stakeholders, we were able to give them examples of projects and institutions where we had dealt with similar issues and solved similar problems. As we met with others throughout the institution, we also identified the "gate keepers" whose approval was needed if we were to proceed. We knew that ERP projects are more about people than technology, and that for a project to be successful there must be campus-wide buy-in and support. This was especially true with large, complex colleges and universities.

When we would read our competitors' proposals, we used to smile when they referred to a prospective client as a "university" when, in fact, it was a community college. We knew that the client would immediately notice that error and conclude that the company was inexperienced in higher education. In referring to personnel, commonly our competitors would use the term "employee" (a corporate term from a higher education perspective) rather than referring to personnel as faculty members, staff, or administrators. Such nuances carried the subtle message that the company was unfamiliar with, and inexperienced in higher education.

In colleges and universities many critical decisions, or at least strong recommendations, are made by committees comprised of members who are representative of the various organizational units and personnel domains throughout the institution. Lacking this understanding, many of our competitors used an executive-oriented sales and marketing approach, in which they assumed that, if they positively influenced the president and executive sponsor, they were well-positioned to win the business. While our competitors likely understood executive issues, we knew that relying on only that source of information yields a distorted and incomplete picture of the issues. Most traditional sales managers ask their salespeople, "Have you talked with the C-level people?" Our sales managers asked, "Have you talked with all of the stakeholders?"

We were careful in our proposals and marketing materials to make sure that we used language and examples that were appropriate to each institutional type. Our approach was particularly advantageous during the early years of our success story. Once we proved that we had successfully completed comparable projects for peer institutions, our prospects and clients did begin to view us a 'trusted advisor," even though we lacked the extensive PeopleSoft experience of many of our competitors. They realized that while we were not "in" higher education, we were "of" higher education—and that made all the difference.

Advantage 3: Effective Staffing Model. We hired consultants with extensive experience in higher education, who understood the unique nature of higher education business processes. Our staffing model was structured to use as many of our own consultants as possible, although from time to time we did use independent contractors for some specialized consulting needs. Because our culture was aligned with higher education, our clients did not have to train us in the business of higher education!

Our competitors' project staffing typically included the use of smart, but junior, consultants with little or no higher education experience. Despite the large size of most of the PeopleSoft implementation partners, many of our competitors were not staffed to provide all of the consulting services required by a large PeopleSoft software project. Their staffing models were structured to use their employees for the higher level project roles and to use subcontractors or independent consultants for many of the other project roles. Their reliance on subcontractors minimized their ability to generate a common culture aligned with higher education.

Advantage 4: Lower Cost Structure. Because we knew that in the culture of higher education, executives were generally unaccustomed to the high hourly rates typical of other markets, we maintained a lower cost structure than most of our competitors. We understood the protracted sales cycle, and viewed it as an opportunity to conduct stakeholder analyses to determine client issues. We provided complimentary executive sponsorship and account management services delivered by professionals with extensive higher education experience. Using an integrated approach, we embedded change-management into our methods as we involved stakeholders in designing and implementing change. For the many clients who had serious concerns about the significant risk of undertaking an ERP project, we shared the risk by making payments dependent upon achievement of critical go-live milestones, such as the generation of financial aid award letters and 24X7 course registration. Although never wanting to be the low bidder, we could comfortably position ourselves under the high cost model of most of our larger competitors.

Some of our competitors were large, hierarchical companies with complex approval processes that were focused on sales opportunities that were likely to close within the next ninety days. Most used cost-plus pricing that resulted in high hourly rates, especially for mandatory executive consultant participation in each project. Some of our competitors viewed change management as a separate expense for which they brought in change management experts. They also usually required that each project include a high-priced executive sponsor or account manager. We took a completely different approach.

Advantage 5: Nimble and Responsive. Fortunately, we understood the importance of reacting quickly when the call to action came. With our non-hierarchical, nimble organization, we reacted quickly during all phases of sales and delivery. Our rapid decision-making process allowed us to be more responsive to requests for information from clients and prospective clients than was typically the case with our competitors, who frequently requested deadline extensions. We were able to expedite the entire contract review and approval process because of our flat organizational structure—and we were fortunate to have a corporate lawyer who always responded immediately.

I have noted previously that the higher education decision-making process is slow; however, once they have made a decision, they want action immediately. Most of our competitors were slow and lumbering in their response, a result of their bureaucratic, hierarchical structures in which decision-making authority was closely held. Their legal review and approval processes took weeks, not days—or so our clients told us.

Advantage 6: Process-centric Approach. Our methodology was based on understanding and redesigning the business processes across the student life cycle. We first sought to gain an understanding by working with the subject matter experts who best knew the business processes within their domain. We did encounter an expectation from the client that project teams would be structured according to software modules rather than business processes. They had been conditioned to think that way by software vendors. While we accommodated this preference, we did a lot of "cross-module" integration based upon the life cycle of the business processes.

Our competitors typically staffed projects with cross-industry consultants using a common method across industries focused primarily on contractual deliverables. Their projects were structured according to software modules, not business processes. Many business processes in higher education, especially student administration ones, cross multiple organizational units. For example, a student may have to go to the registrar's office to solve an issue related to his/her registration, locate the financial aid office to ask why he/she hasn't received financial aid yet, find the Bursar's office to make a tuition payment, and track down a faculty advisor who needs to make an exception and let him/her into a required pre-requisite course. From the student's perspective, each of these actions is a part of a single process of getting into class. Yet, staff and faculty members who perform some segment of this process can be in separate organizational units with differing processes and procedures and sometimes even policies. We referred to this condition as a silo mentality, and it certainly impeded business process innovation and improvement.

Advantage 7: Successful Track Record. When the PeopleSoft student information system was released to the market, there was considerable skepticism about this "new technology" (client server architecture). The legacy systems were functionally very robust, but operated on an aging technological platform. Some of the PeopleSoft beta sites for the student information system were not fully implemented. There was an early disastrous implementation of the system that was featured the Chronicle of Higher Education, a trade publication read by most higher education executives, administrators and faculty. Thus, the market generally was timid about proceeding. We were the first company to successfully implement the full suite of PeopleSoft administrative systems in higher education, doing so within an un-heard of timeframe—eighteen months. We proved that it worked.

Some of our competition had mixed client outcomes, resulting from a combination of immature software and a lack of consultants with higher education experience. As we developed a positive project track record, with client testimonials to substantiate our ability to deliver on-time and within budget, we increasingly found that we were being selected as an implementation partner, as well as being called in to "finish" what the competition couldn't complete.

To validate our successful track record, we featured client testimonials on our booth display at professional conferences and the PeopleSoft user group meetings. It was not uncommon for some of our clients to come up to us and say, "Why isn't my testimonial up there?" We had so many that it was difficult to limit the number to what could be accommodated on our booth display. That was a nice problem to have!

We knew that we had to focus on those competitive advantages that were of high value to the higher education market. These advantages could be thought of as factors that would expand the breadth of our moat to protect our soon-to-be constructed business castle. These advantages became the basis for the differentiation strategies that helped us overcome our primary competitive disadvantages, including small size, lack of PeopleSoft experience, minimal brand recognition, and the presence of Oracle as a competitor.

"Oracle as a competitor" refers to the competitive disadvantage we encountered when competing against Oracle Consulting for services work. Some prospective clients perceived an advantage to "having one throat to choke," by selecting the software vendor as their implemen-tation partner. This was not a big issue at the beginning of our jour-ney; the demand for PeopleSoft services exceeded supply, and there was plenty of work for all qualified consulting firms. Also at that time, PeopleSoft/Oracle was much more focused on the higher margins of software sales than the lower margins of professional services. Later in our journey, as software sales began to go flat, Oracle Consulting be-gan to leverage their competitive advantage much more aggressively by promoting their own in-house professional services offerings, which threatened to reduce the size of our moat.

OUR EXPANDING MOAT

At any time during our journey, the size of our protective moat was determined by the strength of our competitive advantages as compared to the negative impact of our competitive disadvantages. In **Figure E** below, and the accompanying table, I depict the changes in the size of our moat by comparing the competitive advantages and disadvantages of year one compared to year twelve. In the table, I list our moat expanders (competitive advantages) and moat contractors (competitive disadvantages) and depict their impact with arrows either up (expanding influence) or down (contracting influence). I state "little change" for those factors that did not impact a change in the size of our moat during this time period. As the illustration depicts, our student system experience, positive track record, and hosting capability were the most influential competitive advantages that expanded our moat. Although we did not have hosting capability in the early years, once we did offer these services, our moat greatly expanded.

Figure E: Relative Moat Size – Year 1 Compared to 12

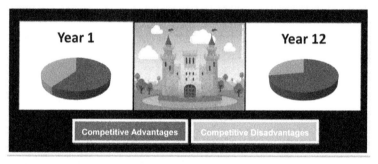

MOAT EXPANDERS	12-YEAR TREND	MOAT CONTRACTORS	12-YEAR TREND
Student System Experience	⬆	Lack of PeopleSoft Experience	⬇
Higher Education Experience	Little Change	Small Company Size	⬇
Staffing Model	Little Change	Minimal Brand Recognition	⬇
Low Cost Structure	Little Change	Oracle as a Competitor	⬆
Nimble and Responsive	Little Change		
Track Record	⬆		
Hosting Capability	⬆		

PROOF OF PERFORMANCE

"The CedarCrestone team is made up of higher education veterans who know PeopleSoft. They understand the day-to-day business of managing a college or university, which in turn helps them come up with solid, workable systems solutions with a PeopleSoft implementation. For our engagement, they gave us what we were looking for - a fair and objective evaluation of PeopleSoft functionality. Their knowledge, expertise and professionalism were superb. They brought such a great level of experience to the effort, and are a great addition to any PeopleSoft implementation."

Director of Administrative Computing
Research University within a Multi-campus System

LESSONS LEARNED

- Mind your moat! Your foes are watching.
- Strong competition strengthens your muscles.
- To take advantage of market gaps, be willing to shift your paradigm…and do it quickly.
- Because they are dynamic, competitive advantages have to be leveraged quickly and adeptly.
- It's the expansion of your moat that determines sustainability.

6. Was it Time to Attack?

Borrowed Wisdom

> "Good ideas are more often the stringing together of experiences, observations, and thoughts in a way that no one has done before."[34]
>
> Bill Russell,
> Eleven-time NBA Champion

Guiding Principle

> Be willing to be different. It makes a difference.

To protect our business castle, we created personnel, marketing, sales, pricing, and delivery strategies. The manifestation of our strategies in action evolved as we leveraged our success and learned from our mistakes. We quickly learned the difference between a "hold your ground" strategy versus one that "attacks the market." And we liked attacking the market a whole lot better than holding our ground.

Personnel Strategies

Our personnel strategies were developed to support our market leadership goal, to leverage our very deep experience and understanding of the higher education market, to attack the primary weaknesses of our competitors, and to focus on our hedgehog concept. From the outset, our leadership team continually focused on our personnel strategies. We threaded these through all of our other strategies, both formally and informally. As our business evolved we tested these strategies, and found they stood up well despite changes in our ownership, market, and competitive landscape.

Initially, our most important personnel strategy was to establish an attractive work environment for higher education professionals. To help off-set our difficult travel requirement, we knew we had to create a high-trust work environment supported by principled leadership and clear expectations. The following quote from the *Great Place to Work Institute* supports this premise: "Our approach is based on the major findings of twenty years of research—that trust between managers and employees is the primary defining characteristic of the very best workplaces."[35] High-trust relationships also helped to reduce the stress that can be caused by aggressive implementation deadlines.

Our second personnel strategy was to be prime contractor. There were several reasons that we decided to do so. First, being a successful prime contractor would significantly enhance our chances of earning a trusted advisor relationship with our clients. Second, it was the only way to fully leverage our higher education credentials and satisfy our passion for serving the higher education industry. Third, and perhaps most importantly, we knew that it would help us attract the best talent in the industry. We often heard one of our consultants praise their colleagues and talk about how our great people made our company an enjoyable and challenging place to work.

Being creative when it came to selecting people and staffing projects was at the core of our third most important personnel strategy. Edward de Bono, physician, author, inventor and consultant, introduced us to the concept of lateral thinking and thinking creatively by "breaking out of established patterns in order to look at things in different ways."[36] For me, this meant being willing to challenge conventional wisdom and think about things a little differently. Had we not been able to do so, we would have been just another subcontractor in the PeopleSoft consulting world.

Judie was one of our more creative leadership team members. I first became aware of her ability to look at things differently when she was vice president for business development at IA in the late 80's. Fresh out of higher education, she was making her first sales meeting presentation. Judie's futuristic presentation to the sales force included concepts and illustrations that none of us had ever envisioned. For example, she showed a slide of a university president wearing special glasses that allowed him to bring up a display of his management information. She also showed a slide and talked about a holographic version of the president walking up and down stairs in the bar chart that depicted enrollment trends. These two slides and others with a similar futuristic orientation were Judie's introduction of the new product and services for an Executive Information System for higher education, which was a product offering designed to convert data from the IA administrative software into meaningful information for higher education executives.

There were two influential factors that interfered with our execution of personnel strategies: the travel requirement and the stress that accompanied meeting critical deadlines. The most difficult challenge in our recruiting process was the requirement of a heavy travel schedule. The typical consultant workweek consisted of four ten-hour days at the client's location, typically Monday through Thursday. Weekly departure and return times varied, depending on proximity to the client, but it was not uncommon for a consultant to leave home Sunday afternoon and return late Thursday evening. Of course, that schedule assumed there were no travel delays or mishaps…and there always were plenty of those. It was not unusual for our consultants to stay over the weekend at the client site when it was necessary to support a critical go-live milestone. Compared to the life of a typical college or university administrator, consulting was a much different lifestyle that impacted not only the consultants, but also their families. This lifestyle change was exacerbated by the stress of working with aggressive deadlines and the severe consequences of project delays. These factors could certainly put a chink in our armor.

Marketing Strategies

Promoting the success of our clients was our number one sales and marketing strategy. One of the most important ways in which we could execute this strategy was through case studies. As our client list grew, so did the number of client case studies illustrating the success of our clients. We were very careful to not promote a new client until there was a success story to tell. Occasionally, this would frustrate our corporate marketing people and business partners, who were trained to promote new sales wins or new delivery capabilities without the benefit of a real client success story. However, these success stories were the proof of our capabilities: we knew that a peer-to-peer reference approach was the most valuable marketing campaign that we could ever have in our kind of market. We posted the case studies on our website by institutional type. For example, someone from a research university could go directly to the research university case studies. This website structure was another subtle way in which we illustrated that we understood the importance of peer institutions and references.

Client success in the software implementation business takes patience. Market leadership takes even more patience. Although we had some significant competitive advantages that allowed us to address some critical market gaps, it still took us the better part of a decade to emerge as one of the market leaders. The good news was that there was plenty of time for our client whisperers to engender trusting relationships that fueled a variety of client success stories, including many testimonials that reinforced our differentiated approach. We had testimonials, authorized by our clients, that explained the value of our approach from the client's perspective, which is always much more powerful than a glossy brochure containing our self-proclaimed corporate capabilities. Client feedback, including testimonials, provided both useful constructive criticism to help us with our faster, cheaper, better quest, and validation of our consulting efficacy.

Our proposals were written by very skilled people, some with doctorate degrees, who knew how to appeal to the diverse higher education audiences. From the feedback that we received, prospective clients viewed our proposals as responsive to their needs, and as being clearly written by experienced higher education professionals. In the early years, when our company was a virtual unknown in the market place, we often were selected as a finalist based solely on the quality and responsiveness of our proposal.

Because each of our implementation projects was unique, the value of creativity was high when developing proposals, presentations, and implementation strategies for these unique projects. Replicable, boilerplate verbiage had little value. However, many of the implementation activities that occur during a project were much more routine, which allowed us to benefit from those replicable tools and methods that could be deployed in an efficient manner from project-to-project. By design, we had no canned marketing brochures or corporate capability brochures. Our early clients told us that the contrast between our custom materials, which focused on the needs and concerns of our potential customers, were dramatically different from the high quality, but corporate focus, of our competitors' marketing materials.

I note that our ability to write creative, responsive proposals was often limited by the requirements set forth in the RFPs. On numerous occasions, we longed for the latitude to write what we thought would be most helpful to prospective clients in their decision-making processes rather than respond to the numerous less important, requirements set forth in the RFP. We regretted that many institutions issued requests that would not result in proposals that would provide them with the critical information they needed to select the vendor who could best provide what the client most needed to succeed.

There were three factors that adversely impacted our ability to execute these marketing strategies: corporate marketing alignment, appropriateness of marketing materials, and low cost model. Generally these factors were subtle, although over time some became more overt. Given the expertise that is present in higher education, we tried to be as appropriate and accurate as possible in all of our marketing materials, and respectful when interacting with the experts. However, in one instance in which we were using our generic corporate marketing template, we found out that we weren't as accurate as we thought we were. Here's what happened. During the time when our company was named Cedar Consulting, we made a presentation to an evaluation team for a public university, using our company slide template which had a logo with tree rings in the upper right hand corner to depict a cedar tree. To our surprise, during our presentation one of their selection team members abruptly interrupted us and said, "That's not a cedar tree!" He was a faculty member in the College of Forestry…and he knew our logo was not of cedar tree rings. No detail is too small to be noticed by an expert in the field!

Once we became part of cross-industry companies, we had to address how best to align our marketing strategies with those of corporate marketing. There were occasions when some corporate strategies were more appropriate to the commercial and public sector markets than to higher education. In these situations, we had to determine whether to use the cross-industry marketing programs, or craft our own program with the accompanying effort and expense. In those instances in which we felt strongly that we needed to develop and execute our own program, our corporate marketing staff lent what assistance they could, given they had to put most of their efforts and resources into the marketing programs that could be leveraged across multiple industries. However, as they came to know and understand our marketing approach to higher education, there were fewer times that we had to craft a marketing program specific to higher education.

SALES STRATEGIES

Our sales strategies were highly effective in expanding our moat. Most were based on the *solution selling* method offered by Bosworth (Solution Selling by Michael Bosworth. Copyright 1995. By permission of McGraw-Hill Companies). It was at this early stage of making contact with potential clients that we tried to build the foundation for a trusting relationship, even though we recognized the higher education audience felt a strong general distrust of vendors. We knew that if we could listen to and understand their issues at this stage, trust would develop. Five of our sales strategies are listed below, beginning with the all-important one of trust.

- Focus on developing trusting relationships.

- Fill the voids created by our competitor's weaknesses.

- Promote the success of similar clients with similar needs.

- Focus and customize all sales collateral on the needs and issues of each prospective client.

- Leverage existing industry relationships.

There were several influential factors that expanded our moat in the sales domain: the right salespeople, an attitude that everyone is a salesperson in our company, and trusting relationships. All of the salespeople we hired shared the common traits of being genuinely nice people of high integrity, and were comfortable with the culture of higher education. Prospects tended to like them, and many times they acted as our inside sponsors because they wanted us to win. The most effective salespeople were skilled at establishing trusting relationships as the foundation for the successful execution of our differentiation strategies. Their strengths included asking great questions, empathetic listening, and patience in dealing with the protracted sales cycles of our market. In support of our strategy of being the most responsive vendor, their qualities included common courtesies such as being on time for all meetings and conference calls.

Our salespeople were focused 100 percent on sales, especially with new potential customers. They also got help from just about everyone else in our company. We liked to think that we actually had about five hundred salespeople, some with more sales activity than others. Our account managers and executives spent considerable time supporting sales to both existing clients and new name possibilities. Many of our consultants were involved with sales support activities, including contributions to proposal development, sales calls, and need-development for add-on contracts with existing clients. Client whispering was required for all of these activities, irrespective of title and primary role within our organization.

All of our large deals required a team selling approach. These ad hoc sales teams were configured to align with the needs and issues that appeared to be most important to each individual prospect. Typically, these sales teams included one or more consultants whom we had proposed to play significant leadership roles in the prospect's project. Many times these people made the difference between winning and losing a big contract. It was always a good sign near the end of the buying process when a prospect asked, *"If we select you as our implementation partner, will so-and-so be assigned to our project?"*

The person who helps their prospects discuss and understand what it is they need as part of the initial buying process will be regarded as helpful; if, during that experience, they also demonstrate that they care about the buyer's problems, they have a solid foundation for building a trusting relationship. In his book *The 7 Habits of Highly Effective People* (Copyright 1989. By permission of Fireside Press) Stephen R. Covey says, "If you want to interact effectively with me, to influence me, you first need to understand me."[37] This is particularly true when you're the salesperson.

Covey then explains the key to developing a trusting relationship. "The real key to your influence with me is your example, your actual conduct. Your example flows naturally out of your character, or the kind of person you truly are—not what others say you are or what you may want me to think you are. It is evident in how I actually experience you... But unless I open up to you, unless you understand me and my unique situation, and feelings, you won't know how to advise or counsel me."[38]

PRICING STRATEGIES

In creating our pricing strategies, we considered what many of our friends in the higher education community were saying about the pricing-related issues that they were encountering with some of our early competitors. As we considered our pricing strategies, we wanted to ensure that we could avoid those issues, which included the following "pain" statements. They were tired of having to pay their consultants high hourly

rates while they taught the consultants the business of higher education. Although the original cost estimates of our competitors appeared
reasonable, the add-on change orders were causing significant cost
overruns and project delays (i.e., "low ball pricing). This concern was
reinforced by the EDUCAUSE Center for Applied Research (ECAR) finding that "33 % of all ERP implementations go over budget."[39] Although
prospective clients were impressed with the competitor's sales support
team of consultants, the majority of consulting services were being delivered by less experienced consultants (i.e., "bait and switch").

We continually studied the Gartner Publications, in which they identified the following "cautions" about some of our competitors:

- "...clients sometimes cite limits in the ability of the company to
  resource effectively in an engagement..."

- "...investments in accelerators and industry templates have
  been substantial; however, traction with clients has not yet been
  proved, and examples of significant reductions in the time to
  market of solutions are limited."

- "...client cites cost structures, turnover and higher price points
  as issues."

- "...consulting clients sometimes cite inflexibility with regard to
  contracting and pricing for ERP services."

- "...is limited in business consulting and organizational change
  management offerings required of transformational ERP
  engagements."

- "...clients and prospects sometimes cite challenges evaluating
  a proposal response, as the scope of the proposal may be
  broader than requested or the pricing may be unfamiliar."

- "...focuses on 'out-of-the-box implementations' and clients
  sometimes cite lack of process and industry understanding as a
  challenge in an engagement."[40]

Our resulting pricing strategies were based upon the following approaches: shared risks, (about which I will speak in greater detail in a
later chapter); the principle of reasonableness; and high value services.
We experienced three influential factors that made it difficult to execute
our pricing strategies: internal risk management; consultant resistance;
and low bidding mentality.

Our aggressive approach to fixed-fee pricing was met with some resistance each time the company changed CEOs, which occurred five times during our journey. Each new CEO had a significantly different management style, and expressed concern about our practice of not including a "risk premium" in our fixed-fee calculations. The primary cause of this concern was that each of these CEOs previously had at least one bad experience resulting from an unprofitable fixed-fee that was tied explicitly to contractual deliverables. However, once we explained that all of our fixed-fee projects had been completed successfully and profitably, the CEO's concern began to subside. The concern virtually disappeared once the new CEO understood that our approach was both fixed-fee and fixed term and not tied to contractual deliverables, other than meeting go-live milestones. The only contractual risk of not meeting the go-live milestones was in the event that we were the sole cause of the missed go-live, which never happened.

Occasionally, we would get some pushback from our consultants, who were concerned that our staffing plan and fixed-fee timeline (i.e., fixed term) were unrealistic and would cause consultant burnout. This response created an opportunity for us to reinforce our commitment to client success, which included adding consultants to our project team as was required to achieve client success. Periodically augmenting our core consulting team with additional staffing was necessary with almost all of our large, complex projects. We were able to make these periodic staff augmentations without significantly eroding our profitability. However, there also were times when our consultants had to work long hours as critical go-live milestones were approaching. When this occurred, we attempted to compensate the consultants with time off at less critical times, with performance compensation, and with high praise for all client successes that resulted from the extraordinary effort from our consulting teams.

Our consistent recognition of each client's success was a significant part of our strategy. Each time we celebrated a new client success story, we gave the credit to the consulting team that produced the desired results, and identified each member of that team. We believed that this recognition was like additional performance compensation for our consultants. According to speaker, writer, and consultant, Peter de Jager, "Think of credit as a coin of immense value, people will do almost anything to get it, so...if we want to get things done, and we're willing to give up credit, then we can 'achieve' the very best of everyone around us. We do it by giving credit of achievement away."[41] I attempted to begin our celebrations with a focus on the accomplishment and then slowly transition the celebration to a focus on the next big opportunity.

Low bidding by one or more of our competitors sometimes led to tough price negotiations, and occasionally we lost a sale due to price. We always attempted to address these pricing concerns by highlighting the risk-mitigation value of hiring consultants who had a consistent track record of completing similar projects on time and within budget. Usually, we could reach a win/win agreement that included some price reduction in exchange for the client's commitment to shore-up a project risk issue, such as agreeing to a well-defined decision-making process for resolving issues during the project.

During the early years of our journey, we encountered a credibility issue with a very large public research university that had previously used several of our large competitors to implement their human resource and financial management software. When I suggested that they should budget about $20 million for their upcoming implementation of their student information system, the CIO quickly responded "That won't get it done at this institution. Based on our previous experience, we know that it can't be done for less than $40 million." Even after I provided cost information from some of our large, public research university clients, he was not convinced. He just seemed to believe that we did not understand how large and complex they were. They viewed anything but a high bid as unrealistic for their institution.

Fortunately, there were a number of factors that facilitated successful execution of our pricing strategies: a high price umbrella, our successful track record, trust, and risk-sharing approach. During most of our twelve-year story, we worked under the price umbrella of the large consulting companies. We were very seldom the high or low bidder on an opportunity. However, in slow economic times our market became much more price sensitive, and we had to adjust to the aggressive pricing of our competition.

By far the most consistent factor supporting our pricing strategies was our track record of successful projects supported by our positive client references and testimonials. Many times these references translated into a discussion with a prospect about which consultants would be assigned to the project. It was not uncommon for a prospect to insist on getting the same consultants who had worked on comparable projects for peer institutions—at least that was the case until they actually got to know our proposed client whisperer. At that point, the consultant's resume took a back seat to the consultant's whispering skills.

Given that the biggest cost factor in an implementation project is how many people are assigned for how long a period, we knew that we had to find ways to do it in as short a time period as possible. Most vendors tried to do the faster part by using technology tools, pre-packaged deliverables, and prescribed methods. We realized early on that while these "boilerplate" approaches had merit, the most important factor in delivering our solutions faster was trust. The greater the level of trust with our clients, the more harmoniously our teams worked together to achieve key milestones on time, the more creative our solutions were in overcoming challenges that may have impeded our progress, and the more expeditiously we worked through issues that could have impacted reaching that on-time project objective.

Our willingness to craft creative risk sharing vehicles was a key factor in winning some of our largest and most complex projects. This approach was especially true during the first half of our journey, when our track record was still a bit thin. In a subsequent chapter I discuss risk sharing in greater detail, and explain the risk partnerships that we developed with our clients.

SERVICE DELIVERY STRATEGIES

Our service delivery strategies were some of our most important differentiating features. As executed, they were our "face to the client," and translated the brand promise of our proposals and presentations into the reality of the work performed by our client whisperers. Here is where "integrity walked. There were two strategy decelerators that negatively impacted our strategy to deliver services: protracted issue resolution and staff turnover.

The decentralized nature of higher education institutions and their collaborative culture militated against rapid decision-making. During a software implementation, many issues surfaced that, if left unresolved, made it difficult to stay on schedule. At the beginning of a project, we attempted to get the client to commit to a well defined issues resolution process with predefined decision criteria. We tried to identify an executive sponsor who was willing to make decisions and who was respected by the campus community.

Most large implementation projects consume at least 24 months. It is not uncommon to experience unplanned turnover of project staff, both client staff and consultants during that time. The causes of this turnover were many, including illness, burnout, retirement, promotions, call to military duty, and poor performance. Unfortunately, when key persons depart from a project, they take with them much knowledge and insight that cannot be immediately replaced. If that departure occurs just prior to a critical go-live date, it can significantly increase the risk of production issues arising. On these occasions, the higher education experience of our consultants came in very handy as we helped the client to fill the voids created by departing staff and administrators. Several times during our journey, we had to assign a consultant to temporarily fill a client vacancy and take managerial responsibility for the client's operational unit. For one client, we actually ran their financial aid office for an extended period of time. This type of work was outside of our hedgehog concept, but it was in keeping with our long-term goal of becoming a trusted advisor.

There were two very important service delivery expanders: achieving both relationships and results and insulating project teams from internal distractions. At the time of our entry into the PeopleSoft services market, we took a much different approach to service than was prevalent at the time. The almost immediate success of our sales strategies created some high expectations among our initial clients. At a minimum, we needed to avoid the delivery issues experienced by some of our competitors, as mentioned earlier in this chapter. To have any chance of reaching our long-term goals, we felt compelled to go "above and beyond," especially if we were to achieve our long-term goal of the "highest client satisfaction in the industry." To that end, we started with our guiding principle of "focusing on enhancing relationships and achieving desired results." The solid relationships developed during our solution selling sales process, especially during the need development phase, gave us a running start.

The best way to leverage and enhance those relationships and get started on achieving results was to "seek first to understand." To do so, we took a deep dive into the client's desired results, doing so in a collaborative manner that built positive working relationships. Although desired results were discussed during the sales cycle, we found that deep dives are much more productive once a contract has been signed, and we moved from relationship development to partnership development -- with the objective of earning the status of "trusted advisor."

When my son Glenn's marriage to his fiancée Heather was approaching, I wrote a poem for the rehearsal dinner that contained the following line: *"Make Heather happy, and you'll be happy too."* We shared this philosophy with our consultants, telling them that if they kept their client happy—by making the client successful—they too would be happy.

Our philosophy appeared to be much different than the "company success first" orientation used by some of our competitors. The approach of company success first focused on contractual deliverables and the expansion of project revenue via costly add-on change orders. Our approach of pursuing client success first focused on creating trust among all parties as a means of reaching mutually beneficial resolutions to all project issues. These two differing approaches typically produced different results, in both the short and the long term. Our leadership team centered its attention on the long-term goals of client satisfaction, profitability, and revenue growth. We balanced the need to have both client and company success by having at least one of our senior managers stay very close to each project and assume responsibility for resolving any conflict that surfaced between achieving client success and company success.

Our approach to internal communications was consistent with our client-focus strategy. While attempting to communicate openly about all aspects of our business, we also tried to make our internal communications clear and concise, in hopes they would provide some transparency without creating much distraction from serving the needs of our clients.

Most of our internal communications began with some reinforcement of our guiding principles and strategies, and concluded with at least one client success story. Much like the contents of this book, the majority of our internal communications contained many of the same words to reinforce their importance to our success. These strategic words and phrases included "relationships and results," "focus on the needs of the client," "seek first to understand," "promote the success of our clients," "client success," and "similar projects for similar clients," (i.e., relevant experience). As an illustration, I share one of our internal newsletter articles.

INTERNAL NEWSLETTER: CLIENT SUCCESS

Creating a culture of disciplined thought about client success is most certainly resulting in company success as we experience the growth of our revenue and backlog and the continued profitability of our business. However, I was once asked if our commitment to "client success" could be in conflict with our priority for company success. I think not. In fact, I believe that "client success begets company success." Using client success as the fuel of our primary marketing strategy, we have seen how it differentiates us from most of our competition and engenders win-win relationships with our clients.

Without question, our projects need to be on-time and within budget, but the most important measure of client success is how our clients describe their success, or lack of same, to their colleagues both within their institution and to those in other colleges and universities. This is especially important to us because higher education is such a small industry in which people share information frequently and openly.

The following example illustrates how one client described his experience with CedarCrestone to other colleagues. Recently, we offered to conduct a go-live readiness assessment for a public university system. Recognizing that a successful go-live is in the best interest of both parties, we agreed to not charge consulting fees and the University agreed to pay our travel and living expenses. After the first week of on-site assessment work, the CIO called me to express his satisfaction with our work and insisted that he pay our normal hourly fee for the remainder of the assessment. I have since talked with two other CIO's who heard about our great work from the CIO at this university system.

When compared to the precise internal metrics upon which we regularly monitor company success (e.g., income statements, balance sheets, and other financial reports), client success can be validated only by the client based upon mostly subjective factors that typically are beyond our direct control (e.g., working relationships, responsive issue resolution, go-live decisions, and system response time). Although timely payment of invoices, client acceptance of deliverables and requests for add-on service contracts are client success indicators, in actuality, they tell us more about consultant success than they do about client success. Even with well documented project objectives, achieving a high level of client success typically requires a consensus among a large, diverse end-user community. It is possible for CedarCrestone to meet all of our contractual obligations and receive timely payment for our services without achieving a high level of client success. In other words, client success is as much about people and perceptions as it is about deliverables.

Client success is like PeopleSoft Vanilla. It is an attitude more than a measurable objective. Although usually not 100 percent achievable, it is an attitude that can engender an excellent result. Client success is an attitude that makes people know that we understand their needs and care about their success. It is an attitude that creates a foundation for good working relationships that are essential to achieving long-term results for both CedarCrestone and our clients.

Just as PeopleSoft Vanilla requires us to think differently about how we design, develop and deploy our project deliverables, client success requires us to think differently about how we work with clients on all aspects of a project. Although our project scope and timeline may not allow us to address all of a client's needs, it is important that they believe that we both understand and care about the success of both the project and the people who will ultimately determine client success.

By definition, thinking differently requires a new perspective that is perhaps not completely consistent with the training and mentoring that we have received in the past. To illustrate this point, I offer the following examples from two domains, each one very different from our own. At age forty, Greg Maddux continues to be one of the all-time great major league baseball pitchers (sixteen Gold Glove Awards, four Cy Young Awards and more than three hundred victories) even though none of his pitches is considered overpowering. A few years ago, I read a newspaper article in which

> Greg credited much of his success to being able to "think like a hitter rather than like a pitcher." The lesson for us in this example is that perhaps we should spend more time thinking like our clients, rather than thinking like consultants.

In summary, the execution of our collective strategies resulted in the positive differentiation that we needed to steadily grow our business and become a market-share leader. They leveraged our competitive advantages and minimized our competitive disadvantages. Individually, none of these strategies could have achieved the requisite amount of differentiation. Executed as a set of integrated strategies, they produced the desired result in the marketplace. Sun Tzu stated, "The art of war teaches us to rely not on the likelihood of the enemy's not coming, but on our own readiness to receive him; not on the chance of his not attacking, but rather on the fact that we have made our position unassailable."[42] Were we unassailable? I doubt it, but we definitely became well-positioned through the execution of our integrated, differentiation strategies focused on client success.

PROOF OF PERFORMANCE

> "After a lengthy analysis of possible partners, we engaged CedarCrestone for our recent project. It became clear to us early and remained clear throughout the project that our needs and the success of that project were paramount to CedarCrestone. They worked collaboratively with our project management team to structure a project plan that addressed our unique needs and desires. Thanks to CedarCrestone, we were able to successfully complete the project on-time and in-budget. CedarCrestone fully embraced its partnership role, and we could not have been happier with their positive and collaborative spirit and with their responsiveness to our needs. CedarCrestone was a major factor in our success."
>
> Vice Provost
> Private Research University

Lessons Learned

- Your castle will always be vulnerable. Be sure you have a wide moat

- Seize upon market gaps, but do it differently.

- Execution of differentiation strategies determines the width of your moat.

- Short-term marketing campaigns do little to expand your moat.

- Client success is a lifelong quest.

7. How Do Whisperers Compete?

Borrowed Wisdom

> "Everyone has the will to win, but few have the will to prepare to win."[43]
>
> Bob Knight,
> Hall of Fame Basketball Coach

Guiding Principle

> First get inside...then listen and learn.

Not long after we began to build a sales force, I made a sales call with one of our new salespeople, who had previously worked for two very large consulting companies. We were meeting with a chief financial officer (CFO) with whom I had a long-standing relationship, which was probably the reason he agreed to meet with us. Following some good interaction on a personal level, the CFO launched into a candid description of his concerns about their upcoming implementation project based on his less than satisfying experience with one of our competitors.

After a few minutes of this very informative conversation, our new salesperson interrupted the CFO and said, "We are the perfect implementation partner for your institution." At that point, the CFO stopped talking about his needs and concerns and replied, "Oh really, how did you make that determination?" Our new sales person, who had been trained in the traditional selling techniques of his previous employer, started to give his "pitch." After only a few minutes, the CFO interrupted and said he had to cut our meeting short because of some other pressing priorities that required his immediate attention. Needless to say, we did not win that sales competition! Obviously this was a huge missed opportunity for us.

ALIGNING WITH THE PROSPECT'S BUYING PROCESS

During my solution selling training, Bosworth emphasized the importance of conducting need-development prior to any attempt at differentiation. By doing so, you eliminate the risk of unintentionally creating negative differentiation. Ignorance of the prospect's needs, concerns, and biases makes differentiation a risky proposition. Once you have successfully completed need-development, you can position your differentiation as a benefit rather than just an advantage that may or may not have value to the prospect. For example, if on the first sales call the prospect's gatekeeper, who probably has no buying authority, asks you what makes your company better than your competition, your response needs to be a question, not a sales pitch. Hopefully that question will be the beginning of a need-development conversation that might result in a powerful benefit statement that sets you apart from your competition.

As we began to immerse ourselves in the PeopleSoft consulting business, we used Bosworth's solution selling in every phase of our sales process. His methods were designed to be precisely aligned with the prospect's buying process. Bosworth's training stressed the importance of knowing where each buyer was in their Buying Process. Using the alignment below, we advised our salespeople to stay focused on the same concerns that were at the front of the buyer's mind. **Figure F** below illustrates how we adapted Bosworth's three-phase buying process to our market, as reflected in the questions that we asked in each of these phases. The situation described above would not have been so bad if the CFO had been in Phase III of the buying process. In fact, he was still in the very early stages of Phase I, and his focus was on need and cost (budget)—not on vendor evaluation. In retrospect, he wanted us to understand his needs and concerns so that we could provide some useful input for his budgeting process.

Figure F: Sales Methods - Alignment with the Buying Process

Phase I	Phase II	Phase III
The Buying Process:		
Determine Needs:	**Evaluate Alternatives:**	**Take Action:**
Do I need to change? What do I need? How much do I need it? How much does it cost?	Is there really a solution? Which one meets my needs? How do we justify it?	Should I do it? What are the consequences? Is it the best price?
The Selling Process:		
Develop Needs:	**Provide Proof:**	**Close the Sale:**
Listen empathetically. Make it personal. Qualify buying process.	Demonstrate how our capabilities meet buyer's vision. Help with value justifications.	Why CedarCrestone? Why now? Help buyer deal with fear, uncertainty, and doubt (FUD), and "buyer's" remorse."

It is easy to determine when the buyer moves into Phase III of the buying process. It's when you start getting "buying questions" that reflect the buyer's focus on risk and price. The relationships developed during Phases I and II of the buying process help the buyer to be comfortable in Phase III. Buyers then realize that you really do understand and care about their needs, and will help them mitigate risk and complete the project as planned. It would have been easy for us to be viewed as different from our competition during the CSU buying process; if for no other reasons, we were much smaller and our corporate capabilities paled by comparison to the other finalists. However, by diligently doing our need- and relationship-development prior to proposing a solution, we were able to create some compelling differentiation based on our potential value to the prospect.

The time to involve the expert is when the prospect moves on to Phase II of the buying process and his/her focus moves from need-development to evaluation of alternative solutions. This is the time for experts to design a solution that addresses all of the needs, concerns, and issues that surfaced during need-development. Our best solution designers not only crafted service solutions that addressed the prospect's stated needs, but also anticipated latent needs not yet identified by the prospect. **Figure G** illustrates how the buyer's concerns shift during the buying process.

Figure G: Shifting Buyer Concerns[44]

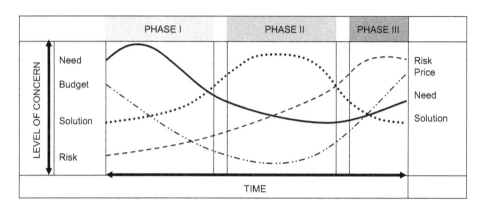

In his book *Making Ideas Happen* (Copyright 2010. By permission of The Penguin Group), Scott Belsky quotes author and marketing guru, Seth Godin who says the source of buyer's remorse is caused by the "lizard brain." Anatomically, the lizard brain exists in all of us at the top of our brainstem. "All chickens and lizards have is a lizard brain." Godin explained. "It is hungry, it is scared, it is selfish, and it is horny. That's its job, and that's all it does. As it turns out we have one too."[45] Belsky asserts, "The lizard brain interferes with execution by amplifying our fears and conjuring up excuses to play it safe...While the lizard brain stays quiet when we have monotonous jobs with a paycheck for dong what we're told, it becomes riled when we start to challenge the status quo."[46] The primal tendency of the lizard brain to keep us safe by avoiding danger and risk usually appears during the buying process. However, cultivation of a trusting relationship during the need-development phase of the buying process helps the prospect have a quieter lizard brain when it comes time for action and vendor selection decisions.

When CSU made the decision to hire our small consulting firm for their very large project, it was an emotional decision—they felt good about the interaction they had with our client whisperers. When the selection committee made their recommendation to the CSU executives, they developed a refined logic to support their decision.

Getting Through the Proposal Funnel

When we received an RFP, or a prospect/client informally requested that we present them with a proposal, we initiated our *proposal development process*. Our first step was to conduct a strategy call with the business development manager (salesperson), the vice president of sales, the general manager, the executive sponsor for the prospect/client, and the proposal lead. During these calls we reviewed the prospect's issues and needs, discussed our relationship with the prospect/client, identified potential competitors, and considered what would be the best staffing and most competitive pricing approaches. Out of this call came our proposal strategy. Sometimes we determined that we would not respond to an RFP based on alignment with our hedgehog concept, staffing capability and/or the relative strength of an existing relationship that a competitor may have had with the prospect under review.

We made our go/no-go decisions quickly. If we determined that we should bid, our proposal lead developed a detailed action plan to complete the proposal, doing so in keeping with our agreed upon strategy. The proposal lead developed a proposal development plan (PDP). It included all of the tasks to be completed, a timeline for completion, a designated person responsible for preparing the required information for a given section(s), and subject matter experts to serve as resources. Whenever a PDP was sighted, it was "all hands on deck."

Within the requirements (and restrictions) of the request for proposal, the proposal lead incorporated our understanding of the client's issues and needs, doing so in consideration of the prospective client's context, such as institutional type (public, private), mission (research university, masters, community college), governance structure (single or multi-campus) and size. Our proposal leads were writers who understood and effectively executed the art and science that were necessary to produce a quality proposal.

Over the years, the RFP timelines seemed to shorten. In the early years, we typically would have a six-week period in which to respond; toward the latter part of our journey we encountered some RFPs that had only a two-week period in which to develop our proposal. Obviously, the tighter the deadline, the greater the pressure—and we had lots of that.

However, we never requested a proposal deadline extension, as did many of our competitors. We thought it sent the wrong message. So our "whispering writers" just stepped up to the task at hand and made it happen. They used to joke about planning a vacation, because invariably when they did so a large RFP came in with an unreasonable timeline. More than once, Tim worked on a proposal in his car as his wife Melanie drove them from Phoenix to Montana for a much deserved fishing vacation. Fortunately, Melanie was a sales vice president for a software company and understood the importance of meeting proposal deadlines. All of us knew that writing a competitive proposal was essential to our success, and everyone, including spouses, helped in whatever way they could.

We always began our proposals with an executive summary intended to get the attention of key decision makers. We knew that we had just a few pages to make a positive impression on this audience. We did so by summarizing our understanding of their needs, citing any previous relationship/success with them, referring to relevant experience with their peer institutions (these would always get their attention), our approach to help them be successful, and pricing for the proposed services. We knew that we had to connect with them in no more than three pages—and that meant there had to be something in those pages that spoke to them. It was more than a matter of meeting RFP requirements.

When we thought it was appropriate, we crafted executive summaries with an "extra twist of differentiation." The following is an example of one of our more creative executive summaries in a proposal to a large, multi-campus community college which requested professional services to implement a student information system. Because the proposal authors had higher education experience, they knew that a friendly, innovative approach was appropriate for this community college system. The authors also knew that "everyone loves a story." Now, imagine that you are a selection committee member having to "pile your way" through numerous ERP vendor proposals of three hundred or more pages each—and then you come to this executive summary.

Imagine that you are embarking upon a "neighborhood revitalization" project. You recognize that individual homes and the neighborhood as a whole are dated; and because the infrastructure is aging, it is becoming more expensive to maintain. Even the appearance of your neighborhood could use some improvement. You are aware of new home features that are more "energy efficient" and perform functions that you don't currently have in your homes. Most importantly, your family needs and expectations have changed. You know that something must be done; it's time to change.

As you contemplate and envision what a revitalized neighborhood would be like, you also consider what the cost would be to do so. To undertake such a revitalization project individually could be unaffordable for some homeowners. You've consulted one another and agree that you could overcome this challenge if you did the project as a neighborhood. There could be cost and time savings. You could help each other by sharing new ideas, innovative tools and expertise.

You recognize, no doubt, that there will be challenges in doing this project. How difficult will it be, for example, to quickly agree on a design feature? Although you are all members of the homeowners association and have worked and socialized together, you've likely not undertaken such a complex, integrated project where the homes are of differing size, age and style. Family sizes and composition vary greatly too. Yet, you recognize that both your individual homes and the neighborhood as a whole would benefit from a new common infrastructure and appearance. Who knows, you might even enjoy the experience of working together on a project like this. Others have…with our help.

We think that your idea of beginning the project with just two homes as a pilot is a great idea! In fact, we've worked with other neighborhood projects where that approach worked very well. It's like experiencing a microcosm of the bigger project without all the complexity, dynamics and challenges of doing the whole neighborhood at the same time. Your other idea of having swat teams involved in the pilot is also a good approach that will take advantage of the expertise that you'll learn from revitalizing the pilot homes. This way, you will be considering the needs of the whole neighborhood as you design and build during the pilot phase. With your collaborative development of common business processes, you already have taken a very important step toward building a strong foundation.

Since we've successfully completed over fifteen similar neighborhood projects, we thought that you would be interested in learning about how we could help you be successful. But first, we want you to know that we've met all of your mandatory requirements, accurately completed the information in the statement of work and have priced out what it would take to realize your vision. We've completed all of the required forms—have to do that, of course. Now, how about meeting some of our people? On paper, that is. We'll briefly introduce some of our crew in this letter and provide more detailed information about all of them in our proposal.

Meet "Bill," your experienced and creative "architect." He has been working on another complex neighborhood project, not far from here. Like your project, this one had two pilot institutions, who were the first to be finished. Because all the "families in the neighborhood" wanted input into what the neighborhood would look like, during the design phase, "Bill" and his team of builders conducted on-site and remote interactive sessions (using a video conferencing system) with every house in the neighborhood. Here's what the vice president for business & administration had to say about the project that Bill managed,

"With a great deal of help from CedarCrestone, we have overcome some significant implementation issues. The combination of CedarCrestone's higher education experience and their commitment to our success has created tremendous value for us. When the pressure is on, it comes down to people and money. CedarCrestone has been just great."

Speaking of understanding community college neighborhoods, we thought that you might be interested in reading what the executive director of enrollment management at an institution similar to yours had to say about working with us,

"In our first meetings, the CedarCrestone team impressed us with their knowledge of community colleges. How refreshing to have someone who understands our pain points and then offers up new ideas. Better yet, they took those ideas and, along with our team, helped design processes and systems that fit our needs. In a culture adverse to change, the CedarCrestone team helped us work through the roadblocks and kept projects on schedule. As the project lead, I have watched our team reach goals that many thought unattainable. Yes, our team worked hard, but our success could not have been realized without the exceptional talent and expertise of the CedarCrestone team."

Now, let me introduce you to some of the other crew members. Dr. "Peters" knows both community college and multi-institution neighborhoods really well. He was the CIO for another multi-college system, and spent four years at PeopleSoft, working to incorporate the needs of community colleges into PeopleSoft's higher education suite of applications. He's been involved in projects for many multi-institution neighborhoods. Here's another crew member who knows what it's like to work in multi-institution neighborhoods: "Linda." She's one of the proposed project managers, even has her PMP certification. We think she likes working in your neighborhood area the best since she's worked at five institutions nearby. Many of our other proposed consultants like to work in your area too. The Campus Solutions Project Manager at one of these institutions had this to say about our crew,

"CedarCrestone consultants helped us in formulating creative strategies to overcome our challenges of limited staff and aggressive timeline so that we were able to achieve an on-time, within-budget implementation. CedarCrestone's adaptation of a Collaborative Model fit our unique situation and helped us to generate user buy-in and accelerate knowledge transfer."

We hope that we can meet with you to learn more about your needs and to share our experiences that would help you to be successful in this important project. But for now, read on, we have lots more to share with you in writing.

About a year later, this prospective client selected CedarCrestone as the implementation partner for their large multi-campus implementation project. Undoubtedly, there were many other factors other than this initial proposal that were taken into consideration throughout the lengthy evaluation and selection process, but at the outset we surely presented ourselves differently from the competition.

SURVIVING THE ORALS CHALLENGE

When a prospective client had narrowed the potential vendors to a limited number of finalists (those vendors who made it through the proposal funnel), they invited the vendors to come to their campus for what we called the orals challenge. Typically, the prospective client required vendors to make a formal presentation about company qualifications and to answer a set of specific questions. Many of the prospective clients, particularly public institutions, standardized the orals presentations to help them do an "apples-to-apples" comparison of vendors' services and pricing. For many years, vendors had conditioned the higher education audience to expect a sales presentation, not an informal discussion. Furthermore, within the context of higher education, the traditional lecture approach is still the dominant mode of disseminating and processing information.

While we much preferred to have a "sit-down" discussion with our prospective clients, rather than a traditional "stand-up" slide presentation, we had to be prepared to do a formal presentation, particularly if the lead person on the client side was a procurement officer. Our general approach was to transition from this formal presentation to a discussion mode as quickly as possible during our allotted time, which could range from two hours to a couple of days. The transition was not always easy, given the audience was pre-conditioned to expect a formal lecture presentation.

Selection committees were usually large and diverse, especially for ERP projects and student information system implementation projects. We recognized the importance of getting to know our audience, or at least the decision-makers and influencers in the audience, in advance of the presentation. However we also knew that in the collaborative culture of higher education, all of the people in an audience of fifty people could be decision influencers, especially faculty members.

The book *Brain Rules* (Copyright 2008. By permission of Pear Press.), authored by developmental molecular biologist and research consultant John J. Medina, and the work of scientist Michael Posner were especially helpful to us in preparing for these presentations and making them as effective as possible, given the expectation that it was to be a formal PowerPoint presentation (yes, with lights dimmed) and would be given to a large audience with differing backgrounds, roles, and issues. In particular, he gave us an understanding of how the mind works (or doesn't) during a lecture and what the presenter can do to gain and retain the audience's attention. We knew if we couldn't do at least that, we wouldn't be "in the game."

According to Medina, "Before the first quarter-hour is over in a typical presentation, people usually have checked out. If keeping someone's interest in a lecture were a business, it would have an 80 percent failure rate. What happens at the 10-minute mark to cause such trouble? Nobody knows. The brain seems to be making choices according to some stubborn timing pattern, undoubtedly influenced by both culture and gene. This fact suggests a teaching and business imperative: Find a way to arouse and then hold somebody's attention for a specific period of time. But how?"[47] Medina refers to the research of Posner, who hypothesized that our brain uses its Alerting or Arousal Network to monitor any unusual activities. "This is the general level of attention our brains are paying to our world, a condition termed Intrinsic Alertness."[48] Based on Posner's research, Medina then shares his five guiding principles for regaining the attention of his audience for a typical fifty-minute lecture, as summarized below.

THE 10-MINUTE RULE:

First the plan, then each part within the plan: "It is key that the instructor explains the lecture plan at the beginning of the class with liberal repetition of 'where we are' sprinkled throughout the hour. This prevents the audience from trying to multitask."[49]

Emotions get our attention: "Emotionally arousing events tend to be better remembered than neutral events. An emotionally charged event (usually called an ECS, short for emotionally competent stimulus) is the best-processed kind of external stimulus ever measured."[50]

The brain cannot multitask: "Multitasking, when it comes to paying attention, is a myth. The brain naturally focuses on concepts sequentially, one at a time."[51]

Meaning before details: "Studies show that emotional arousal focuses attention on the 'gist' of an experience at the expense of peripheral details. Many researchers think that's how memory normally works—by recording the gist of what we encounter, not by retaining a literal record of the experience. With the passage of time, our retrieval of gist always trumps our recall of details."[52]

The brain needs a break: "The most common communication mistakes? Relating too much information, with not enough time devoted to connecting the dots. Lots of force-feeding, very little digestion..."[53]

Medina developed the following model for giving a lecture. He was named the Hoechst Marion Rousell Teacher of the Year—no doubt for his effective execution of this innovative lecture model.

LECTURE DESIGN: 10-MINUTE SEGMENTS

"I decided that every lecture I'd ever give would come in discrete modules...Each segment would cover a single core concept—always large, always general, always filled with 'gist,' and always explainable in one minute. I would use the other nine minutes in the segment to provide a detailed description of that single general concept. The trick was to ensure that each detail could be easily traced back to the general concept with minimal intellectual effort."[54] We used Medina's teaching model as we planned and executed our presentation in the orals challenge.

We always began with strategy: which meant, we needed to find out who the audience was and what was important to them. We asked the salesperson to request from the prospective client's contact person who would be in attendance at the orals session and the nature of their roles. Usually, the prospective client would provide this information, though not always, which made it especially challenging to strategize. We asked what questions would be asked of us, and if they had a pre-determined agenda. Most orals sessions had a client-specified agenda. With this information and anything else we could glean about the prospect, we conducted a strategy call with our executive team and the proposal lead.

Our orals strategy was consistently based on demonstrating client success, but it had to be based on clients whose projects and institutional type were most relevant to the prospective client's. In the early years this was difficult, given our limited number of clients. However, after our CSU success and the rapid expansion of our client base thereafter, it became easier to feature our success at a private research university to a prospective client who also was one. We eventually came to have representation among all institutional types, particularly public masters-granting and research universities, for which the PeopleSoft software was especially fit. For our relevant case studies, we would have a slide that highlighted the institutional profile, their issues, and our solutions. It was the words of our clients on the testimonial slides, though, that validated our strategy of client success.

In keeping with the strategy of knowing the audience, we used images that were appropriate to the higher education audience, which meant few suits, more women, and ethnic diversity. We developed a slide for each issue that had been identified during need-development. We followed each issue with a case study of a similar project that we had successfully completed for a peer institution. We then featured a slide with our proposed solution for addressing their unique needs and goals. As suggested by Medina, we integrated hooks into our presentation in the following ways: our presentation outline depicted what we would be discussing and what we had discussed; we used client testimonials to elicit attention and emotion, and always elaborated upon them with anecdotal comments; we used interesting images and colors, rather than words, to illustrate our key points. We spent days developing these custom slide presentations that complied with the requirements of the orals, but were infused with our issue/solution approach and differentiation.

We understood that the topics which constitute a sales presentation fall into one of two categories: satisfiers and motivators. Satisfiers, or checklist items, are those things that the prospect expects, or insists should be included in the presentation. These typically afforded little or no opportunity to differentiate our company in a positive way. However, if we had not included these items, they could lower our ratings or even eliminate us. Our approach to discussing these topics was to display them conspicuously, but not spend much of our presentation time discussing them. Typical examples of satisfiers included corporate history, number of clients, partnership status with Oracle, consultant experience, and required references. Our slides that covered these items were very similar for each orals presentation (i.e., "boilerplate). We made them visually appealing in the hope that at least having something eye-catching on the screen would keep the audience's attention when the lights were dimmed.

Motivators differed greatly from satisfiers, because they were opportunities for positive differentiation of our company. These were topics of greatest interest to at least some of the prospect's stakeholders and decision-makers, which meant they would be different for each sales presentation. The slide content was customized to the needs and concerns of each prospect. No boilerplate was allowed with these motivators! Hopefully, the needs and concerns covered on these slides had been validated with the key stakeholders, which ensured that the proposed solutions were of great interest to our audience.

In support of the validity of our proposed solutions, we would typically present brief case studies containing similar needs and concerns with similar projects at peer institutions. It was easy to infuse what Posner referred to as ECS—emotionally competent stimuli—into these actual client experiences. The case studies were proof that we both understood the prospect's needs and concerns and had successfully completed comparable projects for their peer institutions. Typically, the presentation of these case studies engendered many questions, which in turn led to more detailed discussion about many other aspects of our case study projects. Sometimes, we would use break-out sessions to allow our expert consultants to meet with smaller special interest groups to discuss in greater detail those topics that were of particular interest to them but not the larger audience.

Over time, we developed a number of templates that could be customized to each unique orals situation and prospective client. An overview of the presentation contents and various dimensions of that content are presented in the table below. For each agenda item, I state our primary purpose (satisfier or motivator), the number of slides used, approximate time used during the presentation, number of attention stimuli, and the calculated number of stimuli per ten minute period, as advocated by Medina. Our goal was to make an orals presentation more like an action movie rather than a typical college lecture. An outline of our agenda is presented in **Table 1** below.

Table 1: Orals "Action Movie" Agenda Profile

Agenda Topic	Primary Purpose	# of Slides	Time Span	# of Stimuli	Stimuli /10 Min
Introductions (with credentials)	Satisfier	8	10	0	n.a.
Overview of CedarCrestone	Satisfier	4	10	2	2.0
Prospect Issues and Concerns	Motivator	21	30	5	1.2
Break	Satisfier	n.a.	15	n.a.	n.a.
Similar Project Case Studies	Motivator	26	50	8	1.6
Break	Satisfier	n.a.	15	n.a.	n.a.
Proposed Solution	Motivator	16	40	4	1.0
Break	Satisfier	n.a.	15	n.a.	n.a.
Group discussion(s)	Motivator	n.a.	45	8	1.8
Why CedarCrestone?	Motivator	1	10	3	3.0
Totals and Avg. Stimuli per 10 Minutes *		76	240	30	1.5

Although every orals audience was unique, we expected that by using this architecture for a sales presentation, each member of every audience would use what Posner refers to as the three mental faculties of alerting, orienting, and the executive network (which controls the "oh my gosh, what should I do now" behaviors) as they listened to and evaluated our presentations.

Once we had finalized our orals presentation, the salesperson assumed responsibility for making color copies of the presentation as a handout for the selection committee. We had some interesting tales regarding this step in the preparation process. For example, on one occasion early in our journey, we debated about whether we should go to the expense of printing the slides in color. We opted to not do so, except for one color copy for the prospective client's project director. Although we won that engagement (largely because of our relationship with the client project director), she told us afterward that she received feedback from the selection committee raising doubts about our "financial viability" as a company if we couldn't afford color copies for everyone. Needless to say, we never again raised the question of "black and white or color?" Color copies thereafter were considered a "satisfier."

Another interesting occasion occurred when we were preparing for an orals presentation to an audience of approximately one hundred people. When we arrived with our boxes of handouts, we were informed that we could not distribute anything in writing. The first vendor had done so; however, when the state attorney general got wind of it, he advised the institution that they couldn't have any written materials other than the original proposal. Unfortunately, many members of the audience had not even seen our proposal! We gulped and sighed as we discarded $5,000 worth of color handouts. To make matters worse, we didn't win the account (no cost recovery on that one).

Generally speaking, we experienced more benefits than liabilities when preparing and distributing our orals presentation handout. There clearly was an expectation that we would have copies. We imagine that these hard copies were helpful to them when comparing the vendors and deciding who would be their partner. We found that the most valuable aspect of providing copies of our orals presentation was when we discussed the timeline and pricing slides, which sometimes included more detailed information than our other slides.

On the evening before an orals presentation, we always huddled together with all of our team to do the final "dress rehearsal" for our orals challenge. We found that these in-person preparations were the most helpful and seemed to put our client whisperers at ease for the orals challenge. Once they could discuss the issues of the prospective client, you could see them shift their concerns about themselves (their stage presence" in this competitive situation) to the needs of the prospective client and how they could help them. We never had a prepared script. Although we were well prepared, we wanted our client whisperers to draw from their natural spontaneity during the orals session. We also used a little levity during that evening to ease the evitable tension associated with "the night before" a competitive challenge.

Hopefully, the topics on our agenda slides sent an initial message to the audience that we knew what was important to them and that most of our planned presentation was primarily about those important topics. Of course, having the right items on the agenda depended on whether we had done a good job with need-development during the first phase of the prospect's buying process. If things had gone well throughout the orals sessions, this segment was a very short summary of the relevant sales points that had been well received during our time with their selection committee.

As our competitors gained higher education experience and positive client references, and some started to emulate our winning tactics, differentiation became more difficult. However, by that time we had developed two areas of high achievement (AHA): multi-institution implementation and PeopleSoft hosting. Once again, the critical success factors included our successful track record with comparable projects for peer institutions and the higher education credentials of our consultants. Our client whisperers' actions consistently revealed that they knew how to successfully compete: they listened, they understood, and they made the audience feel comfortable.

One of our most creative differentiation tactics was developed pursuant to being selected as one of four finalists for a large student system project at a public university in the Pacific Northwest. Our selection as a finalist followed our submission of an eighty-page proposal in response to a "blind RFP," which meant that we had no interaction with the prospect prior to receiving their RFP. Obviously, they were impressed by our proposal, since we made it through the "Proposal Funnel." However, we did not have any insight into what aspects of our proposal had captured their attention. At this point in our journey, we had no salespeople and our lack of both contact with any of the stakeholders and understanding of their pain put us at a big disadvantage. Nervous? Yes. We felt we were on the outside. Could we do it? Yes—but only with an unexpected approach.

We decided to make a presentation that would attack our competitors' weaknesses, highlight our higher education experience and clearly differentiate us from the other three finalists. Our presentation team consisted of one management consultant with a Ph.D., a project manager, two functional leads, a technical lead, and me, as the executive sponsor. The average higher education experience of these six people was more than 17.5 years and the average PeopleSoft experience was 5.3 years. After presenting our higher education credentials, we launched into a comparison between the challenges of the Lewis and Clark expedition of 1804 to hiring an implementation partner with little or no experience implementing student information systems. We made the following salient points in our presentation:

FAULTY ASSUMPTIONS:

- The Rocky Mountains are very similar to the Appalachian Mountains.

- The Indians in the West are as friendly as those in the East.

- The Grizzly bears in the West are the same as the bears in East.

- The illnesses of the West were the same as those in the East.

- The Missouri River connects with the Columbia River.

- Their expedition plan is realistic because the above assumptions are valid.

LESSONS LEARNED

- Even strong leaders need guidance from those who have been there before (listen to the Indian guides who have been there before).

- Before prescribing a solution, seek understanding (what the Indians needed/wanted was much different than the solution that was offered).

- A project plan based on faulty assumptions can be dangerous to your health (the expedition experienced an additional year of severe personal hardship).

- When the plan goes wrong, rely on relationships and focus on critical survival needs (the teamwork of the friendly Indians and the Lewis and Clark expedition got them home safely).

Clearly, this was not what the selection committee had expected from a vendor presentation in an orals challenge! At first they looked at us with some suspicion, as evidenced by the body language of folded arms and no smiles, whatsoever. However, once we started into the Lewis and Clark analogy, some of them started to lean forward, arms began to unfold, and then we had their full attention—even the procurement officer's (although he still didn't smile).

We were both surprised and elated when they awarded this contract to us. Their award notification included an assessment of the presentations used by each finalist. We had met all of the requirements (the satisfiers). However, their anecdotal feedback to us was all very positive. It also included the statement, "You were different." Of course, if we had lost, this would have been bad news resulting from negative differentiation. Because we won, though, we assumed that the artful execution of our strategy did in reality help to differentiate us in a positive way from our competition and motivate them to select us as their implementation partner.

My typical role in our orals sessions was to take the lead in the beginning and ending of our presentation and act as facilitator throughout, to ensure that we stayed focused on our competitive advantages, highlighted the strengths of each of our participants, and responded appropriately to all questions. When needed, I also provided anecdotal comments in support of our client success case studies as further proof that we had solved similar issues for similar institutions. Internally, we called these "war stories;" and if presented artfully, these tended to be good audience alerts, especially if they were discussed in the context of a powerful client testimonial. The more I could relate our previous experience to the prospect's issues and

Lyon's Pride

As point guard on my basketball team, I was responsible for highlighting the strengths of my teammates. This meant getting the ball to them when they had a competitive advantage and high probability of scoring. At times when my teammates' competitive advantages were minimal – against the better defensive teams – I had to become more of a scorer. This required important judgment calls on my part depending on the many dynamics of the game. My general approach was to be a "pass first" player against the weaker opponents and a "shoot first" player against the tougher teams. These decisions made the difference between winning and losing.

concerns, the more effective these "war stories" seemed to be. Many times these anecdotal client success stories resulted in some of the best interactions with our audience, as they probed for more insight into how we helped other clients achieve success. As facilitator of these sessions, I typically fielded questions from the audience and made the decision whether to pass them along to a teammate or respond myself.

Although our orals presentations required a tremendous effort, were very stressful, and immensely challenging, I enjoyed them. The focused preparation, emotionally charged execution, intense competition, effective teamwork, and the joy of winning were similar to my days competing on the basketball court. Like basketball, the relationships with my former teammates are lifelong.

WHISPERING IN THE NEGOTIATING PROCESS

Our strategy to be the most responsive and cooperative sales organization in the industry was based primarily on our experience with and sensitivity to the collaborative culture of higher education. We expected the biggest challenge to this strategy to surface during the sometimes intense negotiations over contractual terms and conditions; but that expectation turned out to be false. In most situations, being responsive was an advantage, especially when we were competing with some of the large consulting companies. They typically had a lengthy corporate approval process and a rather formal, sometimes even adversarial, approach to negotiations. While that may have been effective in other markets, it was not in higher education.

One of the residual benefits of most of our contract negotiations was the strengthening of our relationships with the executives of our new clients. Many times these negotiations marked the beginning of the transition of our client relationship from a low-trust vendor to a high-trust partner—a type of business transformation. One such transformation occurred in the final contract negotiations with a large multi-institution client. The client's team included the CFO, provost and internal legal counsel. Although not official members of their negotiation team, there was a large group of interested parties in the room during these negotiations. After resolving most of the legal issues with the Master Agreement, we were making good progress reaching win-win resolutions to some tricky issues with the six-thousand-word Statement of Work (SOW). However, after several hours of negotiations, the provost expressed concern about the wording of the following sentence: "Client shall be responsible for the overall project management and support during the implementation including, without limitation, knowledge, and experience of the operating environment and database."

As I probed for more insight into her concerns and suggested some wording changes, which were quickly rejected, what surfaced was her need to know that we were willing to take responsibility for the success of the project even though we would not have control over many critical project decisions. Her position was that we were far more qualified to take responsibility for such a complex project than their staff, because that was what we do every day.

Once I understood the emotional basis of her concern with our wording, I said, "I can see that this is a big concern for you, so let's just delete this sentence from the SOW." I could almost feel her relief as the tension in her voice immediately disappeared, and she thanked me for our willingness to address her issue. As it turned out, this was the beginning of a trusting relationship that helped us complete this very challenging project on-time and within budget. The budget for the software fees and implementation services was $29,800,000. Shortly following the completion of this project, the Board of Regents of this institution passed a resolution of appreciation expressing their "deep appreciation and gratitude" to the implementation team that consisted of approximately one hundred and fifty employees and fifty consultants who "completed the two-year contract on time and within budget for all scheduled milestones and all critical path functionalities." Such a positive outcome was most gratifying.

After a corporate merger with one of our toughest competitors, we began using new legal services, most of which were provided by one lawyer, Dale, who was with a law firm in Boston. Her personable style and professionalism were perfectly consistent with our "most responsive and cooperative" strategy. Dale was an important addition to our team. For one of our largest opportunities, with a multi-institution client that used a high-powered attorney from Chicago, who was conducting simultaneous contract negotiations with both us and one of our competitors, our new lawyer became a competitive advantage that helped to get us over the finish line. I guess we should have called her our "legal whisperer."

THE OUTCOMES?

For the first few years of our journey, we always had to be well-prepared to respond to the question, "Do you have the resources to handle a large project like ours?" Incredibly, our win rate for large opportunities for which we submitted a proposal exceeded 50%. Amazingly, the larger the deal, the higher was our win rate. To put this in perspective, typically at least ten companies submitted a proposal for these large deals. It was not unusual for that number to be much higher. When we were selected as one of several finalists, we won more than 70% of them. Over time our sales pipeline and skillful need-development became very predictive of future revenue. These lead metrics allowed us to focus on the activities that had the highest probability of producing the desired results, both quantitative and qualitative. They also helped us establish realistic short-term objectives (revenue and profit) and plan for longer-term goals (reputation and market trust).

Client-focused execution was our primary critical success factor, from sales and marketing efforts through the delivery of our services. We knew that effective execution would leverage our competitive advantages, especially our higher education experience and expertise. Conversely, poor execution would minimize our competitive advantages and make us just another opportunistic vendor. Fortunately, all of us were eager to take action on our strategies, doing so through need-development preparation and client-focused execution; although this wasn't as easy as we thought it was going to be. We felt the squeeze of going through the proposal funnel, the adrenalin surge of the orals challenge, and the intensity of negotiations. But winning? Well, that was just downright exhilarating!

PROOF OF PERFORMANCE

"After an exhaustive selection process, we determined that CedarCrestone is the most qualified implementation partner for our project. All of their client references were very positive about their experience with CedarCrestone, which made them a clear choice for us."

Former Senior Manager
California State University System

LESSONS LEARNED

- Need development begins during the sales cycle and affects all subsequent phases of the client relationship. Do It as thoroughly as possible at the "get-go."

- If you talk like an ordinary salesperson, you'll be treated like one.

- When responding to a cold RFP, you have to be extraordinarily creative to overcome the lack of need-development.

- Every message in an orals presentation should relate in one or more ways to achieving client success. It's not "all about you."

- You must build the prospect's confidence that you can help them because you've done it before—on similar projects with similar organizations.

PART II :
FASTER, CHEAPER, BETTER

8. WHISPERING WAVES OF TRUST?

BORROWED WISDOM

> "...trust is a pragmatic, tangible, actionable asset that you can create – much faster than you probably think possible."[55]
>
> Stephen M. R. Covey,
> CEO, CoveyLink Worldwide

GUIDING PRINCIPLE

> **Wave good-by to sleepless nights – that is, if you trust your teammates.**

One of my gratifying experiences occurred early in our success story with a large, public research university. We had just been awarded a big implementation project, but I had not yet met the new client's executives. My first meeting with the CIO began with some cordial comments. He quickly shifted to the project ahead and said, "Based upon my previous experiences with consulting companies, I don't trust consultants." All I could say in response was, "When we complete your project, I look forward to revisiting this topic with you." When that time came, this same CIO authorized us to use the following testimonial

> "The CedarCrestone consultants have more than exceeded our expectations. Both the technical and functional consultants have proven outstanding throughout our PeopleSoft implementation. We have established a true partnership that has allowed us to develop our own personnel under the guidance of CedarCrestone's senior consultants."
>
> Chief Information Officer
> Public Research University

Covey's insight regarding the "what" of trust might be best summarized as the ability to establish trust with all stakeholders, including clients, business partners, and coworkers. In his book *The Speed of Trust*, Covey posits, "There is one thing that is common to every individual, relationship, team, family, organization, nation, economy, and civilization through-out the world...if developed and leveraged, that one thing has the potential to create unparalleled success and prosperity in every dimension of life. Yet, it is the least understood, most neglected, and most underestimated possibility of our time. That one thing is trust."[56]

We found that the highest value projects resulted from high trust at every point in the process and at all levels of the project, including the following:

- The self-trust of our each individual client whisperers
- Trust within consulting teams
- Trust within client teams
- Trust between consulting and client teams
- Trust within the decision-making team
- Trust between our executives and our client's executives
- Trust between our company and the higher education market

OUR FIRST WAVE: WHISPERER'S SELF-TRUST

Covey probed into what characteristics are required to possess self-trust and identified key elements, or cores. The one that was most essential to our consulting business was what Covey called Capabilities. The solid capabilities of the people on our bus were the only reason that we survived our first few years and produced twelve consecutive years of double-digit revenue growth. Our collective ability to inspire confidence in our prospects and clients regarding our capabilities was a major contributor to our success. Vince Lombardi once said of his star offensive lineman, "Jerry Kramer did not know how good he was when he first joined the Green Bay Packers. You'd be surprised how much confidence a little success will bring."[57] The same probably could be said for our confidence in our capabilities between the time we decided to bid on the CSU opportunity (unsure of our capabilities) to the time we successfully completed that project (confident in our capabilities).

An example of this confidence occurred with a proprietary school client that had a year-round, open enrollment structure, not the typical rigid semester structure of traditional higher education institutions. The PeopleSoft software had been designed to support only the typical semester structure. Our consultants knew that for this non-traditional client, it was critical that they have the flexibility to register students at any time and award financial aid on a monthly, rather than annual, basis. Our consultants took it upon themselves to design an innovative modification that met this client's business requirement. Consequently, the client was able to process these non-traditional students expeditiously—and with some new features as well.

OUR SECOND WAVE: TEAM TRUST

As is the case with basketball, our business progress could be measured by the effectiveness of our teamwork. And teamwork requires trusting relationships throughout an organization. Covey calls his second wave re-

Lyon's Pride

My first big encounter with self-doubt occurred as I was making the adjustment to college basketball. I was eager to please my new coaches. In our preseason workouts, the head coach observed that my shot did not have the proper amount of backspin, which is required to draw the ball down through the net. I was a bit confused by his comments since shooting accuracy had always been one of my strong points. I immediately experimented with a variety of adjustments to my shooting mechanics, none of which produced the desired result. My shooting proficiency diminished. By the time we were preparing to play my first college basketball game, my "self-trust" was near rock bottom.

During warm-ups for our season-opening game, I was very nervous. My anxiety was exacerbated by the unexpected arrival of my brother who was one of my heroes and mentors. He had driven two hours just to see me play. Somehow, when I entered the game, my instincts kicked in and I scored 14 points, and we won the game handily.

This experience gave me an understanding of what it was like for our consultants when they left higher education and started in a new league: the consulting world. I knew that some would experience a similar lack of self-trust as I had years before. We knew the importance of using our experienced people as mentors. It worked!

lationship trust, but we called it team trust, because our story is all about teams and the relationships that exist within every team. He says that it is "…about how to establish and increase the 'trust accounts' we have with others. The key principle underlying this wave is consistent behavior."[58] He presents key behaviors common to high-trust leaders around the world. He claims these behaviors are validated by research and can be learned by anyone. We share the applicability of some of these to our company.

Show Loyalty. This was a major factor in our low employee turnover rate. We had a section in our company newsletter entitled "Kudos," in which employees could submit descriptions of how other employees had done something noteworthy the previous month. When the electronic newsletter was disseminated you could easily see the employee's name printed in bold font. Typically, there were pages of kudos. As a follow-up, there was a flood of one-on-one congratulatory emails among our employees. These kudos reflected the level of team trust that existed through our consultancy. The following are examples of employee-to-employee kudos that appeared in our newsletter during our journey.

"Eric, thanks for all of your work, professionalism, availability and for being a pleasure to work with."

"To Terry for always being willing to help and go the extra mile. You are such a pleasure."

"Thanks to Marianne, Lois, Angie and Tamara for all your help during an unusual fit/gap. Sometimes it takes a village … and I am grateful to be part of this one."

"Once again Tim came through in his usual extremely professional capacity. He is unbelievable in his quest to make everything rise to his extremely high standards."

"Thank you Mary for working weekends to get all of these proposals out – your efforts are very much appreciated!"

"Thanks to Brian for coming to the rescue when I had a seriously dangerous auto issue. He is always willing to lend a helping hand to those in need and his assistance is much appreciated."

I was on the receiving end of some loyalty benefits as a result of my brief time working with Coach Bob Knight at Willis Reed's summer basketball camp. Coach Knight was very loyal to the people in his inner circle. He did me a big favor when he agreed to speak at the all sports banquet of the small Upstate New York high school that employed me as their head basketball coach. His generous words of support during that banquet gave a much needed boost to my nascent coaching career.

Deliver Results. This was our most important behavior, and our performance indicated that we did this very well. Beginning at the proposal stage, we set expectations for our performance. We included performance measures in our contracts in the form of milestones and tied payments to achieving these milestones. Many of our clients included in their testimonials how pleased they were that we delivered on time and within budget. Our client executive sponsors were especially pleased that we delivered what we promised given "their necks were out" at the executive level and campus wide for the success of the project. Our guiding principle of "focusing on enhancing relationships and achieving desired results" paid big dividends in the form of high levels of client satisfaction and wonderful client testimonials. And what better way to measure success than to listen to the voice of the client.

With nearly all of our clients, we were able to develop a high level of trust. However, at the outset some were skeptical and were hesitant to trust. Here is one client experience that illustrates initial reluctance to trust, followed by the results that we achieved—and the recognition for doing it.

One of our hardest fought sales wins occurred with a large state-wide system of higher education. After years of sales activities, they issued a very lengthy, complex RFP to which we responded with a correspondingly long and complex proposal. There were many on-site negotiation sessions. Finally they conducted a day-long, public Board of Regents meeting. Three companies, including ours, made our final presentations. After much discussion, the system executives recommended CedarCrestone as their implementation partner. Following more discussion, the Board approved the recommendation—much to our delight. During a break following their approval of our award, one of the regents cornered me in the back of the crowded room and said, "Look me in the eye, and tell me you can really do this." Obviously, he still had some concern about our selection for this very complex project. I then looked him straight in the eye and replied, "Yes, we can definitely do this." Two years later, the vice chancellor of that same state-wide system approved the following testimonial for use in our promotional programs.

> "The CedarCrestone team of project managers and consultants are experts in Higher Education business processes, knowledgeable about all aspects of PeopleSoft Campus Solutions, innovative and creative in their approach to modifications; but most importantly, they are completely focused on achieving our project vision and goals. We found our ideal partner in CedarCrestone."
>
> Vice Chancellor
> State System of Higher Education

In late 2003, we hired the Customer Loyalty Research Center to conduct an independent client satisfaction survey that gathered information about our clients' procurement process. The results were outstanding and included the following quantitative conclusions:

- 100% rated our service as good or excellent, of which 88% rated our service as excellent.

- 77% of our clients considered at least three other firms during their selection process. Companies named included IBM, Arthur Andersen, PeopleSoft Consulting, KPMG, Price Waterhouse Coopers, Crestone, Ciber, Io Consulting, Deloitte and Touche, Ernst and Young, and EDS.

- 72% of our clients worked with other system integrators and/or IT consulting firms prior to selecting us.

- 94% said they were "extremely/very likely" to recommend our company to others. The other 6% said they were "somewhat likely" to recommend us.

- 87% said they were "extremely/very likely" to use our services again. The other 13% said they were "somewhat likely to hire us again.

This research also included some insightful qualitative comments from our clients:

- "We're very pleased with the consultants they provided, their responsiveness, and their good knowledge of the services they're providing to us."

- "It's a feeling of a partnership, common interests, and us being successful."

- "They bent over backwards to hit the ground running."

Another reliable client satisfaction metric is accounts receivable. When a client is not happy with your work, one of the first things they do is stop paying. Although higher education institutions are notoriously slow payers, it was rare that our invoices went much beyond 60 days past due. This was an important aspect of our belief that client success begets company success. Revenue is great, but cash is essential.

Clarify Expectations. With every all-employee communication, I attempted to make a link to at least one key guiding principle or business strategy. Examples include the newsletter articles contained in this book. The vast majority of our recognition programs focused on team contributions to client success. Many of our communications made reference to our overarching guiding principle of "relationships and results."

Practice Accountability. As part of freedom with responsibility, we encouraged everyone to take responsibility for outcomes, not just activity. Stephen R. Covey called this creating a "Cadence of Accountability."[59] For many of our people who came to us directly from higher education, this was the most difficult part of their transition. From the beginning, one of our strategies was to establish clear lines of authority and responsibility. For example, salespeople were measured and compensated on new sales, project managers were accountable for client success, and our executive team was accountable for revenue and profitability. Every month, I reported on each of these critical success factors to our CEO.

Extend Trust. On occasion, our senior people made judgments that we did not agree with, but as long as they erred on the side of client success we gave them our support. We wanted the people on our bus to know that we would not throw them under the bus. Michael Skapinker, associate editor for *Financial Times*, has some relevant insights regarding trusting within an organization: "There is no point in hiring people with specialist knowledge if you are going to monitor their every move. That is where trust comes in. People not only have to be trusted to do their jobs. They have to be able to trust each other. Successful knowledge work requires collaboration."[60] When it pertained to sales management and executive oversight of our large projects, my approach was similar to one made popular by President Ronald Reagan: "Trust, but verify." And verification always included an assessment of how our prospect and sales team or client and project team were feeling. On our monthly internal sales pipeline conference calls, we probably drove some of our salespeople crazy with all of our questions about their stakeholder analyses and need development activities.

Attempting to master all of these behaviors was formidable and a bit overwhelming. However, our guiding principles and strategies were consistent with each one of Stephen M. R. Covey's core behaviors.

One of the ways in which we attempted to infuse our values, principles and strategies into our culture was through the internal company newsletter. An example of one of the articles that I wrote, entitled "Doing Right," is presented below.

INTERNAL NEWSLETTER: DOING RIGHT

As a young boy, I always enjoyed the bedtime stories my mother read to me. Many of those stories were contained in a wonderful book entitled Doing Right, which I have now passed on to my daughter and grandchildren. My favorite story from that book was "Billy and His Friends." Billy was a star pitcher on his youth baseball team, and he liked to eat lots of donuts before his games, especially when it was a big game in which he would be on the mound. On one such occasion, his body parts (e.g., brain, lungs, heart, stomach, muscles) decided to teach him a lesson. Just as he began pitching in the first inning of his big game, his stomach began to ache and his muscles became so sore that he struggled mightily to throw the ball over the plate. Billy became very unhappy as his team fell behind in the first few innings of the game. However, about midway through the game, his body parts decided that he had learned his lesson about eating too many donuts. They all began to work together to help him regain his strength and lead his team to victory. Very shortly after this happy ending, and sometimes just before, I would fall into a peaceful sleep, knowing that if I could just do things right and keep my body parts all working together, someday I would be able to play baseball like Billy.

Throughout my teenage and early adult years, I participated in several team sports, including baseball, which reinforced the value of teamwork [and trust] and doing the right things to ensure the success of the team. This appreciation of teamwork has continued throughout my adult life, especially during the difficult economic times such as we are experiencing today—or during an important baseball game against a worthy opponent.

Now in a much different domain, it has never been more evident that doing the right things with effective teamwork has been, and will continue to be, essential to the success of our consulting business.Doing the right things for our prospects and clients, and doing those things right, includes helping them deal with the economic downturn and funding issues that are now among their most severe challenges. To do so, we need to create teams of people who have skills and who have a common focus on those things that are-most important to our client. The primary benefit of this approach is a better outcome. We have many examples of the value of teamwork [and trust] combined with a focus on critical client needs.

No longer a young boy, or even a young man, I am experiencing a steady decline in the teamwork of my "body parts." I can easily relate to how Billy felt pitching during those initial innings of his big game. However, the older I get, the more I appreciate the teamwork [and trust] that makes our work so productive and enjoyable. That teamwork [and trust], combined with a clear and consistent focus on doing the right things for our clients, will serve us well, both now and during the better economic times that surely lie ahead. I close this article with a BIG thank you to all who have contributed to our higher education success stories and a reminder that none of us is as good as all of us.

OUR WAVE THREE: ORGANIZATIONAL TRUST

Of this next Wave of Trust, Covey states, "As a leader, you can be successful at the Self Trust and Relationship Trust levels so that people trust you as a person, but then fail at the Organizational Trust level by not designing and aligning systems that promote trust."[61] His chapter on Organizational Trust highlights the "Principle of Alignment,"[62] which results in high trust organizations that are efficient and agile. Covey quotes organizational design expert, Arthur W. Jones, "All organizations are perfectly aligned to get the results they get."[63] Covey suggests his own modified version of Jones' statement as, "All organizations are perfectly aligned to get the level of trust they get."[64]

Our organizational guiding principle, adapted from Stephen R. Covey, was, "Rather than focusing on things and time, focus on preserving and enhancing relationships and on accomplishing results."[65] Throughout our entire journey, we attempted to appropriately balance our focus on relationships with our need for results depending on where we were in the client life cycle with each of our clients. Although hindsight always surfaces lost opportunity for improvement, we attribute most of our success to organizational alignment around our concept of client success, which was well aligned with Stephen M. R. Covey's four cores and thirteen behaviors, and with his concept of win/win.

Covey also introduces the concepts of low-trust taxes and high-trust dividends. He believes that "if you don't have a high-trust organization, you are paying a tax, and it's a wasted tax. While these taxes may not conveniently show-up on the income statement as 'trust taxes,' they're still there disguised as other problems."[66] Examples of his "Trust Taxes" include internal redundancy, bureaucracy, politics, disengagement, turnover, churn, and fraud. We avoided most of these taxes with our externally focused, flat organization and our version of freedom with responsibility culture. However, our most important tax avoidance factor was hiring and retaining the right people on our bus.

Even with three changes in company ownership, we were able to minimize the bureaucracy associated with our higher education practice. All pricing decisions were made by one of our higher education executives, unless some aspect of the pricing exceeded our authority in which case we were able to quickly get approval from either the company CFO or CEO. During our twelve-year run, I reported to four different company C-level executives. Each time that reporting relationship changed, I had to spend more time with the pricing approval process. In each case, we were able to quickly establish enough trust to reduce the amount of time spent on approving the pricing of our large deals. However, establishing that trust was far easier when we were generating fifty percent of the company's revenue than it was in the beginning when we were responsible for less than ten percent of the company's revenue. As our track record improved, so did the level of trust with the other company executives, which increased our ability to avoid bureaucracy.

TRUST IS THE GLUE

According to Wikipedia, "Laminins are a family of proteins that are an integral part of the structural scaffolding of basement membranes in almost every animal tissue."[68] Laminins are what hold us together. They are cell adhesion molecules. Without them we would fall apart. And interestingly enough, laminins are shaped exactly like the letter "t." Could that "t" stand for trust? We came to believe that trust is to success as laminin is to our bodies.

In the parlance of former Cornell professor Carl Sagan, "Science is a way of thinking much more than it is a body of knowledge."[69] In that context, the art of our story was simply creative and imaginative ways of thinking about and building upon trusting relationships to effectively differentiate us from our competition. It is interesting to note that laminins are involved with cellular differentiation, which is defined as the process by which a less specialized cell develops or matures to possess a more distinct form and function.

During a relatively low-trust time in our business, that inevitably comes when companies merge, we conducted a face-to-face meeting of our higher education extended leadership team (about thirty people) to talk about the importance of trust glue, and discuss the adjustments required to return to a high-trust organization. We then concluded that we needed to focus our efforts on the things that could help get us back to a high-trust organization, but we needed to pick our targets carefully. At the end of the meeting, I gave each participant a desk-top version of the Serenity Prayer as a summary of our day-long discussions and to emphasize our need to stay true to our guiding principles with courage and wisdom.

> "God grant me Serenity to accept the things I cannot change,
>
> Courage to change the things I can,
>
> And Wisdom to know the difference."

PROOF OF PERFORMANCE

"The CedarCrestone implementation team was integral to our success. They integrated with our team members, creating an environment in which we could creatively design approaches that fit our unique situation. They demonstrated a continuous commitment to our success through their effective project management, problem solving skills and open communication. All of us in the CedarCrestone Workgroup were extremely satisfied. I respect and trust them as a company and as individuals."

Associate Vice Provost
Public Masters University

LESSONS LEARNED

- Trust is the yeast of client success.
- If clients don't trust their consultants, they won't trust their consultants' company.
- At the heart of most issues is a lack of trust. You may need a stent for trust to flow.
- You can't observe trust, you just feel it.
- Each wave of trust is a forerunner of the next—you can't skip one.

9.   Can Whispering Extend Trust?

Borrowed Wisdom

> "The single most important thing to remember about any enterprise is that there are no results inside its walls. The result of a business is a satisfied customer."[70]
>
> Peter Drucker,
> Author and Management Consultant

Guiding Principle

> Fill your market basket with trust. Without it, you'll go hungry.

Covey describes market trust as being "all about brand or reputation. It's about the feeling you have that makes you want to buy products or services or invest your money and time—and/or recommend such action to others. This is the level where most people clearly see the relationship between trust, speed, and cost."[71] Our brand vision was "trusted advisor for higher education." We analyzed market trust from the following three dimensions: client trust, partner trust and the structural balance and imbalance between and among them.

Client Trust

Although not common, some clients used a high-trust approach to vendor selection. Our first example was a private research university that was not a client at the time. The CIO asked us to come to campus to meet with their executive staff. The CIO opened the meeting by saying, "Based on what we have heard about you from other universities, we expect you folks to walk on water." Although we were taken aback by this flattering statement, it was a wonderful way to begin a relationship. A couple of months later, they hired us to help them develop their ERP requirements, conduct some change management, and facilitate project planning activities. Pursuant to a competitive process, they subsequently selected us as their implementation partner and they were an active client for a total of sixty months.

Our second example occurred with a medium sized public university. For the better part of two years, we provided much "good faith, free consulting" during our sales process. They acknowledged the benefit that they received from this pro bono sales support, and we gained the advantage of some high-trust relationships with their key stakeholders. This certainly felt like a win-win approach—much different from the typical arms' length arrangement associated with the usual selection process that exists in today's low-trust procurement approach. For the same amount of time and cost, both parties received more value, and the entire process was much more enjoyable and gratifying. I say this even though the selection committee's recommendation to buy Oracle software and CedarCrestone implementation services was overridden at the state level and, therefore, we received no revenue from this prospect. However, the institution's stakeholders gained much insight into the implementation and change management processes. They also shared many positive comments about us with their colleagues in other institutions. That went a long way.

Trust was the reason that we met all four of the CSU project objectives, made all of their go-live objectives on time, and saved them in excess of $10 million in the process. Similar to a successful basketball team, our small team of highly skilled consultants had very high self-trust, relationship trust, and organizational trust. Although we had to pay some "trust taxes" in the form of additional bureaucracy to offset some trust issues and normal politics for a large geographically dispersed institution such as CSU, our trust dividends grew by the day as we focused on enhancing relationship trust and achieving the results desired by CSU.

CSU's selection of us as their implementation partner came with some significant risks that they had to manage. We slowly saw their initial risk management rules and controls evolve into collaboration and trust as they realized that we were all focused on the same desired results with the same energy level. The greatest risk to the CSU project was in not trusting the project team to do their work well.

PARTNER TRUST

The biggest market trust challenge that we faced during this period was partner trust, although the majority of our partner relationships were in the category of high-trust. Our most strategic alliance was with the Oracle Corporation after their purchase of PeopleSoft in 2005. As the world's largest enterprise software company, Oracle became our most strategic partner—as well as our biggest competitor. This reality made for some very complex relationships and trust challenges.

Our higher education practice supported several very different, but interrelated, relationships with Oracle, examples of which included the following. We worked very closely with one of their many sales organizations to help them win new software license sales. If they were not successful selling their software, we would not have had opportunities to sell our consulting and hosting services. We invested heavily in our sales support for the Oracle application software salespeople, as did most of our competitors. Oracle's software clients also purchased other Oracle technology products, commonly referred to as systems software. They made these purchases from a different Oracle sales organization with which we also maintained an important relationship. Additionally, we were a significant Oracle client because we used their technology for both our internal back-office automation and to support our hosting services for our clients.

As part of our delivery of consulting and hosting services to our clients, we had to coordinate with Oracle to ensure client success. The amount of coordination varied greatly from client-to-client depending on many factors: maturity of the software, client's relationship with and importance to Oracle, and Oracle's involvement in the actual implementation and support of the software. Oracle's consulting and hosting organizations each reported to a different part of their organization than did their two software and technology sales organizations. However, ultimately all of their various organizations rolled-up to a single executive higher up in Oracle's vast organization.

To help their partners navigate their complex organization, Oracle assigned an alliance manager to each of their strategic partners. These alliance managers reported to a different executive than did the software, technology, consulting, and hosting organizations. Complex?

Yes, for sure. They had numerous strategic partners, many of whom competed with each other and also with some part of the Oracle organization. We all accepted the complexity of this partnership because the partnership was good for our clients, and, therefore, it was good for both Oracle and its partners.

RELATIONSHIP STRUCTURAL BALANCE

To better understand the dynamics of our relationship with PeopleSoft/ Oracle, I borrowed some wisdom from Dr. Jon Kleinberg, a computer science professor at Cornell University, recipient of a MacArthur Foundation "genius grant," and co-author of *Networks, Crowds, and Markets: Reasoning about a Highly Connected World*. (Copyright 2010. By permission of Cambridge University Press) Kleinberg introduced us to the social psychological theory of *structural balance* that resulted from studying the dynamics of relationship triangles involving three people, companies, or other entities that are bound together in a network. His research concluded that certain combinations of friendly and antagonistic relationships were stable. Kleinberg describes structural balance as follows:

"The principles underlying structural balance are based on theories in social psychology...The crucial idea is the following. If we look at any two people in the group in isolation, the edge between them can be labeled plus or minus; that is, they are either friends [partners] or enemies [competitors]. But when we look at sets of three people at a time, certain configurations of pluses and minuses are socially and psychologically more plausible than others...Based on this reasoning, we will refer to triangles with *one or three pluses as balanced,* since they are free of the sources of instability, and we will refer to triangles with *zero or two pluses as unbalanced.* The argument of structural balance theorists is that because unbalanced triangles are sources of stress and psychological dissonance, people strive to minimize them in their personal relationships."[72] A summary of Kleinberg's formula using the number of plus signs is:

Balanced relationship: one or three pluses
Unbalanced relationship: zero or two pluses

Kleinberg uses the following diagrams, as depicted in **Figures H and I** below, to illustrate which combinations of partner and competitor relationships are balanced (stable) and which are unbalanced (unstable).

Figure H: Mutual Partner Examples[73]

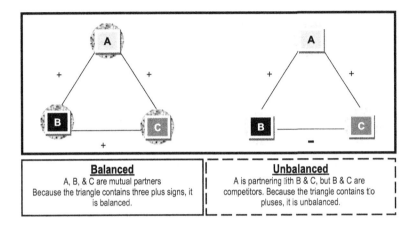

Balanced	**Unbalanced**
A, B, & C are mutual partners Because the triangle contains three plus signs, it is balanced.	A is partnering ⬚ith B & C, but B & C are competitors. Because the triangle contains t⬚o pluses, it is unbalanced.

Figure I: Mutual Competitor Examples[74]

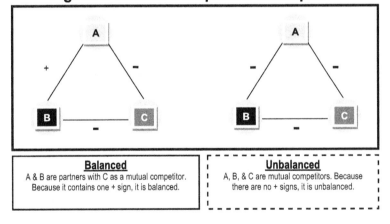

Balanced	**Unbalanced**
A & B are partners with C as a mutual competitor. Because it contains one + sign, it is balanced.	A, B, & C are mutual competitors. Because there are no + signs, it is unbalanced.

Using his relationship triangles as building blocks, Kleinberg then explains structural balance in networks of four or more nodes. He suggests that a network is balanced if every one of its triangles is balanced. In **Figure J below** the network on the right is unbalanced due to the two unbalanced triangles (two plus edges).

Figure J: Structural Balance in Networks of Four or More Nodes[75]

Balanced	Unbalanced
Each triangle has one plus sign.	Two unbalanced triangles: 2 +'s in each

Using Kleinberg's network model above, I represent our network that consisted of four sales entities. I used a "+" label for a business partner relationship and a "−" label for a competitor relationship.

A = PeopleSoft/Oracle consulting services sales

B = PeopleSoft/Oracle software sales

C = CedarCrestone higher education sales

D = Other PeopleSoft implementation service partners that were not subcontractors to Oracle Consulting

In **Figure K** below, I present our perception of this network, displaying it in two distinctly different ways. The diagram on the left shows the network as it existed in the beginning of our journey when market demand for PeopleSoft implementation services exceeded supply, which was the case in the early years of our journey. The diagram on the right shows the network as it existed when supply of qualified implementation consultants exceeded market demand, which was the case in the last few years of our success story. The primary factors that caused the structural balance of this sales network to change were as follows: (1) changes in market conditions, especially the supply and demand dynamics; (2) our emergence as a prime contractor and market leader in the large, multi-institution implementation market segment that previously was Oracle's "sweet spot;" and (3) changes in Oracle's business strategy that led them to more aggressively pursue service revenue opportunities that previously had been left to their implementation service partners, including emerging hosting opportunities.

Figure K: Kleinberg's Network Model Applied to Our Market Trust Relationships

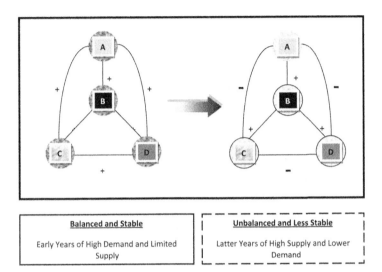

Balanced and Stable	Unbalanced and Less Stable
Early Years of High Demand and Limited Supply	Latter Years of High Supply and Lower Demand

A = PeopleSoft/Oracle consulting services sales

B = PeopleSoft/Oracle software sales

C = CedarCrestone higher education sales

D = Other PeopleSoft implementation service partners that were <u>not</u> subcontractors to Oracle Consulting

It is important to restate that in our adaptation of Kleinberg's model, a plus means a productive business partner and a minus means a competitor—but not an enemy, as in the Kleinberg model.

Once all software and service contracts were executed with a new client and the delivery process began, the network structure changed as we all put the client at the center of our network, as illustrated in **Figure L**. The nodes in this delivery network were:

A = PeopleSoft/Oracle maintenance and client support

B = The Client

C = CedarCrestone

D = Other PeopleSoft/Oracle consulting firms under contract with the same client

Figure L: Kleinberg's Model Applied to Our Delivery Stage with a Client

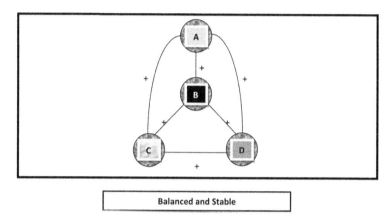

Balanced and Stable

One of Oracle's annual promotions fit very nicely with our "promote the success of our clients" strategy. Each year, they evaluated and recognized select partners for "excellence in developing and implementing solutions based on Oracle technologies." We were always pleased to win one or more of these awards for helping a client optimize their use of technology. Additionally, we were recognized as Oracle's Partner of the Year in 2005. We were even more pleased when one of our clients won a very competitive Oracle award for their successful implementation and use of Oracle software. Although the focus of these client awards was on the client's ability to optimize the value of their innovative technology and not on the implementation partner, this was the best example of "promoting the success of our clients."

It seemed that the service companies that were best positioned to become the ERP trusted advisor to higher education had the most difficult time in maintaining a consistently high-trust approach to servicing this market. For example, most of the large consulting companies have superb in-house training programs. Some of the best training that I ever received came while I was employed by IBM, which has been in business for more than one hundred years. Perhaps the higher education services market is just too small for the very large companies, or the profit margins are too low relative to other lucrative markets, to support the level of commitment that was necessary to become the trusted advisor. Whatever the reason, it created an opportunity for smaller firms to gain market share and move closer to a trusted advisor role in this very specialized market.

THE DIMENSION OF EXTENDED MARKET TRUST

I now explore the dimension of Covey's *extended trust* by envisioning a practical application of his wisdom in our market. I chose to focus on the buying process, because of the high level of trust taxes and low trust dividends present in this business process. If we want to reduce costs, save time, and create greater value for the client, the buying process is a prime candidate for transformation through extended trust.

Most procurement processes in higher education are designed to achieve the following objectives: protect the institution from disputes and litigation that sometimes result after a vendor is selected, ensure that the institution does not overpay for goods and services, and select a vendor that is well qualified to help the institution achieve the desired results. All of these are important, appropriate objectives. However, the typical procurement process used by most institutions of higher education is based on a low level of trust. Trust is actually withheld, and vendors are kept at arm's length, which creates considerable cost for both the institution and the vendors.

You will recall that Covey used the term "trust taxes" to refer to negative consequences that resulted from a lack of trust in a business relationship. There are several examples below of when we felt the impact of trust taxes because of higher education's distrust of vendors in the procurement process. The first occurred after delivering a thoughtful five-hundred-page proposal in response to an RFP. The very next day the prospect informed us that we had been eliminated from the competition in spite of our meeting the requirements, having extensive experience with similar projects for similar institutions, and competitive pricing. We knew that they couldn't have even read our proposal in so short a time. We muttered (and then some) to ourselves, "Who came in the back door?"

The second example was when we prepared a three-hundred-page proposal. We were selected as a finalist, prior to spending large amounts of time on-site with the selection team providing follow-up information and "free consulting." In spite of being selected as the "preferred solution," the executive sponsor ignored the selection team's recommendation, which was most unusual. Sadly, we were not selected to be their implementation partner.

A third example occurred when we prepared a lengthy, complex proposal in response to an RFP from a large multi-campus institution. Within three days of our submission, we received word that they rejected all of the proposals for implementation services. Upon further reflection, they decided that they should first select the software—and then go out with another RFP for implementation services. Arghhh!

As significant as our trust taxes were, they probably paled in comparison to the trust taxes being paid by most institutions during the process to select software and an implementation partner. Some institutions take years of preparation before issuing an RFP. Added to the trust taxes resulting from this inordinately long time in which numerous resources are consumed, institutions also pay various consultants to assist them with vendor selection and the contract negotiations process. This trust tax could be converted into a dividend if the role of these consultants were to help build trust rather than protect the institution from untrustworthy vendors. Although this probably sounds a bit unrealistic, it is worth some creative thought because the financial benefits for higher education could be significant, even if we only find a way to eliminate the failed and distressed projects.

TRANSFORMING THE VENDOR QUALIFICATION PROCESS

In the initial steps in the vendor selection process, the institution could examine each potential vendor using Stephen M. R. Covey's four cores of credibility[76], as stated below:

- Integrity (honesty, walking the talk, being congruent inside out, courage to act in accordance with your values)
- Intent (motives, agendas, behavior, win-win)
- Capabilities (talents, attitudes, skills, knowledge, style)
- Results (track record, performance, getting the right things done)

Very early in the selection process, the institution would conduct the vendor qualification exercise to weed out all potential vendors that are neither qualified nor trustworthy, based on Covey's "Cores of Credibility'" or some other similar criteria deemed appropriate by the institution. These criteria could include some combination of client surveys, reference checks, and vendor interviews. Using the results of this exercise, a short list of the most qualified, trustworthy vendors could be created. This approach could all be done using existing higher education networks and professional organizations. If cost is a significant factor in the evaluation, all interested vendors could be asked to submit hourly rates that would be valid for the remainder of the selection process. With this type of approach at the beginning of the buying process, the low-trust presumption can be changed to high-trust because each of the qualified vendors is now deemed trustworthy.

Stephen M. R. Covey's *principle of behavior*[77] can be used to guide the next step in the procurement process. It would arrange mutually beneficial behavioral evaluation activities with each trustworthy vendor. The purpose of this arrangement would be to determine the relationship orientation of each vendor. These sessions might include some combination of joint need-development and project planning, change management workshops, review of client survey results, and preliminary contract negotiations—the more personal interaction occurs, the better because implementation is all about people and relationships. The best opportunity to extend trust is during contract negotiations. Consistent with Covey's belief, most prospective clients were capable of being trusted, wanted to be trusted, and would run with trust when it was extended to them.

The criteria for evaluation of these activities might be something like Covey's thirteen behaviors, with a special focus on the following ones:

- Talk straight (tell the truth, use simple language, don't spin the truth)
- Demonstrate respect (care for others, treat everyone with respect)
- Create transparency (open and authentic, err on the side of disclosure)

- Show loyalty (give credit freely, acknowledge contributions of others)
- Clarify expectations (disclose and reveal expectations)
- Practice accountability (take responsibility for results)
- Listen first (seek first understand, then be understood)
- Extend trust (have a propensity to trust, extend trust abundantly)

Some who read this approach might question the value of conducting preliminary contract negotiations prior to finalizing requirements, timelines and pricing. It has been my experience that true behavior surfaces during the negotiation of master agreements and statements of work. Additionally, contract negotiations create many opportunities to extend trust.

To the remaining vendors, the institution would issue a brief RFP with clearly stated project objectives, critical requirements and the proposal evaluation criteria, including pricing and risk sharing (i.e., extended trust). The final step of the selection process could be limited to some additional reference checking and final contract negotiations with one or more vendors. Throughout this continuous evaluation process, the institution could involve as many or as few vendors as desired. When vendors are dropped from the process, they would receive feedback based on how they were rated using the well-defined evaluation criteria. The selection of the winner of this competition could occur at any point during the process without the need for the deadline driven production of a comprehensive RFP, proposal, and sales presentation.

The following diagram in **Figure M** below compares the timing of the prospect and vendor interaction during the three primary phases of the buying process for both the traditional low-trust selection process and our proposed more mutually beneficial high-trust process. This comparison is based on the assumption that the actual amount of interaction between the institution and the winning vendor would be identical with either approach. Of one thing I am completely convinced: the better the vendor understands the prospect's needs, issues, concerns, and vision of a solution, the higher the probability of a successful implementation with optimal value to the client.

Figure M: Comparison of Time Allocation in the Buying Process Between High Trust and Low Trust Environments

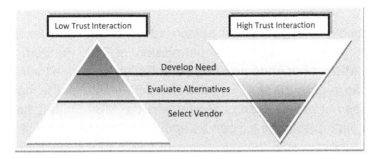

This overall approach could minimize trust taxes and increase trust dividends for both the institution and the vendors, including the following examples:

- Reduce the time and cost of the buying process for all parties

- Enhance need-development, issues awareness, and other knowledge exchange topics during the buying process

- Eliminate the preparation and review of large requests for proposal, proposals and presentations and focus on what is most important for the client to be successful

- Mitigate the risk of disputes and litigation regarding the selection process

- Establish trusting relationships that will result in mitigating the risks of project delays, cost overruns and a failed project

WHAT IF?

Although change comes slowly, especially in the world of higher education, the paucity of trust is something we can change. I agree with Covey's opinion that: "...contrary to popular belief, trust is something you can do something about. In fact, you can get good at creating it!"[78] Perhaps the most important by-product of this extended trust approach is the change in vendor behavior that would undoubtedly occur once they were convinced that trust would be a critical selection criterion instead of just price. If we believe what Covey says about the speed of trust—and I do—then we can be assured that starting with high trust relationships will significantly lower the cost and elapsed time of both the procurement process and the subsequent software implementation for the buyer. I also believe that high trust relationships will result in higher value for the client.

In their book, *The MBA Oath: Setting a Higher Standard for Business Leaders*, (Copyright 2010. By permission of The Penguin Group.) Harvard MBAs Max Anderson and Peter Escher describe their initiative that began in early 2009. "This book is the manifesto for the movement. It provides not only a strong case for why the MBA Oath is necessary but also examples of how it can be applied in the real world. It will help guide businesspeople through some of the toughest decisions they'll make in their careers."[79] Perhaps our industry needs something similar to the MBA Oath. It could be an industry-wide oath like the Hippocratic Oath, which would be difficult to administer, or just an oath that each company is required to sign as a first step in the vendor selection process. Taking it one step further, each consultant could be required to sign an oath that might look something like the following.

> As a professional consultant, my purpose is to serve the greater good by focusing on the success of my clients and working as a team to create value that no single individual can create alone. Therefore, I promise to:
>
> - Focus on the success of my clients
> - Extend trust to all of my teammates, prospects and clients
> - Act with the upmost integrity and pursue my work in an ethical manner
> - Represent the performance and risks of my enterprise accurately and honestly
> - Take responsibility for my actions

What separated the great whisperers from the good whisperers in our business was their ability to engender trustworthiness through their empathy and concern for the things that were most important to the client, their ability to design effective solutions that responded appropriately to client needs and priorities, and their commitment to actually doing what was best for the client. These qualities represent my interpretation of Covey's Principles of Behavior. And what separated great clients from good clients? It wasn't revenue and profit, although they were essential components of good business. However, our best clients always included people who understood win-win and the mutual value of trusting relationships.

OUR WAVE FOUR: GREATER CAUSE TRUST

I derived much gratification from my missionary work during a time when vendor-supplied application systems were in their infancy, with the promise of making life better for those colleges and universities that were willing to form high-trust partnerships. It was especially gratifying when clients such as CSU realized cost savings that exceeded our consulting fees. Of course, our experience pales in comparison to the significant contributions made by the larger corporations that serve higher education, as well as the many philanthropic individuals who are supporting higher education institutions in a variety of ways. Nonetheless, feeling good about our small contribution was an important aspect of our success story.

Even with a heavy travel schedule, many of our consultants found time to get involved with volunteer work in their communities. For the past five years, I have worked as a Court Appointed Special Advocate (CASA) for a local boy from a broken home. My inspiration for this came from an article in our company newsletter about one of our consultants in Chicago. The article described her experiences as a CASA helping needy children overcome behavior issues that resulted from lack of effective parenting. I was impressed by her very important contributions to this "greater cause" activity.

I conclude these two chapters about how trust was such an important influence in our story, by sharing a quote from Stephen M. R. Covey: "Extending trust to others rekindles the inner spirit—both theirs and ours. It touches and enlightens the innate propensity we all have to trust, and to be trusted. It brings happiness to relationships, results to work, and confidence to lives."[81]

PROOF OF PERFORMACE

> "From day one, CedarCrestone consultants and university team members worked cohesively to build and implement our system. As a result, a sense of trust and enthusiasm developed along the way. CedarCrestone's continuous guidance and commitment to the project were clearly evident and made a lasting impression."
>
> Project Manager
> Public Masters University

LESSONS LEARNED

- People and companies naturally gravitate to balanced relationships.
- Balancing is a challenge when a partner is also your biggest competitor.
- Extending trust may be risky, but without it you'll not reach your full potential.
- When the market shifts, hold on to trust.
- You don't need to have a lot to give a lot.

10. What's a Whispering Win-Win?

Borrowed Wisdom

> "For when the one Great Scorer comes to write your name, He writes not that you won or lost, but how you played the game."[82]
>
> John Wooden,
> Hall of Fame Basketball Coach

Guiding Principle

Invent options for mutual gain. They will compound themselves.

Once we were selected by a prospective client as their implementation partner, we faced the challenge of crafting a contract that focused on terms that would facilitate client success. Throughout the need-development and orals presentation, there was always an undercurrent of risk aversion on the part of the prospect, but this reached its peak at contract negotiation time. This attitude typically was normal for people in the late stages of the buying process, but it was exacerbated by the number of distressed and failed projects that were present in the early years of the nascent PeopleSoft software. A number of companies withdrew from the higher education market because the risks were too high and the consequences of failure too severe in terms of the negative impact on their bottom line—not to mention reputation.

Risk Alignment

In light of the theory of risk homeostasis, it was not necessary to mitigate all risk of an implementation project. In his book What the Dog Saw (Copyright 2009. By permission of Little, Brown and Company), Gladwell defines risk homoeostasis as "…under certain circumstances, changes that appear to make a system or an organization safer in fact don't. Why? Because human beings have a seemingly fundamental tendency to compensate for lower risks in one area by taking greater risks in another."[83] He then offers some examples, including, "Why are more pedestrians killed crossing the street at crosswalks than at unmarked crosswalks? Because they compensate for the 'safe' environment of a marked crossing by being less vigilant about oncoming traffic. Why did the introduction of childproof lids on medicine bottles lead, according to one study, to a substantial increase in fatal child poisonings? Because adults became less careful in keeping pill bottles out of the reach of children"[84]

Another important factor that impacts acceptable risk is competition. The tougher the competition, the more inclined we were to accept risk—as long as the potential reward was high. Typically, we were willing to accept more risk to win the deals that had a high potential of becoming a notable client success story.

The two most significant and interrelated concerns for our clients were the risk of missed go-live milestones and project cost overruns. Some of our clients had actually experienced both with previous projects with other implementation partners. These risks were also our two biggest concerns that could jeopardize our ability to execute our marketing strategy of promoting the success of our clients. Although there were many timing and cost factors that we could not control, and some over which we had very little influence, we wanted our project team to take responsibility for delivering the desired results of being on-time and within budget. It was in the best interest of both parties for us to focus our teams on reducing the risk of project delays and cost overruns. When we did so, our mutual risks were in almost perfect alignment. For all of our projects, the amount of acceptable risk was determined by the level of trust among the project participants—more trust meant more willingness to take risks.

Lacking a trusting relationship with the client, it was difficult to reach agreement on the consequences of cost overruns. The untrusting client wanted severe provisions for cost recovery and dispute resolution in the event of project delays, and our risk management people wanted to limit the amount of liability we had to assume for any significant project issues. In most of these low trust situations, which only happened occasionally, we would have to settle for a compromise solution, which is never ideal, or decide to walk away from the opportunity. Fortunately, compromise solutions worked quite well once our client relationships moved from low trust to high trust. Thus, we had to focus on those relationships to ensure that we could achieve the desired results.

At contract negotiation time, we attempted to convince the client of the benefits of risk alignment. We wanted the client's project team to understand our mutual commitment to delivering the desired results of on-time and within budget. This mutual commitment typically included a fixed-fee, fixed-term contract, which essentially was a performance guarantee for our clients. We committed to complete our work within the prescribed timeline and the client committed to not unreasonably delay the decision to put the new software in production on or near the targeted go-live dates. If we failed to have the software ready for production on those dates, we agreed to complete our work at no additional cost to the client. If the client decided not to put the production-ready software into live production, they would pay us for any services rendered after the go-live dates specified in the contract. In almost all cases, we were able to leave the contract in a drawer during the project and each party did whatever was necessary to achieve the desired results. This was possible because our mutual risks were in alignment and all parties felt responsible for client success.

Our proposed solutions included some combination of fixed-fees, incentive go-live milestone payments and project completion payments. Our approach to calculating these mutually beneficial fixed-fees might have been our most creative sales tactic. Some of the large, complex opportunities appeared so complex that people were inclined to believe that they couldn't be done, and certainly not within an aggressive implementation timeline. Without a way to minimize or eliminate some of the perceived complexities, their perception was probably accurate.

Proposing a fixed-fee for complex projects required some significant risk-taking and placed a premium on risk mitigation. In their book, *Finding the Priority Path*, in which our risk mitigation work is referenced, co-authors Bryant L. Stringham and Jon D. Stephens, discuss ways to "help organizations identify, prioritize, and control risks, deficiencies, and other factors upon which success depends."[85] With assistance from their company, Priority Systems, we used their PriorityPath® process, with its roots in risk engineering, to help some of our clients identify and mitigate project risks associated with software implementation planning and organizational change.

Having now touted the merits of our risk alignment approach, it seems prudent to point out that there always were very difficult issues that surfaced during the course of all of our large, complex projects. However, the root causes for most of these issues had little to do with risk management or risk mitigation. We had no simple answer for the vast majority of these issues given they usually resulted from some combination of politics and poor communication. Almost all of these challenging situations required us to take responsibility for fixing the problems without trying to determine who caused them. However, people in leadership roles cannot please everyone all of the time and often have to make issue resolution judgments based on the priorities of their organization.

Although we used a collaborative approach to issue resolution, the relative weight of the importance of the task to our goal of client success as compared to the importance of relationships varied from situation to situation. It was essential to consider each instance and use the most appropriate issue resolution style. Each of the following styles was necessary during most projects and our most effective whisperers knew how to best use each. At the beginning of a project, collaboration was essential to ensure the development of trusting relationships that would be required during more challenging times later in the project. As project deadlines approached, there were always times when it was necessary to be more directive and more receptive to compromise solutions to ensure a successful project.

FIGURE N: ISSUE RESOLUTION STYLES

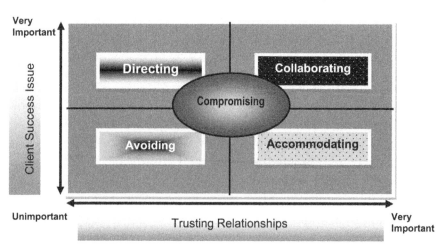

Our guiding principle for client issue resolution was to view each issue as an opportunity to demonstrate our commitment to the success of the client. In a couple of rare situations, we could not find a solution to a polit Ically-centric issue, so we had to create a work around. Each time this occurred, I regretted our inability to find a better practical solution. However, over time our risk partnership approach became a competitive advantage for us, and we earned a reputation for win-win problem solving. The client testimonial below is an example of how we assumed risk for a distressed project and together with our client achieved a successful outcom.

"CedarCrestone salvaged a troubled project on an extremely short timeline. Their ability to work across several departments with a variety of individuals allowed us to complete about eighteen months of work in just over six months."

Vice President for Planning and Enrollment Management
Public Masters University

RISK ROPERS

By their very nature, large, complex software implementations are risky, especially in the higher education environment. Additionally, client whisperers actually increase the amount of risk because, by nature, they are risk takers. They are confident in accepting risk because they are problem solvers. They have confidence in their ability to create solutions that will eliminate potential risks and achieve the desired result. They could deal with a high level of acceptable risk.

It was not possible to identify all potential risks during the planning phase of a large project, so one of the components of our project status reports was a section about project risks. We were constantly searching for new potential risks that could surface during the course of a project. When we discovered a new risk, we then could develop a risk mitigation strategy and include the mitigation status in all subsequent status reports.

In the middle of our journey, we encountered a particularly complex software gap that resulted during implementation planning for a university that followed a unique academic calendar. At that time, the

PeopleSoft software was designed to support traditional academic calendars that were much different than the one used by our client. To address this critical gap, the PeopleSoft software had to be redesigned to accommodate our client's calendar, which had a large impact on the processing and reporting logic of the software. When we discussed our planned gap solution with the vendor's software developers, they strongly advised us to not attempt this solution because it was very complex and risky. However, we decided to take the risk and create this solution because it was critical to our client, which put it in the category of acceptable risk. We also assigned this work to our most creative designers and developers.

In the spirit of thinking differently under the pressure of externally imposed deadlines, I explain our pricing process that uses some of de Bono's parallel thinking concepts from his international bestseller, *Six Thinking Hats.* (Copyright 1985, 1999 by MICA Management Resources, Inc. By permission of Little, Brown and Company). He touts his innovative method as being "simple, robust and effective," which was appealing to me. He believes, "The main difficulty of thinking is confusion. We try to do too much at once. Emotions, information, logic, hope and creativity all crowd in on us. It is like juggling with too many balls."[86] de Bono then explains the limitations of traditional Western thinking and contrasts it with his innovative method. "Western thinking is concerned with 'what is', which is determined by analysis, judgment, and argument. That is a fine and useful system. But there is another whole aspect of thinking that is concerned with 'what can be', which involves constructive, creative thinking and 'designing a way forward.'"[87]

THE PRICING PROCESS

In search of a way forward, I used the following seven-step pricing process that was based on de Bono's thinking method. However, there were times when the turnaround time was so short that we simply had to jump to Step 7 and "trust our gut."

STEP 1. SEEK FIRST TO UNDERSTAND

Using mostly objective thinking, we began our pricing process by gathering all relevant information and validating our understanding of the prospect's priorities, critical needs, and most significant issues and concerns. Before responding to a request for pricing from either a prospective or an existing client, we gathered all easily accessible information about the sales opportunity. In most cases, this included results of in-depth need-development with most, if not all, key stakeholders; validation of the prospect's priorities and preferred implementation timeline; and all other information regarding the prospect and the specific sales opportunity. We also prepared a summary of all similar projects that we either had completed or were in the process of completing to gain insight into hours required, project outcomes, profitability, and lessons learned. Finally, we conducted an analysis of our competitors' proposals for similar sales opportunities.

Step 2. Seek to Be Understood

Thinking with optimism, we then attempted to establish an aggressive project timeline that supported the prospect's highest priorities and was consistent with their academic calendar. The vast majority of the implementation cost is directly related to the duration of the project. The longer the project, the more person-hours will be used by the project team consisting of both client employees and consultants. Ideally, the prospect would have provided a preferred timeline based on their needs, priorities, staff availability, academic calendar, and project budget.

Step 3. Simplify, Focus, and Manage Expectations

In this step, we identified all high value project requirements and defined a solution strategy for each of these requirements. We eliminated all low value/high effort items from the project scope using the assumption that, with an aggressive timeline, these items should fall by the wayside. However, we did not eliminate any items for which the value to the client was not yet confirmed. We created a short list of project objectives that were well defined and feasible within the preliminary project timelines. A critical step in the very complex CSU project was to get all of the key stakeholders to agree to four simple, achievable objectives.

Step 4. Explore Creative Solutions

Now we began to think creatively about faster, cheaper, better ways to address the prospects needs with competitive solutions. Our consultants were very good at focusing on "what can be" and "designing a way forward." I will discuss this ability in greater depth in a subsequent chapter.

STEP 5. MATCH BEST PEOPLE TO BIGGEST OPPORTUNITIES AND GET BUY-IN

We established the smallest and most talented consulting team as appropriate for the situation. Small teams consisting of the right people are much more effective and efficient than large teams. Some very difficult decisions were made during this step of the process that required compromise, prioritization, and judgment. We established buy-in techniques and made adjustments for faulty assumptions based on feedback from the proposed consulting team. It was important to get feedback from all creditable sources, but final pricing decisions were made by the executive team.

STEP 6. BEWARE OF THE "BIG GORILLAS"

With our risk management hats on, we attempted to identify all ill-defined aspects of the project and all potential "black holes" that could increase the risk of project delays and cost overruns. Typically, these included ill-defined client needs, software customizations and ad hoc end-user reports. For all well-defined project components, we established preliminary pricing based on the optimal timeline and consulting team make-up. Our consultants were very good at identifying the "big gorillas" based on their experience with similar projects for similar institutions.

Then, we eliminated or mitigated all high risk factors via pricing assumptions, contract negotiations, project risk mitigation strategies, and alignment of our perceived risks with those of the prospect. Many times we would develop fixed-fee, fixed-term pricing options as part of this step. This approach worked best for projects that had a significant client consequence associated with project delays, which is always the case with student system implementations.

STEP 7. TRUST YOUR GUT

Now was the time to lead with our emotions and "trust our gut." In his *Chronicle of Higher Education* article, "Gospel of Well-Educated Guessing," Tom Bartlett describes how MIT professor, Sanjoy Mahajan, "can start with seemingly zero information and, after some furious scribbling and rapid-fire explanations, come up with an answer that's close to the mark."[88] In his book, *Street-Fighting Mathematics: The Art of Educated Guessing and Opportunistic Problem Solving*, Mahajan explains that trying to be too exact can be paralyzing; or "rigor leads to rigor mortis." Mahajan's principles for "back-of-the-envelope calcula- tions" include "simplify by subdividing (our step three), take out the big part (our step six), and trust your gut." Mahajan emphasizes that "It is as much an attitude as a technique. For MIT students, who are used to getting the right answers, the transition can be tough."[89] This also was true for many of our consultants, who prided themselves on getting precise answers.

Our overall pricing approach included some of the principles espoused by Mahajan in combination with our industry experience and some art- ful creativity. We made final pricing adjustments and added risk sharing components to ensure the following outcomes: a competitive proposal based on the strength of our relationships with the prospect; a commit- ment from the prospect to the timeline, staffing, and issue resolution; all available competitive insight; and our final assessment of project risks. This was not the time for more analysis. For the large, complex proj- ects, there was no perfect price other than in retrospect. We just had to choose between erring on the side of aggressive pricing to increase our chances of winning or erring on the side of risk management to increase the probability of a profitable project—if we won the deal. All of these pricing decisions had to be made expeditiously to comply with proposal submission deadlines dictated by the RFP.

How Did We Actually Determine a Price?

If you asked a team of experienced consultants, most of whom have very little knowledge of the prospective client's needs, to develop a detailed project plan and estimate of the consulting hours required to achieve client success, the typical result would be a project budget that exceeds what any sensible CFO would approve. If that team of consul- tants had been involved with in-depth need-development with most of the client's key stakeholders and had experience with similar projects for similar institutions, that resulting project budget would be lower, but most likely still beyond a CFO's budget for such a project.

The big challenge of pricing large, complex software implementation projects was that I had to juggle too many balls. I often found myself trying to reconcile the logical information provided by our consultants, tame my emotional aspiration of wanting to win the sale, temper my anxiety about the business risks, and harness our creativity to differentiate us from our competition.

In dealing with the challenge of pricing, I found the primary principles underlying Occam's Razor to be useful: The Principle of Plurality—Plurality should not be posited without necessity, and The Principle of Parsimony—it is pointless to do with more what can be done with less. Although these principles certainly were not conceived as a pricing tool, my interpretation of Occam's Razor is "When you have more than one logical solution to a complex problem, choose the simplest one." If you are missing some important facts, which was typically the case with our pricing deliberations, you have to rely on your instincts and trust your gut.

Once we were selected as a finalist, it was common for the prospect to request a "best and final" price. Most of our competitors inflated their initial price in anticipation of this negotiation. In the spirit of "talking straight" with our prospects, we chose not to engage in this practice and attempted to clearly state that our response to the prospect's RFP contained our "best and final" price. Of course, most prospects still attempted to negotiate price as part of contract negotiations. Typically we would respond with only a token price reduction in the spirit of relationship development. However, we always tried to make this a win-win situation by getting something of value to us in return. Many times that quid pro quo was a more precise project scope; a more definitive, rapid issue resolution process to be used during the implementation project; or simply a commitment to a set of issue resolution criteria.

With many of our large opportunities, especially for multi-campus projects, it was not possible to gather sufficient information in Step 1 to complete Step 2 with any high degree of comfort. In those situations, we attempted to develop reasonable assumptions based on our experience with similar projects. Using those assumptions, we quickly moved to Step 6 to determine the potential risks associated with these assumptions. This analysis helped greatly when we ultimately got to Step 7. The more experience we had with similar projects, the more comfortable we were with trusting our gut.

At the time of the CSU RFP, our experience was relatively low, and we felt very uncertain about our pricing for that proposal. Whatever comfort we did have resulted from the expectation that our chances of winning the deal were extremely low and, therefore, the risk of having to deal with all of the CSU "big gorillas" was also very low. As it turned out, we were the low bidder. This advantage, combined with our effective need and relationship development during the sales process, elevated our probability of winning to 100%. Fortunately, at the beginning of the project, we were able to get CSU to agree with most of the assumptions we had developed in Steps 3 and 4 of our pricing process which allowed us to reduce the risks associated with the "big gorillas" that we identified in Step 6 of that process.

For each successive multi-campus proposal, it became easier to trust our gut. We gained confidence that our proposal assumptions were correct. By the time we had completed several of these large projects, we had more substance to our analysis and fact finding; but even more importantly, we had more confidence in what our collective "guts" were telling us.

HERE'S AN EXAMPLE

One of the most interesting examples of how we priced large, complex projects was in response to an RFP from the Nevada System of Higher Education ("NSHE"). They were in need of a fully functional ERP solution for all of the state's seven universities and community colleges. Prior to receiving this RFP we spent a great deal of time doing need development with NSHE people, both in their central administration and in most of their seven institutions.

Their 2006 RFP was for a comprehensive ERP solution that would replace most of their administrative software that used very old technology and was operating on a costly mainframe computer. The overarching objectives were to reduce both the cost and the risk of failure of their existing legacy system and to significantly improve service to their students, faculty and staff. Although in some cases very detailed, the software requirements contained in the RFP were difficult to interpret due to the diversity of the individual institutions and lack of standards across the state-wide system. Furthermore, a strong preference was stated for proposals that included both software and implementation services, which meant that we would have to joint bid with Oracle. This preference was further complicated when Oracle made the decision to joint bid exclusively with one of our biggest competitors, which left us out in the cold. However, we decided to submit a "services only" proposal in hopes that it would be compelling enough to overcome the prospect's preference for proposals containing both software and services.

We began our proposal development process for this very large opportunity knowing that both our implementation approach and our pricing had to be compelling. I took responsibility for the pricing process that went something like the following.

STEP 1. SEEK FIRST TO UNDERSTAND

There was so much to understand about this complex opportunity! Fortunately, our need development that we conducted prior to release of the RFP provided some very useful insight. We also had some knowledge about their legacy system because two of our consultants were part of that implementation project many years ago. However, the information gaps were significant, especially regarding the implementation model, project timeline, and software customizations that would be required to satisfy NSHE's high priority needs and wants. To help close these gaps, a handful of our client whisperers, who had significant multi-institution experience, developed a set of questions that we submitted to NSHE. The responses we received back from NSHE were helpful, but there were still many remaining information gaps. At this point, pricing was a mystery that had to be solved quickly to avoid missing the deadline for proposal submission. The only way to gain enough insight to calculate a fair price was to conduct "deep dives" into the thousands of RFP requirements. However, if we were to meet the proposal deadline, there was no time to conduct a deep dive.

I decided that the most readily available information that I could collect to help us price this complex project would be an analysis of plan versus actual for our completed and in-progress multi-campus projects. I did so with a special focus on those clients that shared similarities with NSHE. While no two of these large projects were ever identical, it was very helpful to search for whatever similarities we could identify. For the NSHE opportunity, the most important similarities with at least one of our previous large projects included the following: a history of using common software and a centralized support organization across all institutions, disproportionate support for the larger institutions, compelling need to get software off the mainframe, some reluctance to participate in a "one size fits all" software implementation, paucity of PeopleSoft experience, strong executive support in central administration, a need to share selected information among all institutions, campus concerns for a state-wide approach to ERP selection and implementation, and limited project funding. We then identified what factors made NSHE different from our previous multi-campus clients. Our primary concern was the academic diversity and differing priorities and imperatives that the software would need to support during a simultaneous implementation for both research universities and community colleges. Another concern was the logistics associated with the geographic dispersion of the individual institutions. The resulting composite analysis gave us a better foundation for our pricing assumptions.

STEP 2. SEEK TO BE UNDERSTOOD

With an aggressive proposal development schedule, we had to begin Step 2 prior to completing Step 1. Recognizing this would result in some rework in subsequent steps, I began developing a preliminary implementation timeline and assumptions to be used as a straw man in my pricing discussions with our internal experts. Using this draft approach allowed me to quickly solicit valuable input from our consultants without them each having to complete detailed analysis based on their individual assumptions about the project. Even with this approach, however, opinions varied greatly about project assumptions, timeline, and staffing. Through an iterative process that included some lively discussions, I was able to complete a preliminary implementation timeline and assumptions based upon input from our most experienced multi-campus project managers and consultants. However, if we had attempted to complete the pricing at this point in the process, we would have priced ourselves out of the opportunity with a price in excess of $30,000,000, which I was certain would not make our proposal compelling.

STEP 3. SIMPLIFY, FOCUS, AND MANAGE EXPECTATION

With the goal of getting to a more competitive price, a small team of our consultants attempted to determine what would be of most value to NSHE and what aspects of the project would likely have the least value for them. Once we got comfortable with this prioritization, which was not an easy task, we created a preliminary staffing plan that focused on high value services and the elimination or minimization of the low value ones. Although doing this without client validation was very risky, our experience suggested that once a project with an aggressive timeline begins, the project team quickly realizes that there is not time to do everything and that some prioritization makes good sense for everyone. We then documented our assumptions so that we could clearly state in our proposal what was within-scope and what was out-of-scope for the project. This delineation was important for setting reasonable expectations for both the client and our consulting team. Using these scope assumptions, we were able to get the preliminary price down to approximately $24,000,000.

When we first entered the PeopleSoft market, some of the large competitors were charging for both consultant travel time and very high rates for mandatory executive/partner project involvement. Consistent with our "trusted advisor" vision, we felt strongly that clients should not pay for this low value time. Our approach created significant cost savings for our clients. For example, during a typical twenty-four-month project with a team of about twelve to fifteen full-time consultants and an executive sponsor participating about eight hours monthly at an hourly rate of about $250, we saved our client almost $2,000,000 over the life of the project. Typically, our hourly rate for project managers and other consultants was at least $20 per hour lower than the rates being charged by the big consulting companies, which added to the cost savings for the client.

STEP 4. EXPLORE CREATIVE SOLUTIONS

We explored ways to meet specific RFP requirements with more creative solutions than were assumed earlier in the pricing process. We knew that some requirements could actually be addressed with creative low-cost solutions, some of which we had developed for previous clients. However, with the limited specifications contained in the RFP, it was difficult to precisely calculate the consulting effort for many of these, so we established a reasonable pool of consulting hours to deal with the items in this category.

One of the mandatory RFP requirements was a facility to allow NSHE institutions to share selected data among all seven institutions while maintaining the integrity of each institution's information. We had developed a customization for a previous client to meet a very similar requirement and our experts felt certain we could provide this type of solution to NSHE at a much lower cost than those that would be proposed by our competition, which turned out to be accurate. These adjustments helped us reduce our preliminary price by almost a million dollars.

STEP 5. MATCH BEST PEOPLE TO BIGGEST OPPORTUNITIES AND GET INTERNAL BUY-IN

We knew that assigning the right consulting team to this opportunity was an important cost factor. A relatively small team of the right people is much more effective than a large team of less experienced people. This is especially true if the team of right people is excited about the opportunity to produce results for both the company and the client. The biggest challenge to assembling such a team was availability of the right people. This challenge was exacerbated by the difficulty of predicting a start date for the NSHE project. However, during the pricing process, we decided that the NSHE opportunity was important enough that we would find a way to assign the right team to the project. Based on this decision, I felt comfortable reducing our price by another $3,000,000. But it was important to get those right people involved in our pricing and project planning activities to get their buy-in to whatever we finally proposed to NSHE.

STEP 6. BEWARE OF THE "BIG GORILLAS"

We asked our proposed team members to validate our pricing assumptions and identify the potential "black holes" that could lead to cost overruns and/or delays during the project. This was the beginning of minimizing risks for this potential project. Most of the high risk items fell into one of three categories: ill defined software customizations, NSHE's inability to staff the project with the right people, and NSHE's willingness to resolve project issues expeditiously. Based on these discussions, we began to craft proposal language to address each risk area. We also formulated negotiation strategies to be used in the event we were selected as a finalist. We decided to propose fixed-fee, fixed-term pricing for all reasonably well defined deliverables with an hourly rate for all yet-to-be defined customizations.

STEP 7. TRUST YOUR GUT

Up until Step 5 above, I was very concerned about our pricing deliberations for this NSHE opportunity. Consequently, my gut was telling me to be conservative and ensure that our price was not too low. At the conclusion of Step 5, however, I began to feel much more aggressive about pricing because I had confidence in our proposed consulting team. Although this was still a real long shot for us, I was getting excited about the possibility of actually winning this deal. My gut seemed to be telling me that $19,000,000 was the right price. That's what we submitted.

After a protracted evaluation process, we were selected by NSHE as a finalist, along with two software vendors – Oracle and SunGard – each of whom proposed both software and services. After a lengthy contract negotiation process with each of the three finalists, NSHE selected us as their implementation partner! We were elated with the news, to say the least. When the NSHE executives presented their vendor recommendations to their Board of Regents, they said of CedarCrestone, "They share project risks with NSHE – gave fixed pricing even in unclear areas." We subsequently executed a $14,000,000 fixed-fee contract for the initial phase of their ERP project. A little more than two years later, NSHE went live with their new software.

With each of our large projects, at least one significant, unanticipated issue surfaced post contract execution, and win-win solutions had to be negotiated while the implementation work was in progress. For example, during contract negotiations with CSU, we reached agreement that there would be no software upgrades until after the completion of all contractual go-live milestones that were covered by a fixed-fee. About four months prior to our first major go-live, PeopleSoft announced the release of Version 8.0 of their software that contained very exciting internet capabilities that could potentially be very beneficial to CSU. Upgrading to this new version would require a large effort for institutions that were already in live production with a previous version of the software. The CSU team determined that the benefits of moving to Version 8.0 were compelling and asked us to evaluate the cost and risk of completing the upgrade prior to completion of all contractual go-lives.

Our team determined that the upgrade effort would be much less if we could find a way to complete the upgrade prior to the initial go-live date. However, to do so we would have to begin the upgrade work immediately. We presented our findings to the CSU leadership team. We then offered to complete the upgrade work at no additional charge to CSU if they would agree to complete a list of tasks by the required due dates and to act as a demonstration site for this new and exciting internet-based software. We also knew that there was much additional consulting opportunity within CSU. We felt that eventually we would get a high return on our investment in our no-charge upgrade work. We had a very happy client when we went live with the functionally rich, latest release of software.

With the help of some creative pricing and service delivery tactics, our multi-institution implementations became an additional competitive advantage. During our journey, we won competitions for large projects with more than twenty large, multi-institution or multi-campus clients. To ensure an acceptable blend of analysis and art, we retained the authority and responsibility for all pricing at the highest level of our higher education practice. However, it always required a team effort to get it right. From an internal perspective, it is interesting to note that although we did not charge premium rates, our higher education practice was more profitable than any of our other company divisions, due mostly to the waves of trust that developed within our project team, within the client's project team, among all project participants, and the collaborative culture of our market.

PROOF OF PERFORMANCE

"The student system implementation effort continues to be one of the healthiest projects Gartner has seen across our diverse client base. With regards to our higher education clients, SSP *is the healthiest.* Since the last review, overall risk has decreased as a result of continued proactive project management and the project team's responsiveness to prior risk recommendations."

Gartner Project Review
Assessment of CedarCrestone's Project with
University of Virginia

LESSONS LEARNED

- Always focus on eliminating the risks that matter most; the others will usually dissipate when you do so.
- Mitigate the risks that matter the most to both you and your client.

- Partnerships, not solo-ships, are the most effective way to mitigate risks.

- Get internal buy-in to the proposed pricing from those who will be responsible for the success of the project.

- Trust your gut—ultimately it is your best calculator.

11. WHAT'S A WHISPERER'S FCB?

BORROWED WISDOM

> "...'trusted' leaders do things better, faster, and at lower costs."[90]
>
> Nolan Archibald,
> Chairman of the Board and CEO,
> Black & Decker Corporation

GUIDING PRINCIPLE

> Trust is the basis for faster and cheaper; artful execution is the basis for better.

Faster, cheaper, better ("FCB") was the mantra of our Client Whisperers. The drive for faster was based on the rationale that: (1) speed has the biggest impact on cost, which then impacts price; (2) technology upgrade releases were always on the horizon; and (3) the stress associated with large, complex projects should be minimized for a client by getting through it as quickly as possible. Delivering our services cheaper than our competitors obviously gave us a competitive advantage. However, we felt that if we could find a way to save our clients money by doing it faster, which meant even cheaper, we also would be contributing to client success. We came to realize that the single most important facilitator of faster and cheaper was trust; and if people were able to be brutally honest about opportunities for improvement, trust was also a precursor of better.

REALITY DISTORTION

It was not uncommon for both our consultants and clients to begin projects thinking that our proposed implementation timeline was much too aggressive–perhaps out of touch with reality. However, based primarily on my experience at IA, I was convinced that we could change the conventional wisdom regarding the time required to implement PeopleSoft software. I recalled hearing about how the people at Apple described Steve Jobs' "reality distortion field" that enabled him to create the sense that the seemingly impossible was possible, and how that often led to the "impossible" actually being accomplished. Although this sounded a bit over the top – the term reality distortion field came from Star Trek – my gut told me that the right strong-willed people working in a high trust environment could indeed accomplish things that the pundits had previously called impossible. Examples of our effective use of reality distortion included our initial CSU project and almost every other multi-campus PeopleSoft implementation project that we completed successfully thereafter. The other factor that contributed to our effective use of reality distortion was the propensity of our client whisperers to treat the ordinary with disdain and seek out the most challenging projects. This phenomenon also helped us recruit some of the best whispering talent in the industry.

TRUST: THE KEY TO FASTER AND CHEAPER

Stephen M. R. Covey created the following simple formula to convey his belief that trust always affects both speed and cost. As depicted graphically in **Figure N**, when trust goes down, speed will also go down and costs will go up; and when trust goes up, speed will also go up and costs will go down.

Figure N: The Economics of Trust[91]

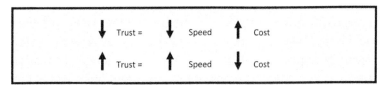

EXCELLENT EXECUTION

In his book *The 8th Habit: From Effectiveness to Greatness*, (Copyright 2004. By permission of Free Press.), Stephen R. Covey makes reference to a five-year study conducted by Nitin Nohria, William Joyce, and Bruce Robertson, as published in the *Harvard Business Review*, July 2003. "In what they called the Evergreen Project, they examined more than two hundred well-established management practices as they were employed over a ten-year period by 160 companies. This research enabled them to distill which management practices truly produced superior results. Their compelling conclusion is that without exception, companies that outperformed their industry peers excelled at four primary management practices."[92] I present these practices below.

- Strategy—Devise and maintain a clearly stated, focused strategy
- Culture—Develop and maintain a performance-oriented culture
- Structure—Build and maintain a fast, flexible, flat organization
- Execution—Develop and maintain flawless operation execution

An example of our fast, flexible and performance-oriented culture is reflected in the following client testimonial.

"CedarCrestone consultants' depth of knowledge in designing efficient modifications to address our campus needs, their strength in bringing campus staff along through the learning curve, and their consistently speedy response to issues have been second to none. They have helped us optimize and migrate our existing processes, which has saved us incalculable re-engineering time."

**Associate Chief Information Technology Officer
Public Masters University**

We felt that our strategies were focused and clearly stated. We had built a culture that was aligned with the performance orientation of our client success goal. The structure of our organization was fast, flexible and flat. However, execution was the most challenging for us because our organization was a virtual one, our projects were geographically dispersed, and we had externally imposed deadlines that were ever present. For our clients to be successful using our faster, cheaper, better approach, we had to overcome our deficiencies. We now share three examples of how we did so, almost flawlessly, with our execution tactics.

PROCESS-CENTRIC: GETTING TO THE HEART OF IT

When the need to replace aging legacy systems and hardware in higher education was coming to the forefront as an issue in the mid-to-late nineties, many institutions viewed this technology paradigm shift as an opportunity for a corresponding business process paradigm shift. In the previous generation of proprietary software, the implementation process was largely one of training the users on use of the software. To make the software support an institution's current business processes required either a change in business processes or customizations to the software. Many institutions opted for customizations that supported their current way of doing business, particularly the larger, more complex research universities. However, as funding came to the forefront of issues in higher education, some institutions looked for ways to reduce the heavy workload associated with maintaining these highly customized legacy systems and cumbersome business processes. A market opportunity emerged for an approach that could integrate business process redesign into an ERP implementation.

Because the PeopleSoft software was designed much differently than legacy systems, the implementation process accordingly was much different. The PeopleSoft software had a great deal of flexibility to accommodate the diverse ways in which colleges and universities conducted business. However, most vendors took the approach of "setting up tables" in the various software "modules," just as they had done with legacy systems using a traditional implementation methodology.

Because of our higher education experience—and our strategy of differentiation—we incrementally developed a methodology that integrated business process analysis and redesign into the implementation process. In **Table 2** below, I contrast a typical traditional implementation methodology used by most of our competitors with our process-centric methodology.

Table 2: Comparison of Traditional Versus Process-centric Methodology

TRADITIONAL METHODOLOGY	CEDARCRESTONE METHODOLOGY
• Software-centric	• Business process-centric
• Methodology-centric	• Human-centric
• Directive	• Collaborative
• Sequential project phases	• Iterative phases
• Large teams	• Small teams
• Few teams	• Many teams
• Short-term training	• Continuous knowledge transfer

To illustrate the evolution of our approach, I present two client vignettes. The first illustrates how our early process-centric approach using The Hunter Group methodology combined with one of our exceptionally talented client whisperers gave us just the edge we needed as we began a dauntingly large project. The second illustrates how an international faculty member teaching in the Marriott School of Management at Brigham Young University "turned on a light" that greatly enhanced our ability to map and redesign business processes and how one of our clients accelerated our approach even more.

CLIENT VIGNETTE ONE: I'M ONE OF YOU

When we first merged with The Hunter Group, we brought together some of our key consultants to meet in Baltimore with their methodology guru. The Hunter Group had recently hired Lindsey, an intelligent, get-it-done person with a vivacious personality who had earned her degree from Brown University. She had been working at Southern Methodist University (SMU), one of the PeopleSoft partner universities that implemented the beta version of the PeopleSoft student information system. Given they did not have any methodology as they made their way through implementing the system, she was elated to learn about the Hunter Group's methodology, particularly the second phase in which Interactive Design and Prototyping (IDP™) was conducted. She quickly became our higher education "IDP advocate and guru."

As we planned for our all-important CSU project planning meeting, it was an easy decision to include her in our team presentation. When we entered the meeting room, we observed the formality and size of the horseshoe arranged room and setup for the PowerPoint presentation. We wondered if our informal approach of talking about their issues and needs, as we had learned from our campus visits, would be well received in such a formal setting—and if our IDP scenario approach would be "too folksy." When the CSU stakeholders came in, we shook hands with a few of the members we knew from our previous CSU activities. However, once the meeting commenced, we sensed an aura of formality.

After we presented the high level project strategy and objectives, we watched Lindsey enthusiastically go up to the front of the room near the flip chart. We held our breath, hoping that her natural, engaging personality and recent higher education and PeopleSoft experience would be well received. In her easy, client whisperer conversational approach, she said that she understood what they must be feeling, because she had felt like that when she worked for her former university and their implementation loomed.

Lindsey explained that when she joined The Hunter Group and learned about its methodology—especially the Interactive Design and Prototyping (IDP)—she realized how much easier it would have been to have used a methodology like IDP when she was implementing the software at SMU. Lindsey explained that if she had used such a methodology, she would have saved a great deal of time and would have experienced much less stress—probably would have even enjoyed it. Then she gave a preview of what it would be like if they were in an IDP session. She moved over to the flip chart and started interacting with the audience as she showed them how we first learn about a client's business processes and then redesign the processes as an integral part of the software design and configuration process. All eyes were upon her. Lindsey explained, as paraphrased, "My IDP sessions begin with discussions of the clients' current business processes and the timing of the processes. Then we match those processes with like or similar processes in Campus Solutions (the student information system). The business processes that exist in the client's legacy system, but are not covered in PeopleSoft, are initially considered gaps in functionality. The goal is to find a way to redesign a current business process to eliminate the gap. If a redesign solution is not possible, we develop a system modification. After business processes for the current system and PeopleSoft are mapped, we then perform system set up. I always tailor the IDP sessions to the participants and their skill sets. We even have fun in IDP sessions!"

During Lindsey's presentation, we sensed the atmosphere in the room shift from a cool formality to a pleasant, friendly one. After the meeting concluded, we received very positive feedback from the CSU leadership team. We gave three cheers—and then some—for Lindsey who had convinced the CSU project team that she knew how they felt—and could do something about it through our process-centric approach.

CLIENT VIGNETTE TWO: IT'S EASIER THAN YOU THINK

Judie and I, along with two consultants from IBM, were involved in a project called VISTA to design a model for World Class Student Services for Brigham Young University (BYU). Part of the scope of this engagement was to evaluate current student administration business processes across the university as a basis for redesigning services to achieve the president's mandate of World Class Student Services. BYU had used the Priority Systems method and tools to evaluate and receive input into the effectiveness and efficiency of their student administration business processes from the perspective of students, faculty, staff, and administrators. Even the president of the university participated! Both undergraduate and graduate students were involved in the project, as either project team members or as analysts performing business process reviews.

It was a Friday morning when Judie and the Vista project team members were sitting in a conference room, eagerly awaiting a presentation from graduate students in the Marriott School of Management regarding their business process analysis work at the university. When the students got up to make their presentations, they confidently explained how they had used the Picture Card Design Method (PCDM), developed by Dr. Markus Gappmaier, visiting professor in the Marriott School of Management. Dr. Gappmaier was a noted pioneer of holistic business process management and had successfully applied his methodology in hundreds of companies in Europe and in the United States. Dr. Gappmaier explained that in his approach, the goal was always to "work toward a solution." As Judie watched the student presentations of their business process mapping and redesign using the PCDM method and listened to Dr. Gappmaier's approach, she said to herself, "That's it! I'm going to try it—and right away."

Judie was concurrently conducting a management consulting engagement at California Polytechnic University, San Luis Obispo, (Cal Poly SLO), one of many campuses within the CSU system that needed to build campus-wide support for a PeopleSoft implementation. The associate vice provost, who was very progressive and understood the importance of building consensus when undertaking a project of this scope, had constituted a campus-wide, representative work group. She knew that the initiative would have high visibility and she wanted broad representation of the campus-wide community. After the initial planning with the work group that had been constituted, Judie was ready to begin the business process mapping of the academic advising processes across Cal Poly SLO's ten colleges.

Judie jumped right into the business process mapping using the PCDM methodology, which she had seen only three days prior. Beginning with the College of Agriculture, Judie and the associate dean of the college mapped the entire academic advising process for the college within two hours, creatively using color post-its on flip charts throughout the room. Judie continued the mapping process, along with the project leader, by meeting with the directors of advising and academic advisors in the other nine colleges. The client project leader identified a way to make the documentation of the business process maps even more expeditious by recording the maps in an MS Excel spreadsheet as Judie was placing Post-its on the flip chart. Lindsey also came to assist in the process, along with a team member from BYU's Vista Project who wanted to see how PCDM was being used at Cal Poly SLO. Todd conducted a day-long session with the work group about the capabilities of the PeopleSoft software and how it could streamline processes and improve access to and dissemination of information. Judie and each of the lead academic advisors then presented the resulting maps of current processes to the work group. Energized by the opportunity to improve these processes, the academic advisors and members of the work group met in small teams to redesign all fifteen academic advising business processes across ten colleges, doing so based upon best practices principles and new features available in the PeopleSoft software.

They eagerly showed the results of their efforts to the full work group, who helped to further streamline the processes and identify policy considerations. Through this project, the academic advisors of the ten colleges formed stronger professional and personal relationships. They laid an important foundation for accelerating the time-to-degree process through redesigned business processes supported by new information systems. I now share a testimonial from the associate vice provost and project leader for this engagement.

"My reason for bringing CedarCrestone in was to help get a group of individuals, who crossed colleges, roles, etc., exposed to PeopleSoft, to be more comfortable with the thought of the PeopleSoft implementation and to gain some advocacy for the implementation in the academic units throughout the campus...The process maps that were done by CedarCrestone were extremely helpful in illustrating what it is we do. They visually showed the complexity of some of our processes without being too technical. It was a great learning tool to illustrate how differently each area does things, to stimulate questions of why we do things, to share ideas on how to do things better, etc. The Picture Card Design Method (PCDM) has a visual impact that is simple, yet powerful. Our purpose for process mapping was not to document exactly how we do things, when decisions are made, etc. but instead to give us a good understanding of how things happen, where decisions are made, etc. so that we could discuss how we could improve. Our results were outstanding!"

After this engagement, Lindsey suggested to our leadership team that we have a professional development program for our consultants, to train and retrain them in our methodology, including the PCDM methodology. In response, we launched our CedarCrestone Academy and proceeded to plan and deliver a series of process-centric workshops for all of our consultants throughout the country. Our process leadership team included Judie; Lindsey; Jill, one of our most effective client whisperers who had a strong background in financial aid; and

Dana, our highly regarded consultant responsible for our internal training program.

In the workshops, Judie and Lindsey gave the consultants instructions on how to use the PCDM as part of the Interactive Design and Prototyping (IDP) phase of our methodology and demonstrated how we had successfully used it with some of our clients. They then conducted mock exercises to map out sample business processes. The consultants eagerly and actively engaged in their small group activity of mapping a current process and redesigning it, all the while having fun using colored Post-its. We were amazed at the heightened level of creativity that they demonstrated, no doubt drawing upon their combined experience in higher education, knowledge of how the software could be setup, and real live situations with their current clients. Time flew! They finished their redesigns in two hours. Each group then proudly shared with the full group what the current business process looked like, and how they had redesigned it based upon best practices principles and optimization of the software. It was plain to see that they were very satisfied with the results that they had achieved, all the while further building their team relationships with fellow client whisperers.

I share a few of the comments that we received from the participants when asked what benefits they received from participating in the workshop. "The Picture Card Design Method was very exciting, and I will use it. It was definitely an 'aha' moment. The amount of information was fantastic!" "I walked in not knowing how to perform an Interactive Design and Prototyping session or use a Picture Card Design Methodology and came out excited to try out the methodologies." "I love that I now have an effective business process mapping technique that will provide that added value that ONLY CedarCrestone consultants can bring to a project and a client. I look forward to sharing with you my use of the business processing mapping technique in the future."

We were greatly encouraged by the feedback from our consultants and clients that our process-centric approach worked even better than before—and faster, which meant cheaper. FCB! And did you detect our client whisperers' eagerness to learn, their desire to bring more value to their clients, and their sense of excitement about trying something new?

SIMPLIFY TECHNOLOGY

We experienced an interesting technology-oriented example of how a trusting relationship with one of our large, multi-campus clients resulted in a faster, cheaper, and better solution. This occurred in the context of a pending decision regarding a technical solution that started during the sales cycle, continued into contract stage, and was resolved in the early stage of our delivery. Our team of consultants willingly embraced emerging technologies, and we had more relevant experience than most of our competitors. However, our experience suggested that embracing emerging technologies was not always the best way to optimize FCB. For example, this large multi-institution client needed a way to ensure that all student data were synchronized and accurate across all of their campuses. They even included the requirement in their RFP. One of our competitors proposed a very sophisticated, but expensive, solution, while we proposed a simpler solution for much less money.

Our solution was focused on addressing the need, as described by the client in the RFP. Our experts believed that the more expensive solution had "too many moving parts;" and, in addition to being more costly, it would be difficult to implement and maintain. During the sales process, we sensed that the institution was a bit skeptical that a much less expensive solution would meet their needs. Our approach during contract negotiations was to give them the option of using either of the two alternative solutions. Once we began the project and our client whisperers established trusting relationships with the client, we explained in more detail how our proposed simplified technical solution would work. The client opted for our approach and, as a result, they experienced a FCB implementation of their new software.

MARKET RESPONSE TO **FCB**

For some, FCB was an oxymoron. If you focused on "faster"-- which always resulted in "cheaper"—there was not much time available for "better." The trick was to identify and document the high value opportunities for "better" as early in the discovery process as possible, which of course should begin with need-development during the buying process. We always sought to prevent rework near the end of the project due to inadequate quadrant of quality discovery work at the beginning of the project.

There were differing client perceptions of, and interest in FCB. For example, in our early years, when we had clients who were concerned about a Year 2000 disaster, faster was definitely better. On the other hand, to one of our large research universities that wanted to optimize their investment in new technology across the entire enterprise, "better" meant taking the time to address change management and business process innovation. Taking the time to "do it right" was more important to them than were either "faster" or "cheaper," because they did not want to miss a big opportunity for improvement in both operating efficiency and effectiveness. In most situations, operating efficiency and effectiveness saved more money in the long run than did skimping on process improvement work during the implementation project.

We continued to explore ways to achieve FCB for our clients throughout our journey—some more successful than others. During that time, the challenges to FCB actually increased. This was mostly due to higher expectations, more robust software, more stringent RFPs, and more detailed contracts. For example, our initial CSU contract was only thirteen pages. The contract for a recent project of comparable size required 260 pages.

We felt confident that if we could keep our team focused on using their experience and skills to enhance client success, that FCB could become our most important competitive advantage. Occasionally we lost a sale when a competitor proposed a "FC" solution that lacked "B." Typically these solutions included a significant amount of remote consulting that expedited the software configuration and modification processes. This approach would make sense if software implementation were mostly about new technology. However, one of the lessons that we learned many years ago is that software implementation is more about people, politics, and process than it is about technology. The only way to focus on these dimensions is to work hand-in-hand with client stakeholders to transfer knowledge and resolve issues on a daily basis.

Losing a sale after being selected as a finalist was one of the most distressing aspects of our business, even though each loss was a great learning opportunity for us. But losing a sale was just like losing a basketball game – you either won or lost – no such thing as a moral victory.

It's either the "thrill of victory' or "the agony of defeat." And each time you experience either, your will to prepare to win intensifies. Our most frustrating losses occurred when the prospect selected a competitor's low bid that we knew was unrealistic based on the RFP requirements (low ball pricing). A number of institutions who initially went with "FC" came to us when their project was distressed. It wasn't difficult at that point for them to understand the difference between "FC" and "FCB." These clients eventually were some of our biggest supporters due to our willingness to get involved with someone else's mess. The distressed projects were never ideal, but turning them into great success stories was very gratifying.

Several times during our twelve-year journey, we were asked to replace one of our competitors as the preferred partner for some very large upcoming projects even though they were not "distressed" in terms of meeting their deadlines. They were highly dissatisfied with the value they were receiving from their original partner. This low value was primarily due to the combination of high consulting rates and inexperienced consultants. In all of these situations, the original vendor was a very large consulting firm with a long history of working with their client. These were wonderful opportunities for us, and each time we were able to develop high-trust relationships that resulted in a new revenue stream for many months and most importantly, another successful client.

PROOF OF PERFORMANCE

"The partnership between our team members and CedarCrestone assisted us in executing a project that is an example of how projects should work. We were on time and under budget, and we had the right individuals involved!"

Chief Information Officer
University Medical Center

LESSONS LEARNED

- Client whisperers are always hungry for more – make sure you feed them.

- You can assess and redesign business processes faster, cheaper, and better if you keep it simple—and colorful.

- Seek out client feedback—they see things you can't.

- Just faster and cheaper may not always be better.

- Faster, cheaper, and better solutions are always works-in-progress.

12. What's the Speed of Whispering?

Borrowed Wisdom

> "The ultimate danger of being victorious is losing sight of how you got there."[93]
>
> Bill Bradley,
> United States Senator and NBA Champion

Guiding Principle

Stay focused on client satisfaction!

Collins describes his concept of the "Flywheel Effect" to illustrate how the good-to-great companies all achieved a period of steadily increasing growth as the momentum kicked into high gear. When asked what caused this phenomenon, none of the companies could recall when it started or what specifically caused their flywheel to spin so rapidly—what Collins called their "breakthrough." Collin's concept of the Flywheel Effect made us ponder about at what point did our business flywheel "whoosh" and how did we become the "the buzz" at professional conferences? We thought about which milestones seemed to have accelerated the speed of our flywheel and fueled the contagion of our success stories. We recalled when technology contributed to our momentum. We certainly had the "best and worst of times" through our mergers and acquisitions, of which there were four.

During my career, I was involved with two management buyouts, five mergers from the seller's side, and four mergers from the buyer's side. With all eleven of these transactions, I continued working for the surviving company and, therefore, experienced the adventures of merging two different cultures into a single entity. Seven of these occurred during the twelve-year journey discussed in this book. That was a lot to endure in just twelve years and we did it without any discernable interruption in our growth curve. To say the least, there were many cultural challenges to overcome, each one different from the others.

Collins goes on to explain how the good-to-great companies dealt with many of the challenges of growth. "We learned that under the right conditions, the problems of commitment, alignment, motivation, and change just melt away. They largely take care of themselves."[94] A key phrase in his statement is "under the right conditions." In our case, this included favorable market conditions that helped facilitate our twelve consecutive years of double digit revenue growth. Cause and effect are always difficult to assess; but our ability to "artfully manage growth" was much easier to accomplish when both the demand for our services and our consultant utilization were very high.

OUR FLYWHEEL

A flywheel image appropriately conveys what our journey was like. There was no single client success that pushed us over the hump—it simply was the cumulative effect of client success. For us, the process of becoming a market share leader was just as Collins described the transformation of the good-to-great companies. There was not a trans-forming event although there were some very significant milestones along the way, examples of which follow.

- Year three: successful completion of two of the first PeopleSoft full ERP implementations

- Year five: selection by CSU as their implementation partner

- Year seven: selection by the University System of Maryland, a large public university system of higher education located on the East Coast, that gave us East/West multi-campus presence

- Year seven: successful completion of the initial CSU project

- Year nine: selection as the implementation partner for ten large implementation projects

- Year ten: selection by Arizona State University, one of the largest public research universities in the country, as their on-going hosting partner

- Year eleven: selection as the implementation partner for three separate statewide systems of higher education

- Year twelve: received marketplace recognition by Gartner, Inc. as a company in the "Magic Quadrant"

Growth: for Better or Worse

Collins writes, "Few successful start-ups become great companies, in large part because they respond to growth and success in the wrong way. Entrepreneurial success is fueled by creativity, imagination, bold moves into uncharted waters, and visionary zeal. As a company grows and becomes more complex, it begins to trip over its own success."[95]

For our higher education practice, steady growth over a period of twelve years created many distractions from our focus on the fundamentals of our business model. The addition of more people also meant more politics, more hierarchy, more complexity, and more internal focus. To off-set these distractions, we intently focused our attention on the fundamentals of our differentiation strategy—and that went a long way to diffuse the liabilities that came with growth.

We stayed true to our belief in the efficacy of small teams which, for us, were talented project teams. Our growth consisted of creating more of these relatively small project teams to support our steady growth in sales. Thanks to Gladwell's "Rule of 150," that he explains in his book *The Tipping Point: How Little Things Can Make a Big Difference* (Copyright 2000. By permission of Little, Brown and Company), I now understand that, "The size of a group is another one of those subtle contextual factors that can make a big difference...people who are willing to go along with the group, who can be easily infected with the community ethos below the level of 150, somehow, suddenly—with just the smallest change in the size of the community—become divided and alienated. Once that line, that Tipping Point, is crossed, they begin to behave very differently."[96] Most of our big competitors had to deal with the ramifications of managing many more than 150 people in one location. Fortunately, we were able to avoid that problem, which helped us maintain a formidable moat around our castle.

We experienced three very different types of growth: organic growth accomplished by hiring more great people; acquisitions, typically of small, boutique firms; and mergers with competitors. We grew our software implementation business organically and our software upgrade and hosting business via a merger with one of our competitors. Our first merger was with the much larger Hunter Group in year three of our story, which expanded our expertise into the implementation of Human Resource and Financials Management systems. The second was with Crestone International, a company that was about the same size as our company, and brought software hosting capability. To expand our student information system staffing capability, we acquired the much smaller Software Armada in year eight. Lastly, in year ten, we acquired a small company that specialized in developing solutions using new technology with the PeopleSoft software—which won them (and therefore us) an award from Oracle for innovative use of technology to leverage PeopleSoft software.

Both Hunter and Crestone were cross-industry companies with higher education practices smaller than ours. However, their cross-industry capabilities and strategies created a conundrum for us. Our higher education differentiation strategies had been developed to help us compete against cross-industry companies, and now we had become part of a cross-industry company. Adding to this conundrum was our new corporate strategy of leveraging cross-industry resources, including Crestone's highly regarded hosting capabilities. To unravel this conundrum, we promoted our combined strengths of a deep pool of higher education functional and technical consultants, cross-industry consultants with extensive experience in the "back-office systems" of finance and human resources, and our strong hosting capability. We also found that there were advantages in responding to RFPs when we could demonstrate a stronger balance sheet now that we were a larger company. There also were advantages with our partner, Oracle, because of our increased size and ERP marketplace presence.

Technology: Under the Right Conditions

Collins reported that although technology was important, it was never a primary cause of greatness. This finding reinforced our long-standing opinion that staying on the leading edge of technology was not as critical as staying focused on optimizing mainstream technology for our clients. Collins's research also revealed that technology could be an accelerator of growth if it were linked to the company's hedgehog concept.

Early on, we recognized that some form of outsourcing service would be required to reach a market leadership position. Although not yet a factor during those initial years, it seemed clear to us that the need for new technology would continue to increase, and that clients' ability to acquire and manage the latest technology would be their biggest limiting factor. When the underlying PeopleSoft technology became web-based, people began to talk seriously about the concept of externally hosting the PeopleSoft software as a more cost effective way to optimize the value of both the software and the underlying technology. Prior to our merger with Crestone, a few of our competitors were making salvos into that arena. We considered doing so as well, but we lacked the necessary resources and skills to jump into the hosting business. We began to explore partnerships with a few large companies who had significant experience with technology outsourcing, but their cost structures made hosting services prohibitive for most of our clients.

Fortunately, our equity partner was very supportive of our business, and we acquired one of our competitors, Crestone International, that had a PeopleSoft hosting business, some higher education clients, and a sound reputation in various commercial markets. As a result of this merger, our company became approximately twice its previous size and was well positioned to become a marker leader in PeopleSoft hosting services as a complement to our combined PeopleSoft consulting capabilities. During the next few years, we earned large, long-term contracts for PeopleSoft hosting services in support of more than twenty institutions of higher education, which made us a clear market leader in this service domain. Thus, hosting and supporting PeopleSoft applications in our computing center in Atlanta became our technology accelerator that helped us extend our breakthrough period. Additionally, we were able to help some of our existing clients to address some chronic technical challenges, and we even significantly improved service to internal clients.

> "When we looked for an application hosting partner, we wanted a partner that has a thorough understanding of PeopleSoft. We wanted a partner that can deliver high-performance and availability at the lowest possible cost. We wanted a partner that understands our organization and mission. And we wanted a partner that was financially stable and will continue to provide service in the future. We found that partner in CedarCrestone."
>
> Executive Vice President
> State College System

THE BEST AND WORST OF TIMES

The last two years of our story were both "the best of times and worst of times." With software hosting as our technology accelerator, a longer list of clients, and more great consultants, sales activity was extremely high. However, internal conflict was also higher as we attempted to support two different cultures, operating styles, and execution strategies associated with merging two comparably sized companies that had competed hard against each other during the previous decade.

To mitigate the potential negative impact of these conflicts, we had to execute the following internal tactics. At the executive level, we validated the company's commitment to an industry-specific business model. We continued to generate at least forty percent of the company's total revenue and used our revenue and profit contribution as proof of the efficacy of our differentiated approach to the market. We had to educate the rest of the company on the fundamentals of our differentiation strategy, especially those aspects of the model that conflicted directly with those in other internal business units. We confirmed and communicated the lines of authority and responsibility for each critical client facing activity (e.g., sales, pricing, proposal development, account management, service delivery, etc.). And finally, we reengineered/negotiated the cross-industry business processes that were essential for the continuation of our high level of client satisfaction (i.e., teamwork).

During the lower-trust period directly following the Crestone merger, all these steps were difficult. Fortunately, this low-trust period did not last long because we established credibility by producing the desired financial performance, which then allowed us to develop trusting internal relationships. From time to time prior to our Crestone merger, someone would suggest that I should push to become CEO of our company since we generated the majority of the company profit. However, my passion was with our higher education practice, not corporate leadership. That being said, I always understood that we needed to exert our influence on corporate leadership to ensure that we maintained our quest for market leadership.

Near the end of our journey, we also had to overcome the curse of competence. As Collins points out, "To go from good to great requires transcending the curse of competence."[97] And "good is the enemy of great.[98] As our client success flywheel spun faster, client feedback became increasingly more positive, and our market share growth received external validation, it was more difficult to stay humble and focused. As a result, we started to see more hyperbole creeping into our proposals. Salespeople and consultants were becoming more prescriptive, and our leadership team was less vigilant about differentiation. However, whenever we lost a big opportunity to a competitor, we quickly revisited our strategies and tactics in an attempt to be "brutally honest" about changes in our competitive advantages and position in the market.

TRUSTED ADVISOR VISION

Warren Bennis said, "Leadership is the capacity to translate vision into reality."[99] Although we did not actually reach our vision/dream of becoming "the" trusted advisor of higher education by the end of our twelve-year journey, our high profile client success stories resulted in a very positive reputation and, as Stephen M. R. Covey points out, "...another term for 'reputation' is 'brand,' and another term for 'brand' is 'trust with the marketplace.'"[100] We saw how this trust powered our marketing and sales strategy of "promote the success of our clients."

One of the most credible sources regarding market presence is Gartner, Inc.'s annual publication of its Magic Quadrant for ERP Service Providers, North America. Through most of our twelve-year journey, we were not mentioned in Gartner's publication. However, in our final year, Gartner included CedarCrestone as one of the twenty-three leading providers of ERP services for all industries. During our journey, we frequently competed with seven of the other twenty-two companies in Gartner's Magic Quadrant, and all of them were many times larger than CedarCrestone. Gartner identified the following strengths of our company:

- "CedarCrestone has a strategy focused on a specialized supplier of skills related to PeopleSoft applications for the healthcare, higher education, public-sector and commercial segments. This positioning combined with a solid track record has seen it carve out a defined area of expertise."

- "CedarCrestone's strategy allows it to have scale in terms of resources, technology capability and client references to be a credible provider although its absolute size is smaller than other top-tier provides."[101]

PROOF OF PERFORMANCE

"CedarCrestone's willingness to listen to us and meet our needs – from top level management down to our individual consultants – guaranteed our success. I would strongly recommend CedarCrestone as a trustworthy partner.

Chief Information Officer
Public Masters University

LESSONS LEARNED

- It's not just one thing that makes it happen, and you won't recognize it when it does happen.
- Be careful when you get too big or too good; while it's an asset, it can also be a liability.
- Start with trust, build on trust, and then honor trust.
- The cultural conflict of mergers and acquisitions will dissipate when teamwork kicks in.
- The best validation of mergers and acquisitions is success in the market.

PART III: THE CLIENT WHISPERERS' WORLD

13. What's a Whispering Culture?

Borrowed Wisdom

> "I've learned that people will forget what you said, people will forget what you did, but people will never forget how you made them feel."[102]
>
> Maya Angelou,
> Renaissance Woman and Author

Guiding Principle

> Who's responsible for outcomes? Every single person!

Our overarching, long-term competitive advantage emanated from our client whispering culture. It was built inside-out and outside-in to ensure its enduring—and endearing-- appeal to the higher education market. Our culture was based upon an all-pervasive commitment to client success. In Geert Hofstede's book, *Cultures and Organizations, Software of the Mind* (Copyright 2010. Third Revised Edition, McGrawHill, By permission of Geert Hofstede.), he defines culture as mental programming and makes the distinction between what is innate and what is learned. "Every person carries within him - or herself - patterns of thinking, feeling, and potential acting that were learned throughout the person's lifetime…Culture is learned, not innate. It derives from one's social environment rather than from one's genes…The human ability to feel fear, anger, love, joy, sadness, and shame; the need to associate with others and to play and exercise oneself; and the facility to observe the environment and to talk about it with other humans all belong to…mental programming. However, what one does with these feelings, how one expresses fear, joy, observations, and so on, is modified by culture…The personality of an individual…is based on traits that are partly inherited within the individual's unique set of genes and partly learned."[103]

During my volunteer work for CASA, I was introduced to the concept of a cultural sensitivity lens (CSL) used to better understand the family culture of disadvantaged children. This same concept applied to our client whisperers. Unlike my CASA experience, our client whisperers came to us with a highly developed CSL as a result of their in-depth understanding of the culture of higher education.

OUR CULTURAL CONTINUUM

The roles of our employees were spread along a cultural continuum, ranging between the not-for-profit culture of higher education to the typical bottom-line culture of a for-profit business. I share in **Figure O** below an illustration of our cultural continuum by role.

Figure O: Our Cultural Continuum by Role

As illustrated by this continuum, our functional consultants had the greatest degree of alignment of all of our company roles within our higher education practice. This alignment is not surprising, given they spent from Monday through Thursday on campus—and came from the ranks of higher education prior to becoming a consultant. They realized that the client's vision was to achieve "positive educational outcomes"—not a robust profit. Client whisperers naturally seek out new knowledge and are eager to learn—traits that flourish in a "learning and research enterprise" like higher education.

Our salespeople were in the middle of the cultural continuum. When compared to our consultants, they spent less time with individual clients. Although they may not have understood the specific cultural idiosyncrasies of a given client or prospect, they did understand the overall culture of higher education based on sales calls to many colleges and universities. Because they had incentives for sales and revenue, however, they also understood and felt comfortable in a for-profit culture.

Our senior leadership team spanned the full continuum from the not-for-profit to the for-profit culture. At the not-for-profit end of the continuum, we conducted numerous visits to client and prospective client sites. On the for-profit end of the continuum, we spent countless hours on internal conference calls and occasionally participated in face-to-face company meetings to monitor our business performance. We easily spanned the cultural continuum because we had extensive experience not only working in higher education but also in software and professional services firms serving higher education. We knew that we were the "cultural integrators" responsible for hiring people and aligning their roles in a compatible manner with the culture in which they would work. Throughout our organization, we understood that the higher education culture is based on "The Greater Good"—and all of us wanted to contribute—it was synergy at its best!

The impact on our clients of our culturally synergistic roles meant that our consultants quickly understood how to work within and communicate effectively with the varied constituencies in a college or university. Within the client's organization, we were always looking for what Gladwell calls "*Mavens,*" people whom we knew could provide new information about how to get things done in their environment. They collect information and share it with others, which can influence software and service decisions and help resolve issues during an implementation or upgrade project. I called these people *thought leaders.*

The cultural synergy of our consultants with our clients was made even stronger by our understanding of the cultural nuances among differing institutional types. For example, we knew that our community college clients were very focused on student success, and dealt with a more diverse student population than universities typically did. We understood that our research university clients were heavily influenced by a mission that encompassed research, particularly as research factored so heavily in evaluating and awarding faculty tenure.

Some of the most rewarding manifestations of our cultural synergy with higher education were the many "random acts of culture" that occurred during our journey. Most of these random acts resulted from one or more of our client whisperers going above and beyond the call of duty to help achieve something of great importance to a client, even if it was not explicitly required by the contract. For example, one of our early clients faced political challenges because there was faculty resistance to purchasing and implementing a student information system. Their resistance was informally expressed by one academic dean when he said, "There go the dollars for faculty salaries and classroom equipment into yet another administrative project." When we got word of it, we worked with the provost and his deans to design a prototype of an academic "Deans' Desktop" using information from the new student information system that was relevant to academic deans, department chairs and ultimately faculty. The client was surprised by this random act of culture and most relieved when faculty attitudes shifted from resistance to support, or at least moderate support.

CULTURAL CHALLENGES: MERGERS & ACQUISITIONS

In his book, *The Corporate Culture Survival Guide* (Copyright 2009. By permission of John Wiley & Sons.), Edgar Schein discusses what he calls the "The Multi-Culture Problem." He describes the problem as follows: "Cultures meet any time there is a merger of two companies, when one company acquires another, when two companies engage in a joint venture, or when a new group is created with members from several cultures. A merger attempts to blend the two cultures, without necessarily treating one or the other as dominant.

Each culture is, from the point of view of its members, the correct way to perceive, feel about, and act on daily events. Each culture may have opinions and biases about 'the other,' but by definition our own culture is always the one that is 'right.' Getting cross-culture organizations, projects, joint ventures, and teams to work together poses a much larger cultural challenge...Often overlooked until too late is that the means by which the goals are accomplished in the two organizations may be very different, and the underlying assumptions about business and human processes may actually conflict with one another. Rarely checked are those aspects that might be considered 'cultural:' the philosophy or style of the company; technological origins, which might provide clues to basic assumptions; beliefs about its mission and future; and how it organizes itself internally. Yet a cultural mismatch in an acquisition, merger, or joint venture is as great a risk as a financial, product, or market mismatch."[104]

A subtle, unanticipated market reaction occurred after The Hunter Group was acquired by Renaissance Worldwide. It seemed that just the name "Renaissance," and the associated imagery on marketing templates, which we used when submitting proposals, resonated very well with our higher education audience, especially research universities. Of all the names we had, marketplace reaction to "Renaissance"—intellectual transformation—was the most culturally compatible with higher education.

When The Hunter Group was acquired by Cedar Group, a United Kingdom software and services company, they restructured the company from a regional to an industry organizational structure. Within this industry structure, they gave us full latitude in leading and managing our higher education practice. To some extent, we were like a cultural cocoon within the larger Hunter Group organization. We were able to effectively engage a number of The Hunter Group's functional and technical consultants in our higher education projects, using them to implement the "back-office systems" of finance and human resources. We observed that it was in these back offices that our higher education clients aligned somewhat with a for-profit business, rather than the higher education culture.

With subsequent changes in ownership, we did not experience any cultural incompatibility, primarily because these acquisitions were financially based, rather than the merger of cultures. As long as we performed well financially, which we did, we managed our culture somewhat independently within the corporate structure.

Our Software Armada acquisition gave us the closest cultural alignment of any of our mergers and acquisitions. They were from higher education and focused only on student information system implementations. Their consultants became some of our very best client whisperers. We made Elizabeth, who had been a Software Armada founding partner, a member of our executive team—and she was a perfect cultural fit!

The Crestone merger was our first real experience of having to deal with the challenges of merging two different cultures. The Crestone executives were great managers, which Steven R. Covey defines as having the skills necessary for "...the breaking down, the analysis, the sequencing, the specific application, the time-bound left-brain aspects of effective self-government[105]...Management is a bottom line focus. How can I best accomplish certain things?"[106] We were focused more on leadership, which Covey defines as "...primarily a high-powered, right brain activity. It's more of an art; it's based on philosophy. Leadership deals with the top line. What are the things I want to accomplish?"[107] In the words of Drucker, "Management is doing things right; leadership is doing the right things."[108] As former competitors, our initial relationship could be categorized as low-trust. However, once we learned to trust each other, our synergy and collective capabilities worked quite well as we managed diligently from the left and lead with artful differentiation from the right.

A recent experiment conducted by the University of Pennsylvania's Wharton School of Business highlighted the "power of why." They determined that employees get much better results if they understand why they do what they do as compared to employees who understand just how to do what they do. Understanding the importance of their work – "the why"— motivates people to get better results. Our leadership was focused on "the why" (achieving client success) and our management was focused "the how" (creating contractual deliverables). Author and New York University professor Diane Ravitch believes, "The person who knows 'how' will always have a job. The person who knows 'why' will always be his boss."[109]

Blending cultures is difficult work, but the following insight from Schein appropriately describes the approach that worked best for us. "Blending is most likely to occur when the separate subcultures face a new common problem that can only be solved by collaboration. When members of the subcultures have to work together in forced interaction, they begin to pay attention to each other, develop understanding of their differences, and create new ways of working that take advantage of both cultures."[110] For us, this typically involved problems that threatened consistent client success and that required the combined strengths of all participants. It was always gratifying to be part of this type of cultural synergy that usually enhanced one or more of our competitive advantages.

I suspect that some of our competitors were frustrated by the Long-term Orientation of the higher education culture. We, on the other hand, understood it well; and although we certainly would have preferred a shorter sales cycle than was most always the case, we knew the lengthy process was intrinsic to the culture and must be accommodated. We used it to our advantage by getting to know the prospects needs, imperatives and diffused power inter-relationships. Now, let's talk about the four cultural characteristics that we fostered to be successful in our market.

DISCIPLINED THOUGHT

The characteristic of disciplined thought is a *prerequisite* for a client whisperer. And "thinking like a client" Is the mantra of a client whisperer. From Linda Elder and Richard Paul's book *Critical Thinking* (Copyright 2002. By permission of Pearson Education Inc. Upper Saddle River, NJ), they state the following wisdom regarding the importance of practicing disciplined thought: "True excellence in thinking is not simply the result of isolated intellectual skills[111]...Good thinking can be practiced like basketball, tennis, or ballet. When people explicitly recognize that improvement in thinking requires practice and adopts some regimen of practice, then, and only then, have they become what we call 'practicing thinkers.'"[112]

We wanted to help our people discipline their thoughts in a way that optimized team synergy and enabled us to deliver faster, cheaper, and better solutions to our clients. We stressed the importance of aligning our selling process with the prospect's buying process to ensure that we were responsive to the issues and concerns on the minds of the buyers...that we were thinking like a client. Similarly, we used those same concepts to ensure that the solutions we were delivering were meeting the client's critical needs as we focused on client success with disciplined thought. Many of our client testimonials validate that our consultants exhibited critical thinking skills in solving problems and bringing value to their clients. Clearly, they had practiced disciplined thought in doing so.

Because our client whisperers' could generally think like a client, they quickly established rapport with our clients. They were aware of the lengthy decision-making process and knew that an inordinate amount of communication was necessary to build and maintain momentum and support for a project. Our consultants collaboratively developed decision-making processes and communication plans with their clients. They recognized the vulnerability that our clients felt when replacing their legacy systems, particularly the student information system that extended to all students and many faculty and staff. These client whisperers had numerous ways in which to address this deep concern, including risk mitigating strategies, go-live readiness assessments, and checklists to avoid any disruption in service.

Many companies confuse disciplined talk with disciplined thought. Some of the traditional sales training programs are more about disciplined talk than disciplined thought. Disciplined talk without disciplined thought typically results in "salesy" lingo. Mastery of disciplined thought makes disciplined talk occur naturally and exude sincerity.

Much of the marketing collateral used by our competition reflected disciplined talk. Thus, a competitive advantage for us became disciplined thought. We attempted to leverage this advantage by emphasizing the concept of thinking like a client. For example, at professional conferences, we preferred smaller dinners that included our clients and prospects so that there could be peer-to-peer discussions. These more in-depth dinner discussions enabled us to better understand what our clients and prospects were thinking than was the case when exchanging sound bites and social niceties at a large reception, as was typically the case with our competition.

DISCIPLINED ACTION

This characteristic is the Whisperer's "Art Form." "It isn't enough to talk about peace. One must believe in it. And it isn't enough to believe in it. One must work at it."[113] In these words of wisdom from Eleanor Roosevelt, we knew that it wasn't enough just to talk about and promote client success (disciplined talk). We had to believe in client success (disciplined thought). And it wasn't enough to just believe in client success. We had to work at making client success a reality during each of our implementation and upgrade projects (disciplined action).

Collins created the following matrix in **Figure P**. He uses the culture of discipline and the ethic of entrepreneurship to create four quadrants that characterize organizations. Our goal, of course, was to transition from a good start-up organization to a great organization without ever becoming a hierarchical and/or bureaucratic organization. To do so, we had to preserve our high ethic of entrepreneurship and develop a culture that had a high level of discipline.

Figure P: The Good-to-Great Matrix of Creative Discipline[114]

Good to Great by Jim Collins (copyright © 2001)

In 1980, I relocated to Dallas to open a branch office for IA. Establishing an office in Texas was intended to be a strategic move to counter our competitor's success in this geography, much of which we believed was due to their Texas presence and connections. Although we were the market share leader, most of our Texas prospects viewed us as a Northeastern company that did not understand how things were done in the Texas culture, which was pretty accurate at that point in time. My first staffing decision was to relocate two of our experienced employees from the Northeast to Dallas. The first was an experienced project manager with Texas connections. To help jump start our sales activities, my second staff relocation was a sales manager who also had associations in Texas; he even walked and talked like a Texan. Soon after opening the Dallas office, these Texas connections paid off as we learned that Texas Tech University was about to sign a large contract with our biggest competitor, SCT, for a fully integrated, on-line student information system. Texas Tech was a major research university with about twenty-three thousand students and a large Health Sciences Center. Unfortunately, we didn't know anyone at Texas Tech. We began placing calls into the decision-makers in an attempt to slow down their contract signing process with SCT.

Our understanding of the shifting buyer concerns during Phase 3 of the buying process led us to attempt to raise concerns in the minds of the Texas Tech stakeholders about the risks of signing such a contract with SCT without considering our software solution. Unlike SCT's proposed solution, our software had actually been installed at several similar institutions, albeit outside the borders of the State of Texas. However, none of those institutions was yet in live production with our most recent version of the software. We could not get anyone at Texas Tech to return our calls, and we knew that time was running out. The chances of Texas Tech stopping their procurement process with SCT were diminishing by the hour.

And then the phone rang...it was the Texas Tech vice president and executive sponsor for the student information system procurement. My pulse rate quickened, and I instantly realized that I was ill prepared (undisciplined thought) for the conversation that was about to take place. I took a deep breath and quickly tried to recall the "elevator speech" [disciplined talk] that we had developed for use by our salespeople in the event they unexpectedly found themselves in the elevator with the key software selection decision maker for one of their top prospects.

Fortunately, the Texan on the other end of the phone was a straight shooter; and after introducing himself, he explained that a colleague at another Texas institution called him earlier in the day and suggested that he give me a call. His colleague recently participated in one of our software demonstrations at a professional conference, and he liked what he saw. However, my caller then said that Texas Tech recently completed a twelve-month evaluation of all integrated, on-line student information systems and concluded that SCT's system was the only one that would meet their needs. He also said that his selection team never heard of our company, and he could not believe they would have missed our solution if it really could meet their needs. As my pulse rate slowed and my natural instincts started to kick in, I began to develop [disciplined thought] a way to get him to agree to put the SCT contract on hold and allow us to conduct an on-site demonstration of our software [disciplined action]. As I recall my response went something like the following.

"From what you and others around the State have told me, Texas Tech University needs to replace your very old and inadequate software with a comprehensive, on-line, and fully integrated student information system. Your Board has approved the project funding, and your team is committed to begin the implementation of this new software immediately. If I can provide you with peer institution references regarding the capabilities of our software, will you agree to arrange for our team to meet with your team and demonstrate how our software will address the needs of your stakeholders?"

Then I held my breath for what seemed like several minutes of silence before he replied, "If you can get your team out here next Monday and conduct a real time software demonstration, I will delay signing the contract with your competitor to allow us time to evaluate your proposed solution." I then quickly confirmed the time and place for the demo and thanked him for his willingness to consider our solution. I subsequently learned that he had already talked with his counterpart at a peer institution prior to calling me.

With an extraordinary effort by the great people in our new Dallas office, we were able to conduct a successful on-line demo for the selection team at Texas Tech using a slow dial-up connection to our mainframe computer in New York, which in those days was no easy task. The interaction between our team and the Texas Tech selection team was very positive. They were impressed by our software demo, but they liked our people even better. The next week their team came to our Dallas office for a "deep dive" technical review with our vice president of software development. Two weeks later, we signed a contract with Texas Tech University for both software and implementation services. Our implementation team was on-site a few days later to begin a challenging, but very successful, project. Texas Tech University became a wonderful reference for us. They were an important factor in our many subsequent sales successes with other institutions both in and outside of Texas. Our Texas Tech experience in those early days of my career greatly enhanced my understanding of the differences among disciplined talk (rehearsed elevator speech), disciplined thought (natural instincts), and disciplined action (proof of your capabilities).

For our sales process, disciplined action meant not proposing a "solution" when the buyer was not yet in the "Evaluate Alternatives" phase of the buying process. When the buyer was in the Evaluate Alternatives phase of the buying process, disciplined action meant demonstrating our understanding of their needs by discussing our success with similar projects for peer institutions. In our delivery of consulting services, disciplined action meant not having to ask permission to suggest the best way to address a client need, even if it was not covered in the contract. It also meant not having to say you're sorry if you erred on the side of enhancing client success.

As mentioned earlier, it was not uncommon for our clients to experience high stress and panic during a large, complex project. That panic typically resulted in requests for more detailed project plans and status reports that they thought would reduce their stress and help them better understand the unfamiliar circumstances of software implementation. Ironically, the presentation of a detailed project plan tended to actually increase their stress by introducing more unfamiliar terminology and overwhelming them with the magnitude of detailed tasks that were required to complete the project. In a sense, this must have felt a little like "flying strictly by instruments." Thus, we found that redacted project plans were more useful in most situations.

Our approach to reducing this stress and panic was to keep the client focused on risk mitigation, which typically involved circumstances that were familiar to them such as politics, communication, decision-making, change management, and team building. Invariably, at the conclusion of a tough project, the client would talk about one of the most important lessons learned: software implementations are more about people, politics, and process than technology. The vast majority of risk mitigation strategies used during a project were focused on ensuring timely disciplined action on the part of the key stakeholders. For our clients, disciplined action meant "faster, cheaper, better" implementations, upgrades, and hosting solutions. Additionally, it meant having a trusted partner who would listen and respond appropriately without the necessity of contract amendments and costly change orders.

Our client whisperers used their industry knowledge and experience to fuel their disciplined action. When issues arose during the sales and delivery processes, they typically were able to react instinctively and address the issues. In contrast, some of our competitors' consultants who had a reputation of being very bright, but inexperienced, could use only disciplined thought—choking and thinking too much—to deal with difficult situations that surfaced during complex implementation projects. Thinking too much typically causes inexperienced consultants to resort to talking too much (undisciplined talk). If the situation worsened, they could not use their intellect to overcome their panic, and then even the talking would stop.

We heard many stories from our clients who had previously worked with some of our competitors and witnessed first-hand the panic and choking behavior during stressful periods in which issues invariably arose. Consultant panic resulted in no issue resolution while choking sometimes resulted in bad implementation decisions that led to costly rework down the road. Our client whisperers experienced many stressful situations, but their experience with similar situations allowed them to avoid the pitfalls associated with choking or panicking.

FREEDOM WITH RESPONSIBILITY

This cultural characteristic is a requirement of client whisperers. Collins explains that one of the challenges of growth is the perceived need for bureaucracy. He states, "...the purpose of bureaucracy is to compensate for incompetence and lack of discipline—a problem that largely goes away if you have the right people in the first place."[115] Elder describes what she calls "The Problem of Bureaucracy." She explains, "Bureaucratization is a state in which employees work increasingly by fixed routine rather than through the exercise of intelligent judgment. With bureaucracy, narrowness in thinking emerges. There is a proliferation of hard-and-fast rules and fixed procedures—wrongly thought to contribute to efficiency and quality control."[116]

In our higher education practice, we enjoyed much free-

Lyon's Pride

During my college days in the mid-1960s, my alma mater had an academic concept that was similar to our business concept of "freedom with responsibility." This freedom was designed to "foster personal discovery and growth; nurture scholarship and creativity across a broad range of common knowledge; and pursue understanding beyond the limitations of existing knowledge, ideology, and disciplinary structure." I was able to use this "freedom with responsibility" to explore diverse academic disciplines without the constraints of stringent degree and attendance requirements or even standardized majors. With a few exceptions, such as engineering and architecture, each student was free to develop jointly with an advisor an individualized degree program that best served his/her needs. For those who respected this symbiotic relationship between freedom and responsibility came the reward of graduating from a prestigious institution with a degree in an academic program tailored to meet their individual abilities and interests.

dom and independence. But…it was based on trust. None of us was tied to a physical office and many of us seldom met face-to-face with our supervisor. Each of us was responsible for supporting our guiding principles and business strategies. However, we would not have had such freedom in our culture without a corresponding sense of responsibility.

Our salespeople had the greatest freedom of all of our employees. They worked out of their homes, typically traveled according to their schedule, and worked the hours that they preferred. We never questioned how our salespeople handled their time because they had the most measurable outcomes of all: sales. We did have a few salespeople who likely took advantage of this freedom; however, if they did not accept responsibility for and achieve their sales goals, they didn't last. What was most frustrating with our salespeople was when we received a blind RFP for one of the prospects whom they supposedly had been visiting. Their being unaware of this opportunity quickly revealed that they had not assumed responsibility as they enjoyed their freedom.

We continuously worked to find flexibility in our methodology so that our consultants had sufficient freedom to create needed solutions and solve unanticipated client problems. Although our methodology was based on industry standards, we didn't let those standards be interpreted so rigidly that our consultants couldn't do what was right for the client.

During our early years, I received many questions from our project managers and consultants regarding how they should deal with specific implementation issues and opportunities. Many of these questions fell into the category of, "The client needs this capability, but the contract is not clear about who is responsible for doing it." As we continued on in our journey, I got fewer and fewer of these types of questions because our consulting teams were beginning to answer their own questions as they focused more on client success and less on the contract. Typically, they would tell me about their decision after the fact and say, "Time was short, and I knew this is how you would have responded if I had asked you what we should do."

Some of our very talented technical consultants took the liberty to develop a modification if they knew it had great value to the client. In many such cases, the client had experienced difficulty getting buy in and/or making it through their lengthy decision-making process. When our consultants took the initiative and developed a solution, the client enthusiastically responded because they had what they needed to be successful in their implementation. The detractors quickly embraced the solution. Our consultants knew that they had the freedom to bring value to their clients—they didn't need our approval for that! Fortunately, our project managers understood where to draw the line between the freedom to make their own decisions and the responsibility to keep the management team informed and involved.

These are just a few of the benefits of an organization in which bureaucracy was minimized. Upon my retirement, I received the following generous compliment in an email from one of our most experienced client whisperers, "In this business it is rare to find senior management who care more about the quality of work and satisfied customers than billing hours. It is also rare to find people with your kind of integrity in the consulting world."

Our mantra of faster, cheaper, and better solutions emboldened our consultants and salespeople to flourish in a culture of freedom. Time and again, we found a competitive advantage in our ability to respond quickly in both delivery and sales. In the delivery world, we heard many times about our competitors "change order" process. For them, it seemed that anything above and beyond the specific contract terms required creation of yet another document—and approval process. Our consultants, on the other hand, did what was needed to make our clients successful. There were only rare occasions when clients took advantage of our willingness to go above and beyond. In the end, they became some of our strongest supporters and more than returned in subsequent business what we may have initially lost in profitability. An example of client feedback that illustrates our approach is presented below.

> "The CedarCrestone consultants assessed critical problems quickly, developed a plan of action, and told the hard truth in language that people understood and accepted. The project manager has worked hard to train our staff on how to remain disciplined and to focus on critical priorities. In fact, he has helped to change the culture of our campus."
>
> President
> Public Research University

MATURE JUDGMENT

This cultural characteristic is essential to "freedom with responsibility." Noel M. Tichy and Warren Bennis' book, *Judgment: How Winning Leaders Make Great Calls*, (copyright © 2007 by Noel Tichy & Warren Bennis, Inc. Used by permission of Portfolio, an imprint of Penguin Group, Inc.) includes some very important insights on mature judgment, including the following points:

- "With good judgment, little else matters. Without it, nothing else matters.

- Good judgment results from a whole process that runs from seeing the need for a call, to framing the issues, to figuring out what is critical, to mobilizing and energizing the troops.

- Long-term success is the sole marker of good judgment.

- Winning leaders use mental frameworks to guide good judgment."[117]

Appropriate use of guiding principles is a key element of "freedom with responsibility;" any tendency to view these principles as corporate edicts would have been detrimental to our culture. During the course of a protracted sales cycle or large implementation project, our client whisperers encountered myriad situations that required them to exercise "good judgment." At a high level, we characterized good judgment as any decision that was consistent with our guiding principles.

The more experience a person had, the easier it seemed to be for him/her to make decisions based on our guiding principles. But what does it mean to make decisions based on guiding principles? For salespeople, it meant seeking first to understand stakeholder needs and concerns and developing trusting personal relationships as a foundation for a long-term business relationship with each of our clients. Although this may sound easy, it certainly was not. Our client whisperers were confronted with many difficult situations that appeared to be much more complex than simply staying true to our guiding principles. After all, they were just that: principles used to guide our employees though their professional endeavors. They were not necessarily applicable to every decision they might encounter. The most perplexing judgments were those that were impossible to precisely discern right from wrong—

those conundrums that you could easily make a logical case for choosing either of the alternative decisions.

When faced with a judgment call, we hoped that all of our experienced consultants and project managers would give the benefit of doubt to the client rather than to the contract, because this was consistent with our principle of focusing on client success. We wanted to ensure we did not err on the side of a literalistic interpretation of the contract. Our goal was to achieve both a realistic and humanistic approach to client whispering.

An example of making judgment calls during implementation projects was the decision of when to use an existing solution or an original solution to address the needs of any particular client. We created a repository for our intellectual property that our client whisperers contributed to during our projects. Much of this material was reusable in subsequent projects to address similar client needs. For many clients, this was an important component of faster, cheaper solutions. However, each situation was different. Many times a creative solution was required to make the solution better for any particular client. These judgments were not always easy to make because it was seldom possible to deliver the ultimate solution on-time and within budget. Our guideline for these situations was to provide the client with a cost/benefit analysis and risk assessment of each alternative solution. We made a recommendation of which one to choose based on the objectives for the project and our understanding of the priorities of the institution.

Our personnel model of hiring more mature, experienced people greatly strengthened this cultural characteristic. For example, when we were called in to recover projects that had failed, our more experienced consultants knew how to work within the higher education culture to solve problems and collaboratively bring the project back on track. Because they were experienced, they knew what decisions, particularly bad ones, negatively affected the software implementation "downstream" and jeopardized achieving a successful go-live. With their combination of mature judgment and cultural alignment, the outcomes were very favorable for our clients. As word spread, our positive reputation increased.

PROOF OF PERFORMANCE

> "CedarCrestone always went the extra mile to listen to our concerns and provide the necessary resources and support to complete critical tasks. Their professionalism, breadth of knowledge in project management and higher education business processes, as well as their technical expertise allowed us to complete the project on-time and within budget."
>
> Executive Director
> Large Community College

LESSONS LEARNED

- Deliberately strive for cultural synergy with your clients by thinking like a client.

- Values must be ingrained in everything that you do...and how you do it.

- If you think in a disciplined way and act upon your thinking in a disciplined way, then you will reap the rewards of disciplined accomplishment.

- With experience comes mature judgment; with mature judgment comes freedom with responsibility.

- If you want to be successful in a culture that values the greater good, you and your team must believe in and value the same greater good.

14. How Does a Whisperer Whisper?

Borrowed Wisdom

> "We keep moving forward, opening new doors, and doing new things, because we're curious and curiosity keeps leading us down new paths."[118]
>
> **Walt Disney,**
> **American Film Producer and Entrepreneur**

Guiding Principle

Always wonder why...and why not.

How does a client whisperer actually whisper? They follow the credo: "seek first to understand, then to be understood," as advocated by Stephen R. Covey. This credo is multifaceted and includes at least four important interrelated whispering qualities: observing, listening, questioning, and learning. While some of our consultants innately possessed these qualities, others had to learn them through the mentoring process. Once they experienced the benefits with their clients, the external reinforcement instilled an internal motivation to embrace these qualities.

Observing

Gladwell describes in his book, *Blink: The Power of Thinking Without Thinking,* (Copyright 2005. By permission of Little, Brown and Company) what he calls "The Love Lab" at the University of Washington that is operated by psychologist, John Gottman. "Since the 1980s, Gottman has brought more than three thousand married couples [into his lab]. Each couple has been videotaped and the results have been analyzed according to something Gottman dubbed SPAFF (for specific affect), a coding system that has twenty separate categories corresponding to every conceivable emotion that a married couple might express during a conversation...Gottman has taught his staff how to read every emotional nuance in people's facial expressions and how to interpret seemingly ambiguous bits of dialogue…Then these data from the electrodes and sensors are factored in…and all of that information is fed into a complex equation.

On the basis of those calculations, Gottman has proven something remarkable. If he analyzes an hour of a husband and wife talking, he can predict with 95 percent accuracy whether that couple will still be married fifteen years later. If he watches the couple for fifteen minutes, his success rate is around 90 percent. Recently, a professor who works with Gottman…who was playing around with some of the videotapes, trying to design a new study, discovered that if they looked at only three minutes of a couple talking, they could still predict with fairly impressive accuracy who was going to get divorced and who was going to make it. The truth of a marriage can be understood in a much shorter time than anyone ever imagined."[119]

Gladwell then explains a concept called thin-slicing. "Thin-slicing refers to the ability of our unconscious to find patterns in situations and behavior based on very narrow slices of experience…Thin-slicing is part of what makes the unconscious so dazzling. But it's also what we find most problematical about rapid cognition. How is it possible to gather the necessary information for a sophisticated judgment in such a short time? The answer is that when our unconscious engages in thin-slicing, what we are doing is an automated, accelerated unconscious version of what Gottman does with his videotapes and equations. Can a marriage really be understood in one sitting? Yes it can, and so can lots of other seemingly complex situations."[120]

On a personal note related to observing, when my grandkids came for one of their visits, to help them become more observant, I began giving them the challenge of the Hocus-Focus visual discrimination, as featured in the morning newspaper. As a result, they have become much more proficient at finding six differences between two seemingly identical cartoons—plus they have fun in the process. Another personal example is that I love taking walks on the golf course adjacent to our home. To add a quantitative aspect to these walks, I search for lost golf balls that seem to be everywhere around this mountain golf course. Sometimes I prefer to just take a nature walk and enjoy the natural beauty. On those occasions, I find few golf balls. When our grandchildren visit, they always want to go golf ball hunting with me. Sometimes they get discouraged if we don't find at least one ball every few minutes and they exclaim, "There are no more golf balls out here!" And that is exactly how many golf balls they find for the rest of the walk—not because the golf balls aren't there to be found, but rather because they stop looking. Of course, the moral of this story is that you find what you are looking for—which is an interesting combination of disciplined thought and the power of observation.

Bosworth's solution selling approach was very effective for both selling and delivering implementation services to colleges and universities. There was much to be learned when observing a sales call, conducting a contract negotiations session, or facilitating a project planning meeting. Who influences whom? Who has the high trust relationships with key decision-makers? Who are the decision-makers? Who are the thought leaders? What are the issues that could derail an implementation? Observation is particularly important in higher education because decisions are made by committees and myriad "hidden influencers." These influencers cannot be identified simply by studying an organizational chart. These indirect influencers are everywhere in a large institution. They can be found in academic departments, administrative offices, the student body, and even in informal alumni gatherings. Their scope and extent of influence in the organization can only be detected by observing the respect that others afford them. If you are the one doing all the talking, they may listen, but will not divulge anything. The best way to identify these important people is by listening and observing, two skills that have a close link to relationship development. They also are two skills that many salespeople lack. An example of the impact on our clients of our client whisperer's ability to observe follows.

"Our consultant was excellent at knowing when to take the lead and when to sit back and observe. He was instrumental in the development of our RFP, he made sure we got the most out of our vendor demonstrations, and he ultimately helped us navigate the process of evaluating and selecting the vendor that was the best fit for our needs. At the end of the engagement, he also gave us some best practices for implementation that have been very useful. We've already recommended CedarCrestone to other institutions, and will continue to do so."

Director of Project Services & Technology Support
Proprietary University

LISTENING

In *The Seven Habits of Highly Effective People*, Steven R. Covey emphasizes the high value of diagnosing before prescribing. Covey states that "If I were to summarize in one sentence the single most important principle I have learned in the field of interpersonal relationships, it would be this: seek first to understand, then to be understood." He goes on to say, "Most people…are either speaking or preparing to speak. They're filtering everything through their own paradigms, reading their autobiography into other people's lives."[121] Covey also points out that empathetic listening is not the same as active listening with the following comparison: "When I say empathetic listening, I mean listening with intent to understand. I mean seeking first to understand, to really understand. It is an entirely different paradigm."[122]

We observed that all client whisperers begin with empathetic listening. Many years ago, Bosworth taught me the importance of taking time to listen and diagnose before offering a prescription. He also taught me that people buy from the people who both understand and care about their needs, issues and concerns and have helped them formulate a vision of a solution. Bosworth's theory was that if you spent most of your sales time listening and doing need and relationship development, you would spend much less time closing the sale, because your prospect would know that you understand their problems and sincerely care about helping them solve those problems— with a solution you helped the prospect design. Covey's statement that, "Most people do not listen with the intent to understand; they listen with the intent to reply,"[123] was the more common mode of most salespeople.

Over the years, I have hired a few salespeople who had mastered the art of disciplined talk (i.e., "gift of gab) during their sojourn in large, egocentric corporations. We quickly discovered that we first had to "un-train" them before we could begin to progress toward disciplined thought—and that was never an easy task. The biggest challenge was to minimize what Bosworth used to call "premature elaboration," which typically resulted in the salesperson talking most of the time during initial sales calls. Our rule of thumb was that during a successful sales call at the beginning of the buying process, the prospect should do at least eighty percent of the talking while we listen empathetically and ask probing questions. Of course, with these traditional corporate "client shouters," the prospect did most of the listening and the salesperson learned very little about the sales opportunity.

I recall my first sales presentation, in 1977, shortly after joining IA. I was asked to present the software solution that I had implemented while at Cornell to a large group of interested people at the University of Massachusetts (UMass). My new boss at IA asked if I wanted anyone else at IA to help with the presentation. I said that I didn't think I would need any help, since I had designed the Cornell version of the software that the prospect wanted to evaluate. Although my boss was a little concerned, since I had never made a sales presentation, I proceeded to prepare for my first sales call with great enthusiasm.

When I arrived at UMass just after lunch, I was greeted by a large group of interested parties. After a short introduction by the committee chairperson, I launched into my presentation, which consisted of about one hundred very detailed transparencies that were displayed on a large screen via an overhead projector. I made those poor people sit through every one of those hard-to-read transparencies. About four hours later, I mercifully concluded my presentation. I now understand that, as a sales presentation, it was truly awful! However, we did win the business…due primarily to the lack of competition and the comfort they received from knowing that our proposed solution had been successfully implemented at a very similar institution.

About a year later, I experienced a much different sales call at the University of Kansas (KU), which shared many similarities with the UMass situation of the previous year. I made an appointment at KU just to stop by on my way to an already confirmed appointment for the next morning at Kansas State University. When I arrived at KU, once again just after lunch, the receptionist escorted me to what I believed would be the private office of the person with whom I had confirmed my appointment. However, it turned out to be a large lecture hall filled with people who had just settled in for an afternoon sales presentation, some probably expecting to catch a little "shut eye." However, this time I had no presentation materials and had done very little preparation since I was planning on a brief informal conversation with their selection committee lead. Fortunately, the lecture hall had a large white board that could be seen by all participants.

Trying to appear calm as I recovered from my initial shock, I thanked everyone for coming and began to ask a few questions about their expectations for the meeting and their need for a new software system. Although the responses came slowly at first, the meeting became very interactive as I drew high level flow diagrams on the white board to explain my responses to their questions. During the second half of the meeting, the KU folks did most of the talking as I listened, responded as appropriate, took notes, and asked some probing questions to gain more insight into their needs, concerns, and issues. It turned out to be a very successful session, which was confirmed by their feedback at the end of the meeting. Although the subsequent KU software selection process was quite protracted, which was typical for a large university, we eventually did win the contract. More importantly for me, I learned a great lesson from what began as a very uncomfortable experience, especially when compared to my initial sales call the previous year at UMass. Another example of the impact on our clients of our whisperer's quality of good listening follows.

"The Readiness Assessment process enabled us to collect relevant information and opinions from project participants and campus-wide constituencies regarding the actual and perceived challenges and anticipated benefits of implementing the new software. The CedarCrestone consultants facilitated open discussion in the focus groups, <u>listened to</u> and interpreted opinions from individual interviews and synthesized it all into meaningful recommendations. As a result of following up on these recommendations, we refined our project planning, increased our communication efforts and realigned our staffing plan."

Associate Vice President, Information Technology
Public Masters University

QUESTIONING

Curiosity, the client whisperers' innate propensity toward life, drives questioning. In his books and sales training workshops, Bosworth describes the different types of questions that can be used to develop client need and a vision of a solution. For each pain/need that is identified, he teaches how to skillfully diagnose the reasons for the pain, explore the impact of the pain, and visualize the capabilities that will be required to address the pain. One of the key concepts of his work is the use of nine different types of questions that Bosworth calls "the nine boxes"[124]: Bosworth maintains that you begin open-ended questions to encourage the prospect to do most of the talking and you conclude with questions that confirm your understanding of the impact of the prospect's "pain." He then provides an example of an effective confirm impact question: "It sounds like this is not just your problem, but it is a companywide problem. Is that right?"

Bosworth also suggests capacity questions (open, control, and confirm) to ensure the buyer feels truly enabled. This last series of capability questions should conclude with something like this, "From what I just heard, if you had the ability to communicate product and price changes to all field sales reps within ten minutes, and if those changes could be communicated to all of your field reps at the same time, so no one is left out or gets different information, could *you* meet your sales goals? What would that be worth to you?"

The solution selling questioning and visioning approach applied not only to sales but also to delivery of our services. Because our client whisperers were curious and eager to explore new perspectives, they were skilled at asking probing questions. We found that one of the many positive aspects of having experienced, mature consultants was that they had a contextual understanding of the higher education environment which gave them a foundation for asking relevant, probing questions.

We cautioned our client whisperers to be very sensitive to client comfort when asking questions during the initial phases of need-development and solution visioning. We encouraged them to be well-informed about the prospect/client's institutional profile and their perceived peer institutions. By merely reviewing the institution's website, our client whisperers could gain broad contextual background regarding the institution as a basis for their specific questions. We consistently urged our client whisperers to obtain any available background on key stakeholders prior to meeting with a prospect. This task was relatively easy for our whisperers due to our vast higher education experience and a database that I developed about twenty years ago with a trusted colleague. Long before the emergence of Facebook, Twitter, and LinkedIn, our higher education people database, called PeopleNet, was populated with electronic copies of the Higher Education Directory, which contained information about administrators in all American colleges and universities.

Our concatenation of this directory information for each year since 1985 allowed us to produce some very useful reports. By entering the name of a current college administrator, we could see all available information on that administrator, all of that administrator's current colleagues who were in the database, and all of his/her colleagues in other institutions who previously worked with that administrator at both the administrator's current employer and in all of the administrator's previous employers. For example, I was an administrator at Cornell University from 1970 through 1977. During that time, I had a working relationship with more than one hundred colleagues at Cornell. Some of those colleagues moved on to work at one or more other institutions. Those former colleagues now have working relationships with hundreds of other people in the higher education community, which means that, within two degrees of separation, I am connected with more than one thousand higher education administrators. Many of my co-workers at CedarCrestone had similar industry networks, which expanded our collective industry network to thousands of administrators. Each of us who was a former college or university administrator could enter our own name and see where all of our former colleagues are today with a list of all of their former colleagues at other institutions. At times during our journey, this information became a very useful competitive advantage.

Thus, we had a good picture of our industry people network, which allowed us to leverage our relationships with any of the people in that network. However, we always had to be very careful not to trust second and third-hand information as being completely accurate (i.e., informed skepticism). This is when the art of whispering kicks in and the dual process of relationship and need-development begins by using an appropriate level of questioning etiquette.

For some, this questioning process was mechanical and less effective. However, the true client whisperer turned this questioning interaction into a natural, comfortable conversation that enabled him/her to gain great insight into the client's situation while at the same time developing trusting relationships that became the foundation for many great client success stories.

I have used solution selling techniques in many aspects of my professional and personal life since I first met Mike Bosworth in 1987. My experience supports his statement that, "Salespeople, consultants, entrepreneurs, engineers, Ph.D.s, executives, and husbands and wives who study this technique, practice it, and master it are amazed at the results."[125] When the buyer senses that you are not selling, but just asking questions, the results can be truly amazing.

The majority of our sales wins occurred pursuant to receipt of an RFP from a prospective client. The primary purpose of each RFP was to solicit information from each qualified consulting company, including specific pricing information. This is accomplished via the use of requests for specific information, which typically includes a long list of mandatory questions to which each company must respond. The most effective RFPs were those that resulted in the most useful information upon which to make an informed decision; they contained the most "good questions." The least effective RFP contained few good questions and many "bad questions' that resulted in no useful information and, in some cases, misleading or irrelevant information for the selection committee.

Typically, all interested parties were provided an opportunity to submit questions to the institution before a specified deadline that was set sometime after issuance of the RFP and before the deadline to submit a proposal. These questions and the answers from the institution were subsequently shared with all companies that received the RFP. We viewed this as an opportunity to learn more about both the prospect and their selection process and to demonstrate our insight into and experience with similar projects for peer institutions. However, the lesser qualified companies tended to submit bad questions that reflected their lack of relevant experience. We suspected that it was easy for the buyer to determine who was experienced and who was not based on the nature of the questions that they submitted.

An example of our client whisperer's ability to ask the right questions at the right time follow.

> "The consultants I worked with had direct experience 'in the trenches' of higher education, which gave them an invaluable understanding of our business processes from the user perspective. They encouraged us to think about the big picture, to take a step back and evaluate what we do and how we do it before moving forward with specific implementation details. The first conversation was always a discussion of what we do and how we do it, followed by suggestions of how we might modify our processes both to streamline them and to use PeopleSoft's delivered functionality to our best advantage."
>
> Assistant Dean for Curriculum Management
> Private Liberal Arts College

LEARNING

According to Wikipedia, the Japanese word Shoshin "refers to having an attitude of openness, eagerness, and lack of preconceptions when studying a subject, even when studying at an advanced level, just as a beginner in that subject would."[126] The combination of a "beginner's mind' and the ability to ask good questions can be a powerful learning tool. This became very clear to us as we interacted with our grandchildren and watched them learn. At times we were amazed at the questions they asked, including the following:

- "At what temperature does your spit freeze?"
- "Will cars ever fly?"
- "In what countries do the bad guys live?"
- "Why do you believe there's a God?
- "Where is heaven?"

And then there is the most difficult question of all: "Why do you have to leave now?"

At the beginning of our journey, our collective ignorance about the PeopleSoft software was at times overwhelming. In this context, each of us truly had a beginner's mind with little time to fill our knowledge void. With a just-in-time approach to learning, we somehow managed to stay a step or two ahead of our initial clients by highlighting our strengths—higher education experience, knowledge of student information systems in general, and insight into the business processes that were supported by the software.

We hired very experienced and energetic people, people who liked to learn, especially new technology. With the ever constant learning curve that is intrinsic to continuously changing technology, our client whisperers were constantly learning to stay abreast of emerging technology. When at project sites having dinner with our client whisperers, I was always impressed by their eagerness to hear about and learn of something new related to technology. However, their insatiable appetite for learning extended far beyond technology, due largely, I believe, to their innate curiosity in general.

Our consultants were extraordinarily proficient at learning from each other. They did this daily in face-to-face interactions within their project teams and periodically during the PeopleSoft Higher Education user group conferences. They also learned from each other virtually within the vast informal network of PeopleSoft experts. At the end of our journey, they were doing it via the burgeoning social media and business networks that were bursting onto the scene at that time. This peer-to-peer learning produced dramatic outcomes at a fraction of the cost of the more traditional mode of learning by instructor led group training sessions in a classroom.

Another characteristic that I noted about the knowledge-seeking be-havior of our consultants was their ability to foster this same thirst for learning among our clients. I think because they first built a strong rela-tionship with our client's staff, they were able to engage the project staff in incrementally and progressively learning more about the capabilities of the software. Their synergistic problem solving sessions were won-derful examples of "learning together."

PROOF OF PERFORMANCE

"From the proposal stage onward, CedarCrestone invested in learning our campus business processes, our pain points and the areas where our ERP upgrade could make vital and perceptible differences to our students, faculty and staff. CedarCrestone's consultants kept the team focused on the issues that mattered to us. When problems arose and our staff was faced with 'not know-ing what they didn't know,' CedarCrestone consultants stayed with the issues until they were resolved. CedarCrestone kept the proj-ect both within the budget and on-time. As complex and multifac-eted as our ERP upgrade was, we would not have been success-ful without CedarCrestone—it's just as simple as that."

Vice President for Information Technology
Community College

LESSONS LEARNED

- Watch, watch, watch…there is more going on than you think.
- Don't open the "gift of gab" in a sales situation.
- Good questions, and the sequence in which you ask them, can make or break a sales call.
- Questioning and listening are pre-cursers to learning.
- Learning is the essence of good-to-great.

15. Instincts and Habits: Important?

Borrowed Wisdom

> "Good instincts usually tell you what to do long before your head has figured it out."[127]
>
> Michael Burke,
> Inspirational Author

Guiding Principle

> Making a client successful requires instinctive and habitual behavior. You do it over and over...and over.

Both instincts and habits are things that you just automatically do without even thinking. The primary difference between instincts and habits is that we are born with instincts—they can't be changed; whereas, habits are learned and formed by practice—they can be changed. Given these premises, our strategy was to optimize our client whisperers' instincts while engendering habits focused on client success.

The Conative Dimension

Kathy Kolbe introduced us to the concept of the conative dimension. She explains, "Conation is the part of the mind that drives you to act according to your instincts. These are the natural talents that, when acted on, lead to success and well-being as you use your creative energy to solve problems."[128] In her book, *Conative Connection: Acting on Instinct* (copyright © 1990-2011 by Kathy Kolbe) Kolbe asserts that the human mind consists of <u>three</u> very different, but interrelated, parts. In **Table 3** below, she compares the cognitive and affective dimensions of our mind, which are well known dimensions, with a third dimension: conative.

Table 3: The Three Dimensions of the Mind[129]

COGNITIVE (THINKING)	CONATIVE (DOING)	AFFECTIVE (FEELING)
IQ	Drive	Desires
Skills	Instinct	Motivation
Reason	Necessity	Attitudes
Knowledge	Mental energy	Preferences
Experience	Innate force	Emotions
Education	Talents	Values

According to Kolbe,"Conation is the mental faculty that causes an individual to act, react and interact according to an innate pattern of behavior...Conation is an internal, unchanging, unconscious attribute. Each person's instincts drive them to naturally approach problems in particular ways. These natural abilities can't be altered by education, coaching, counseling, self-help manuals, parenting, or pleading. They are derived from subconscious, unalterable instincts."[130] Kolbe's work reveals that there are four Action Modes with striving behaviors in each Action Mode, examples of which are presented below in **Table 4**.

Table 4: Action Modes and Striving Behaviors[131]

ACTION MODES	STRIVING BEHAVIORS
• Fact Finder	How you gather and share information
• Follow Thru	How you arrange and design
• Quick Start	How you deal with risks and uncertainty
• Implementer	How you handle space and tangibls

Most of our projects, particularly in the very early years, were in the Quick Start Action Mode and required us to take initiative early and often. We had to deal with unknowns, uncertainties and risks. We also had to have consultants on our teams whose primary Action Mode was Follow Thru. It was essential that the projects be organized and the software configuration be designed. Although we were not the "hardware gurus," whose Action Mode of Implementer entailed handling tangibles, mechanics and space, we had to have enough of these striving behaviors represented on our teams to identify problems of this nature that would impact the project. The Fact Finder Action Mode of gathering and sharing information was critical not only to our project teams but also to our salespeople who conducted stakeholder analyses. Ultimately, we found that the near "ideal" synergy came from having all Action Modes and their related striving behaviors represented on our teams.

Drawing on over thirty years of original research, Kolbe has developed fourteen axioms that fall into three interrelated behavior categories: Individual Actions, Relationships, and Group Behavior. It was easy to see how all of the Kolbe Axioms applied logically to our

Lyon's Pride

All of the basketball teams I played on in my four years of high school were very successful. Each season we won far more games than we lost. The depth of talent on our teams in our freshman, sophomore, and junior years was far superior to that of our team in my senior year. At the beginning of that season, having lost five of our top seven players to graduation, the sports writers described it as a rebuilding year. But we fooled them all! With the right players in the right roles – and with much passion, synergy, and team trust—we went undefeated and won three championships—which was likely due to a higher level of conative synergy and more complementary skill sets.

business. I highlight an Axiom in each category that was particularly useful to us and share an example of each as it applied to our business.

In the category of Individual Actions, I felt that Axiom 7 was especially applicable to our client whisperers: "Creativity requires use of all three mental faculties…The conative, cognitive and affective parts of the mind all contribute to the Kolbe Creative Process, which is synonymous with productivity. Each of these three parts of the mind operates independently, yet all three are equally important in contributing to the process."[132]

Our teams had to be creative: it was a given. Understanding that the conative dimension was the part of the mind that contributed to creativity was an important insight for us as we realized we could leverage the innate patterns of behavior of our client whisperers. Key to creatively designing client solutions was the function of the conative dimension that converted the affective faculties (emotions, preferences or beliefs—of both our team and client team members) and the cognitive faculties (learned knowledge and skills—about the PeopleSoft software) into purposeful performance.

For example, some of our clients' requests for software modification were based primarily on replicating in the new software what had been available in their legacy system. In getting at the "root" of this request, the request was based primarily on affective thinking: they were anxious about having to learn new software. A typical consultant response might be to logically show them how much better it could be done with the new software (cognitive thinking). However, because this cognitive-based solution did not consider the affective root cause, client reaction could be negative and team cohesion could erode. However, using the Conative dimension, our client whisperers typically would creatively design a "bolt on" (which didn't get into the code of the software) that preserved some of the best features of the client's old business process while introducing new capabilities of the software and lowering the maintenance effort. By drawing upon the Conative dimension, our client whisperers integrated affective and cognitive thinking and translated it into a creatively designed client solution. While subtle in its manifestation, Conative thinking in these situations contributed to harmonious teamwork.

The Relationship Axiom that we observed the most was Axiom 8: "Conative stress results when obstacles interfere with the use of conative strengths."[133] Some of our consultants experienced burn-out, probably caused by a combination of working against their conative grain, aggressive project scope and timeline, lack of team trust, win-lose client tactics, difficult travel requirements, weather issues, being away from their families for extended periods of time, and perhaps occasional empathy fatigue. To help prevent or address burn-out issues, we expanded the project team by adding consultants who had conative and cognitive strengths that complemented the strengths of the existing consulting team to allow each consultant to leverage their natural talents.

In Kolbe's Group Behavior category, the axiom that was most applicable was Axiom 14: "Probability of team success improves as conative strengths are appropriately allocated. Kolbe explains this axiom as follows: "Having the right people doing the right jobs is a matter of having the right conative fit. Assigning people to tasks for which they have the wrong conative strengths robs them and the organization of their opportunity to succeed...High productivity is predicted in organizations with a high percentage of people who are able to contribute their conative strengths."[134]

I recall being told by the project manager of a prestigious research university that they already had all of the cognitive talent required to accomplish each task in their implementation plan without our help, but each time they attempted to complete a complex project with no external assistance, they failed. After they hired us as their implementation partner; and together we successfully completed the project, we understood clearly why they needed our help. They had an abundance of conative stress and a paucity of conative synergy. Together, however, we had the right combination of conative strengths.

THE MATURITY CONTINUUM

We were keenly interested in Stephen R. Covey's Maturity Continuum because it helped us to understand the process for developing effective habits. As illustrated in **Figure Q** below, he states that we move, "progressively on a Maturity Continuum from dependence to independence to interdependence."[136]

Figure Q: Covey's Maturity Continuum

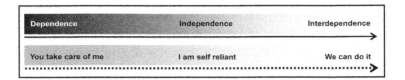

Our business success story was all about the far end of the Maturity Continuum: interdependence and teamwork. Our maturation followed Covey's maturation continuum as we progressed from mastering the fundamentals of individual performance to mastering the execution of team performance. In our consulting business, that team included both consultants and clients as an integrated project team. We periodically used independent contractors to perform a specialized role on a project team. However, sometimes their independent behavior had a negative impact on the performance of the team because they tended to be "limelighters" – consultants with specialized skill sets who were motivated by individual praise and recognition, not by team performance.

THE EFFECTIVE HABITS OF A HEDGEHOG

In striving to achieve a market leadership position, I felt that it was important to align our hedgehog concept with Covey's *Seven Habits of Highly Effective People*. Covey's first three habits deal with self-mastery; the next three with teamwork, cooperation and communication; and the last one with renewal.

SELF-MASTERY HABITS

Be Proactive. As partners in a start-up business with minimal investment capital, we realized that each of us, as individuals, had to be highly proactive. Much of our early work required independent, rather than interdependent, behavior. However, as we started to grow and the size of our teams and clients increased, we shifted our hiring approach to find proactive people who also were interdependent team players. I liken this transition to shifting from a baseball to a basketball team. We encouraged our consultants to blend the best of being proactive with the best of interdependence. I share the following client quote as an example of how our consultants were proactive and interdependent with their client in achieving a successful outcome.

> "Every question I asked, every request I made was responded to immediately. If it could be done, it was done. If not, there were always alternatives proposed to get me to the same place in a slightly different way. More than that, it was often the case that our consultants would anticipate what I was going to want before I even knew I wanted it."
>
> Assistant Dean for Curriculum Management
> Private Liberal Arts College

Begin with the End in Mind. For my basketball teams, the end was winning a championship. For our business venture, the end was becoming the market share leader—a very aggressive goal for a company with zero brand equity. Most of us also wanted to help our team make a contribution to the higher education industry that had been good to us for so many years. At a minimum, that contribution would provide colleges and universities with a "faster, cheaper, better" software implementation alternative to the existing high cost solutions offered by the large consulting companies. We also had a commitment to transfer knowledge to our clients, to further their professional development—all toward the greater good.

One afternoon we met with the chief technology officer of a major research university at a small, off-campus coffee shop. The purpose of our informal meeting was to discuss the vision of the university and how we could help them achieve that vision. He illustrated his technology vision in support of the university vision on a napkin, and said, "Can you do that?" I said, "I think we can, but tell me more about how we can help you." Then, In keeping with our solution selling approach, we discussed how we could collaboratively accomplish the vision—the end—knowing our vision at the outset. The president of the university stated the following at the end of this project.

> "We are integrating and streamlining our business processes to provide the quality of service our students, faculty and staff have come to expect. One of the facilitators of this transformation has been the successful implementation of new information systems and a modern infrastructure. Working in partnership with CedarCrestone and Oracle Corporation, our Information Technology Leadership and staff have successfully completed a rapid implementation of the PeopleSoft Human Resources Management System and Campus Solutions software. This success story was essential for the fulfillment of our vision."
>
> President
> Public Research University

Put First Things First. We believed strongly that if client success was our number one priority, "our first thing," business success would follow closely behind. We realized that for our employees to put first things first required disciplined action on their part. For our sales process, disciplined action meant not proposing a "solution" when the buyer was not yet in the *Evaluate Alternatives* phase of the buying process. When the buyer was in the Evaluate Alternatives phase of the buying process, disciplined action meant demonstrating our understanding of their needs by discussing our success with similar projects for peer institutions.

For all of our employees, disciplined action meant freedom with responsibility without excessive controls and internal bureaucracy. It also meant being able to focus on client success with the understanding that you would get support when needed, both from management and fellow consultants. We stressed that it was important to identify client priorities and work collaboratively to achieve those priorities. For example, with many of our clients knowledge transfer was a high priority, particularly as institutional budgets were reduced. They knew that once they were in production, it was unlikely that they would receive additional funding for consultants. As they envisioned being "on their own," they were very concerned about having sufficient knowledge to maintain the system and provide on-going training of end users.

INTERDEPENDENCE HABITS

Think Win/Win. We first had to get all of our people aligned by thinking win/win, not just talking win/win. Fostering this alignment was more challenging with our salespeople than with our consultants. Salespeople typically were more focused on the potential commission than on the subsequent feelings that our prospective client might have if they did not feel that the contract was a win/win. Our creative approaches to risk sharing were examples of win-win tactics that helped both our salespeople and prospects understand our win/win approach. We also recognized that for our clients to feel a win/win outcome, the project had to yield added value to students, faculty and staff. The following quotes, that were part of a press release issued to a statewide system of higher education, illustrate the power of a win/win approach with our clients. The press release began with a quote from the chancellor.

"On-time and under budget – these are words that are not typically associated with public-sector projects. However, we have successfully accomplished just that with the recent implementation of our integrated student information system. Designed to improve the level of quality of service to students, the new system will transform communications, improve accuracy and timeliness, and make real-time information available to students, faculty and staff. Coming in on time and under budget, this new system not only achieves cost savings through economies of scale, it more importantly improves the student experience and allows faculty, staff and students to invest more of their time in the classroom than dealing with outdated technologies."

The press release concluded with a statement from one of the Regents of the state-wide system. "The entire system should be very proud of what has been accomplished through CedarCrestone's implementation of Oracle's PeopleSoft Campus Solutions...The implementation is an incredible success."

Seek First to Understand, Then to Be Understood. This habit became a guiding principle for all of our client-facing activities. It was the cornerstone of our sales differentiation strategies and our implementation methodology. However, it was also one of our biggest challenges. The natural behavior of expert consultants is to demonstrate their expertise early and often. The other potential problem associated with using expert consultants in a sales situation is giving the appearance of fabrication, which is especially risky if the prospect has a healthy skepticism about vendor veracity. Most people who are fabricating a story are prone to hyper-specificity—way too much detail. The most effective responses to prospect questions are those that are concise, respond to the point of the question, and are delivered with consistent eye contact and open body language.

When a client whisperer is "seeking to understand" during a need-development session, they must be singularly focused on listening to the prospect or client. To do this, the whisperer must clear his/her mind of other thoughts and concentrate on empathetic listening and validation of what they are hearing. An example of the need for focused concentration is when we were called in to make an orals presentation, as described below.

When I first entered the room where the presentation was about to take place, I would always study the surroundings and begin to visualize how the room would look and feel once the session began. This visualization helped me to get focused on the task at hand and block out whatever other unrelated issues I may have had to deal with after an orals session. Once the prospective client attendees entered, I attempted to focus clearly on each participant to gain as much insight into both what their words and their body language conveyed. No multitasking occurred until the session concluded and we were leaving campus. Most of these sessions lasted for at least a few hours, some as much as two days. Typically I felt emotionally tired, sometimes actually exhausted, when the orals sessions were concluded. This single-mindedness was much the same as that of a focused basketball player during the fourth quarter of a big game. Maintaining eye contact, focus, and concentration is hard mental work, but it is key to effective interaction with a client or prospective client. I personally understood Medina's finding that one's attentional ability is not capable of multi-tasking. The most positive feedback we received from our approach to orals was, "You listened to what we had to say and responded as if you understood and really cared."

Synergize. One of our early clients hired us to evaluate and redesign their institutional brand, as presented in the imagery and structure of their website. The project was under the leadership of the University Image Committee. Our proposal called for, and we conducted, a series of interviews and focus groups with representatives from key constituencies and stakeholders as a basis for the evaluation and redesign. Our client whisperer presented the findings with the intention of then facilitating a series of sessions with the Image Committee to create the new brand. As she began, one of the participants said, "I thought that you were going to come in here and tell us what our brand should be. Isn't that what we are paying you for?"

Our client whisperer was taken aback. She had to think quickly and intuitively, given this unexpected question. It was a good illustration of what Stephen R. Covey described as the fear associated with an anticipated creative process: "The creative process is also the most terrifying part because you don't know exactly what's going to happen or where it is going to lead."[138] In response, she said that at the next session the committee members could decide if they wanted to collaboratively create their new brand image or accept her recommendations for a brand based upon generalized best practices.

At the beginning of the next meeting with the Image Committee, our client whisperer first highlighted the differences between an inductive methodology—grass roots up approach—versus a deductive methodology—top down. She shared her experience of using an inductive methodology with other institutions and the synergy that came about when they created a solution together. To illustrate the deductive methodology, she offered her own recommendations that were based primarily upon best practices and research regarding their peer institutions. She then gave them the opportunity to choose which approach they preferred. They quickly—and unanimously—chose the inductive approach. A highly synergistic, creative session took off! The result of this and subsequent sessions was a brand image and website structure that everyone embraced. They had experienced the synergy and excitement that comes from creating something together.

RENEWAL HABIT

Sharpen the Saw. We periodically came together as a team to do some "sharpening," especially when I introduced new concepts from our wisdom providers. To reinforce our approach to implementations and upgrades, we offered a series of internal workshops that over eighty percent of our consultants attended. They were highly engaged and energized as they learned new tools and concepts. We offered a number of other ways in which our client whisperers could engage in learning to complement their personal learning pursuits. For example, we periodically held webinars explaining a new technology that Oracle was releasing, offered project management training, illustrated a unique customization that we had developed, to name just a few. Our consultants were encouraged to contribute to our Communication Center, a web-based knowledge repository, referred to as the "Consultant Backpack," (a metaphor consistent with the prevalence of backpacks on a college campus). The Backpack included a wealth of resources which our client whisperers could easily draw from and contribute to in their continuous pursuit of knowledge.

In terms of how we helped our clients (and our consultants) sharpen their saw, our consultants worked side-by-side with their respective project team members, transferring knowledge and giving them increased levels of responsibility. Our consultants experienced first-hand the adage that one learns most when one teaches. Some of the staff who were backfilling project team members were renewed because of learning a new job or a new dimension of an existing job. Although participating in a project of this intensity and duration could burn people out, many of our client team members were at least partially renewed by the experience, because they were part of the creative process of implementing new solutions.

PROOF OF PERFORMANCE

"CedarCrestone's experienced higher education consultants, using their methodology, have guided us through an effective learning process allowing us to gain confidence in the PeopleSoft student system. They became an integral part of our project team during the implementation phase, offering sound advice and fostering informed decision making throughout the project. With CedarCrestone's help, we feel we're well on our way to taking ownership of the system with a successful, comprehensive implementation that is integrated into our environment."

Assistant Provost & Project Manager
Public Research University

LESSONS LEARNED

- You do best what you do naturally.
- Leverage instincts when forming effective habits.
- Habits are infectious—make sure they are healthy ones.
- Old fashioned mental discipline is still in vogue.
- Trust your gut! It's instinctive.

16. When is a Mystery Puzzling?

Borrowed Wisdom

> "Development of the human mind is quite parallel to the development of the human body. Good theory, good practice, and good feedback are essential."[137]
> Linda Elder and Richard Paul,
> Critical Thinking Experts

Guiding Principle

> Thinking out of the box means that you have never thought of yourself as being in a box.

In conceiving and writing this book, we pondered at length: just what was it about our client whisperers that made us feel their minds were "wondrous," even mysterious at times? Was there anything in their education, training and experience that distinguished the way they thought when compared to other consultants? What qualities should we look for in hiring people so that we could expand our cadre of wondrous minds? We knew that one of the most important skills was critical thinking.

Critical Thinking Skills

Our consulting teams included some outstanding critical thinkers. Without these extraordinary thinkers, we would not have been able to both win and deliver some of our larger projects, most of which required the design and development of complex technical solutions to address unique needs of the client. In other situations, our critical thinkers helped us avoid the need for costly customizations by devising clever ways to use the delivered functionality of the base software to meet the client's needs in lieu of customizations. We were able to set forth such competitive bids because we trusted our critical thinkers to design creative ways to address the diverse needs of both individual campus stakeholders while also meeting the needs of central administration.

The critical thinking skills of our people helped us successfully deal with myriad complexities associated with an ERP implementation project. At the proposal stage of some of these ultimately successful stories, there were external experts who said that what we proposed couldn't be done, especially not in the timeframe in which we had proposed to do it. Contrary to the expectations of these experts, we did indeed do it --- time and time again. Each time that we completed one of these projects on time and within budget, client feedback was very positive and it was easy to solicit client testimonials.

Vickie and her team of quality assurance specialists were particularly adept at thinking critically, as they came in for reviews at key milestones. They interviewed project participants to assess progress and identify any outstanding issues. When reviewing their findings with the project manager, they would think critically and collaboratively about how to mitigate risks and stay on schedule. When our quality assurance specialist met with the client project manager, they were able to further refine these mitigating strategies. This synergy of critical thinking yielded a plan of action that resulted in successful achievement of the client's project goals and objectives. Our clients were able to observe and learn critical thinking skills from our client whisperers. As we continuously mentored our clients' staff, they saw first-hand how we thought critically, especially when confronted with challenging, and even mysterious, technical issues. An example of the effectiveness of Vickie and her team is referenced in the following client testimonial.

"The cohesiveness of the CedarCrestone and our teams was fostered in large part by the Quality Assurance component that sought to focus on project management practices and communications across teams and throughout the various staff levels."

Project Manager
Public Research University

CREATIVE VISUALIZATION

In her book, *Creative Visualization: Use the Power of Your Imagination to Create What You Want in Your Life*, (Copyright © 2002 by Shakti Gawain. Reprinted with permission of New World Library, Novato, CA.) best-selling author Shakti Gawain suggests that, "Creative visualization is the technique of using your imagination to create what you want in your life. There is nothing at all new, strange, or unusual about creative visualization. You are already using it every day, every minute in fact. It is your natural power of imagination, the basic creative energy of the universe, which you use constantly, whether or not you are aware of it."[138]

LYON'S PRIDE

I used visualization to improve my basketball performance beginning as a boy, when I would use a tennis ball and home-made goal in our tiny kitchen. I pretended to out-maneuver defenders and invent new shots not yet tried on a real court. Even today, to satisfy my continued passion for the game, I still play fantasy basketball against make believe opponents on a real basketball court. In the chapter about passion in his book, Values of the Game, (Copyright © 1998, used by permission of Artisan, a division of Workman Publishing Co., Inc., New York, all rights reserved) Bill Bradley wrote, "Country roads mean different things to different people. With a little imagination, young dreamers can transform them into Madison Square Garden."[141] For me, it was not only country roads, but also kitchens, backyards and driveways.

According to a recent New York Times story, "One of psychology's most respected journals has agreed to publish a paper presenting what its author describes as strong evidence for extrasensory perception, the ability to sense future events…The paper describes nine unusual lab experiments performed over the past decade by its author, Daryl J. Bem, an emeritus professor at Cornell, testing the ability of college students to accurately sense random events, like whether a computer program will flash a photograph on the left or right side of its screen. The studies include more than one thousand subjects."[140] Psychologist Dr. Jennifer Hartstein said that Dr. Bem's research "…did find that people who were bigger risk takers tend to have an ability to have better precognition or ESP than other people. Is it that they are taking risks, so will they have to anticipate what might come next? Who knows? But they did find that personality type is more likely."[141]

Sometimes it appeared that our client whisperers were using ESP to anticipate client needs, concerns, and questions. Perhaps the risk-taking personalities of our client whisperers suggest a propensity for ESP skills. This theory also seems to be supported by a series of studies with high school students in India conducted by K. Ramakrishna Rao which has given further insight into the personality traits associated with ESP capabilities. The following adjectives summarize some of the results of this research. The personality traits of their positive ESP scorers seem to track closely with those of our best client whisperers.

Table 5: Positive and Negative ESP Score Characteristics[142]

POSITIVE ESP SCORES	NEGATIVE ESP SCORES
• Enthusiastic	• Suspicious
• Quick, alert	• Threat-sensitive
• Adventuresome, impulsive	• Dependent
• Warm, sociable	• Timid
• Talkative	• Shy
• Cheerful	• Depression prone
• Assertive, self-assured	• Withdrawn, sensitive, submissive
• Good natured, easy going	• Demanding, impatient, frustrated
• Relaxed	• Tense
• Composed	• Excitable

Based on my observation of effective client whispering, I would add the personality traits of "extraversion" and "empathetic" to the left column in the table above. The more you think about the people around you, the easier it should be to anticipate what they will say and do next.

One of the first activities that we would conduct with many of our clients was to facilitate a discussion of their vision for the outcome of the project. Sometimes we would gather information from executives in individual interviews regarding their vision. Interestingly, many executives needed some "idea seeding" given their misperception that this was just a software project, not an organizational effectiveness opportunity. Some had difficulty understanding that the project could contribute to realizing the vision of the institution. Fortunately, our first experience with a client in formulating and achieving a vision was very positive. As one of the first clients to implement the PeopleSoft software just prior to the year 2000, this president had a well-articulated and communicated vision. We just had to be sure we could achieve it. Happily, we did!

For some of our projects, we conducted focus groups with stakeholders to query them regarding their vision for the project. Examples of our questions to help them describe their vision were, "Envision what you'd like this university to be like in three to five years. What would it look like if we came back and walked around campus and talked to students and faculty or went on-line and looked at your website? What would people in your community say about the university? If we asked students what they liked about the university, what kind of comments would we likely receive from them? What would your peers at other institutions have to say about your university? How do you think this project help could help to achieve that vision?" Sometimes we also would share vision statements and case studies from peer institutions to stimulate ideas and illustrate what was possible, an example of which follows:

"The University of Choice"

To further the mission of the University, our PeopleSoft project will collaboratively implement the Student Administration System to build and support the following future environment:

- An enhanced educational and occupational experience through the delivery of innovative, timely, high quality services.

- An empowered student body, faculty and staff through easy access to information resources.

- A strengthened campus community culture through a personalized approach that is complemented and enabled by information technology.

It was during the implementation process that the ability to envision a solution to a challenging problem became especially important. Because our client whisperers typically had experience solving similar challenges and because they were particularly adept at envisioning solutions, the challenges were overcome—many times in unanticipated ways.

GENDER DIFFERENCES

Another very important influence is that of developmental differences between males and females. In that context, Medina refers to the research of Larry Cahill, who studied brain activity of men and women under acute stress. Of particular relevance to our business story was the conclusion that males tend to remember more gist than detail, and women tend to remember more detail than gist. Medina then explains that women have more vivid memories of emotionally important events, and that they are more likely to "tend and befriend"[143] than are men. He also describes the fascinating work of behaviorist Deborah Tannen, that identified the different ways boys and girls talk to their best friends and how they negotiate status. She concluded that girls' verbal skills were more sophisticated and they were more likely to say things like "Let's do this," while boys tended to say, "Do this."[144] Medina then offers the following observations regarding gender differences:

- "Emotions are useful. They make the brain pay attention.
- Men and women process certain emotions differently.
- The differences are a product of complex interactions between nature and nurture."[145]

In her book, *Iron Butterflies: Women Transforming Themselves and the World*, developmental psychologist, Bruite Regine, writes about women in the business domain. "In the business world, emotional strength gives Iron Butterflies an edge. Like all good businesspeople, they effectively engage in strategy, execution, delivery, and bottom-line issues, but their emotional strength enables them to go further and deeper. They ask people how they feel, not just what they think. They notice if people work hard and get results, but they also wonder whether they feel fulfilled by their work. Can they take suggestions or do they get defensive? Are they happy, frustrated, engaged, or bored? Do they enjoy their interactions with their fellow workers or do they feel isolated and ignored? Are they team players or do they bring so much negative energy to the environment that they drain everyone's time and patience?[146]…While dealing with complex feelings takes time and effort, Iron Butterflies make it a top priority because they know that clearing the emotional air opens the way to more effective and creative work…Iron Butterflies are strong in their openness; they are willing to be influenced by others and invite effective dissonance. They are strong because they take their place but make room for others."[147]

According to the 2009-10 Almanac issue of *The Chronicle of Higher Education,* fifty-three percent of the "executive, administrative, managerial" positions in American colleges and universities were held by women. Unlike most other industry segments, women hold the majority of key stakeholder positions that are involved in software implementation projects.

Women were a very important part of our success story. Two of our eight founding partners were women. During most of our twelve-year journey, more than fifty percent of our higher education consultants were women, and seven of our extended leadership team were females. Our acquisition of Software Armada, a small woman-owned and operated higher education consulting company, came with some very talented people, the majority of whom were women. We invited Elizabeth, one of the founders of Software Armada, to join our leadership team. She went on to become a highly effective vice president for business development, setting a good example for our salespeople of how to conduct need development with a prospective client, i.e., a "client sales whisperer." Some of our top salespeople were female.

When IA was acquired by MSA in 1986, our salespeople were invited to participate in a company-wide sales competition. The company's number one salesperson for the year was to receive the use of a Porsche for the subsequent year. At that time, MSA was a male-dominated company, especially their sales organization. As it turned out, the top salesperson in the company was a woman in our higher education practice whose sales manager was also a very competent woman. We were all very excited and eagerly looked forward to the upcoming sales meeting in Atlanta. Just prior to that meeting, however, the MSA sales vice president announced that there would be a second sports car awarded to the number two salesperson in the company, who of course turned out to be one of the many young, handsome, and aggressive men in the commercial sales organization. They just couldn't deal with the notion of a female "salesman" driving away in that red Porsche!

PUZZLES AND MYSTERIES

Gladwell makes an interesting distinction between puzzles and mysteries, and our client whisperers encountered both. "If things go wrong with a puzzle, identifying the culprit is easy; it's the person who withheld information. Mysteries, though, are a lot murkier: sometimes the information we've been given is inadequate, and sometimes we aren't very smart about making sense of what we've been given, and sometimes the question itself cannot be answered. Puzzles come to satisfying conclusions. Mysteries often don't." Gladwell goes on to say, "Mysteries demand experience and insight [whisperers]."[148] Regarding puzzles, Gladwell states "...all require the application of energy and persistence, which are the virtues of youth." To illustrate these points, he states, "Woodward and Bernstein would never have broken the Enron story,"[149] because they were so young and inexperienced. Gladwell's final point is insightful in terms of the differences between solving puzzles and solving mysteries: "Puzzles are 'transmitter-dependent'; they turn on what we are told. Mysteries are 'receiver-dependent'; they turn on the skills of the listener..."[150]

We encountered many puzzling situations that sometimes were even a bit mysterious because data, information and dogma all had to be synthesized and interpreted. Most of our complex projects were much more a mystery than a puzzle. Consultants who were short on experience, particularly higher education experience, were not prepared to deal with the complexities and peculiarities of a higher education ERP project. Our client whisperers, on the other hand, possessed the right combination of experience, knowledge, and skills to guide their clients through the tricky minefields associated with software implementation in higher education.

Pricing could be either a puzzle or a mystery, and many times a combination of both. Pricing for a straight-forward technical upgrade to a new version of the software typically was a puzzle that only required one final puzzle piece: an estimate of effort from an experienced upgrade consultant. However, most of the pricing for large, complex implementation projects was more of a mystery requiring some challenging analysis and interpretation of large amounts of data.

We generally encountered mysteries when it came to software gaps-functionality users needed to conduct business but which was not supported by the software. Every large, complex project had these. Our tasks included identifying these gaps, designing alternative solutions to address each critical gap, and then developing the solution that was approved by the client. These software gaps could present very challenging tasks to perform, and required complex analyses by some of our best functional and technical consultants. Critical thinking and problem solving skills were always required for this rather mysterious aspect of our projects.

One "mysterious puzzle" occurred at the conclusion of a robust implementation project with one of the largest public universities in the country. The timeline for this project was very aggressive, especially considering the complexity of the institution. We had a large team of consultants on-site throughout the project, with all of the software supported in our computer center in Atlanta. The project scope included replacement of the software that supported all of the student services for the university, most notably course registration, financial aid processing, student billing, grading and academic advising. During the last six months of the project we had completed all required testing, examples of which include: unit testing, system testing, stress testing, user acceptance testing and some parallel testing. At the conclusion of this testing, all of the software was performing well. Then, the Friday before the students were scheduled to return to campus for the Fall semester, system performance deteriorated dramatically. The cause of this performance degradation definitely was a mystery. We knew that beginning on Sunday evening, system usage would skyrocket, as sixty-five thousand students would begin registering for classes.

For the next forty-eight hours, we had PeopleSoft experts all around the country doing everything they could to solve the performance mystery. For the entire weekend, we maintained an open phone line to facilitate brainstorming among our onsite project team, our computer operations support staff in Atlanta, the Oracle software developers in San Francisco, and various other experts located in a half dozen additional locations around the country. However, as of late Saturday, system performance remained a big mystery and most people seemed convinced that it had to be a problem with either the software or our computer configuration in Atlanta.

That evening, our computer center people doubled the hardware configuration hoping that expansion would solve the problem, but it had no impact on the poor performance of the system! At that point, we were only about ten hours away from a huge registration disaster and panic was about to set in. And then someone with good lateral thinking skills suggested that the culprit might be an authentication server (computer) being used by the university to check the validity of each person prior to giving them access to the new PeopleSoft system.

Bingo! The client replaced that server with a more powerful one and the mystery was solved. A few hours later, students were registering for classes and the system was performing famously—perspiration finally ebbed! What had seemed all weekend to be a perplexing mystery fortunately turned out to be a relatively simple puzzle with only one small missing piece.

About the same time we were beginning our twelve-year journey, I got hooked on researching my family history. My natural love of discovery was a big asset in this endeavor; but I soon came to understand the importance of lateral thinking as I developed my family tree—a tree that now contains more than twenty thousand ancestors dating back to before the time of Christ. My family history work changed the way I think about solving mysteries and puzzles.

I slowly realized that all perspectives deserved to be analyzed. Who lived with whom and when? Who lived next door? Who else had a similar surname? Were children named after their parents, grandparents or famous ancestors? Who migrated from where and when—and why? What was their culture like and in what type of circumstances did they live? The questions went on and on.

My increasingly creative family research paid big dividends, thanks to lateral thinking. But, you might ask, "What do genealogy and great client service have in common? The answer is: "We should have asked more questions." If I had asked more questions about my family history when my grandparents and parents were alive, I would have saved hundreds of hours of research and would have much more insight into the people who went before me. Likewise, if we had asked more questions about prospect and client needs, issues, and concerns, we would have won more deals and avoided much rework and frustration. Missed opportunity in business is very much like missed opportunity in genealogy.

PROOF OF PERFORMANCE

> From the first day CedarCrestone arrived, they hit the ground running. They always took the initiative to communicate with the functional leads and security team to answer questions and resolve problems while keeping project leaders informed of their actions. I have received nothing but the highest praise from the implementation team about CedarCrestone's professionalism and extreme thoroughness."
>
> Information Services Training Specialist
> University Medical Center

LESSONS LEARNED

- Hiring older, more experienced consultants has more benefits than you might expect. As a starter, their brains are more fully developed.

- The multiple forms of intelligence each have value—if you know how to use them.

- Clever solutions come from clever people. Match your expectations.

- Simulations are stimulating—and they can become reality.

- Gender-blended teams bring out the very best of both flavors.

17. Is There Alchemy in Whispering?

Borrowed Wisdom

"When you combine a culture of discipline with an ethic of entrepreneurship, you get the magical alchemy of great performance."[151]

Jim Collins,
Distinguished Teacher and Author

Guiding Principle

Only the best ingredients...and in the right combination.

Our client whisperers seemed to be natural empathetic listeners. Their sincerity somehow made their clients feel instantly comfortable; their empathetic persona engendered so much comfort that their clients were willing to share both professional and personal pain almost immediately. This type of interaction typically only occurs after a person feels the essence of a trusting relationship. How our client whisperers accomplished this instant relationship building was a bit of a mystery—the solving of which required much interdisciplinary insight.

The Chemical of Liquid Trust

American psychologist, Daniel Goleman, author of Emotional Intelligence *and* Social Intelligence: The New Science of Human Relationships, and American neuroeconomist, Paul Zak, in his work, Moral Markets: The Critical Role of Values in the Economy, have studied empathy in the context of their academic disciplines and concluded that there is a scientific basis for what I came to call the "Alchemy of Whispering." Goleman promoted the vital role of empathy in effective leadership. He believes that, "effective leaders [whisperers] are defined by their ability to empathize with and be sensitive to the needs others."

He defined empathy as, "the ability of leaders to understand what motivates other people."[152]

This definition led Goleman and other researchers to study what happens in the brain while people are communicating. Their research determined that when leaders [whisperers] exhibit empathy and become attuned to others' moods, it literally affects both their own brain chemistry and that of their followers. This revelation has led to leadership enrichment through social intelligence training to help leaders empathize with their followers and listen more attentively.

Zak's research, conducted in 2004, was the first to identify the role of the neuropeptide oxytocin, sometimes called "liquid trust." It has the effect of mediating trusting behaviors between unacquainted humans. He also has shown that oxytocin is responsible for a variety of virtuous behaviors in humans. This research calls into question traditional models in economics that assume people are narrowly self-interested. Through a series of experiments, Zak showed that human brains appear to have "moral sentiments" that modulate the balance between self-interest and prosocial tendencies. His research also showed that using social media such as Twitter raises oxytocin levels. Zak has made a clear case that oxytocin causes a shift in brain chemistry that is evolutionarily important: "the more we trust one another and cooperate, the more we all benefit together."[153]

The website Infinite Mind reports, "In his brilliant book, The Power of Intention, Dr. Wayne Dyer writes about a study that measured Serotonin levels in people during acts of kindness. It was discovered that people who performed an act of kindness received an increase in their Serotonin levels. Furthermore, the receiver of the good act also enjoyed an increase in their Serotonin levels. What was most amazing was that people who had only witnessed the act of kindness also had an increase in their Serotonin levels. In each of these cases the performer, the receiver and the witness all had similar increases in this happy chemical."[154]

I now am confident that it has much to do with the mutual stimulation of their respective "chemistries of empathy." Like most human attributes, the levels of empathy form a continuum that goes from a person suffering from an antisocial personality disorder (no empathy) to a well-trained salesperson (attentive listener) to a universal client whisperer (instant empathy). Based only on personal observations, we became convinced that client whisperers have an extraordinary chemistry of whispering, which allows them to go way beyond active to empathetic listening.

Our proposal director Tim, who had a Ph.D. and higher education experience as a faculty member, was sometimes called in on management consulting engagements. His sincere manner and empathy were critical qualities in those situations when the client's staff were anxious about an impending project or were midstream and some emotional issues arose that impeded progress. The client testimonial below illustrates how his empathetic and trusting nature helped them "clear the air."

> "The CedarCrestone consultant was a pleasant, thoughtful professional who quickly gained the trust and respect of a variety of campus constituencies ranging from senior administrators to highly technical experts to passionate functional staff. His assistance proved invaluable for revealing critical decision points while lowering the emotional threshold."
>
> Associate Vice President Instructional and
> Information Technology
> Public, Master's University

THE POTENCY OF MOTIVATION

ChangingMinds.org suggests, "If you want to motivate people, understand the systems by which they are motivated! There are many theories of motivation. But what if we look deeper? What are the internal structures that lead to us acting (as opposed, perhaps, to not acting)?... It seems that motivation comes from the heart. As long as a person sets goals and expends a reasonable amount of effort to achieve those goals, that person is motivated."[155] Client whisperers are motivated from the heart and work hard to achieve desired results for their clients. This motivation drove them to spend long hours working side-by-side with their counterparts on the client's site.

One of the attributes that made our client whisperers effective was their understanding and application of what prominent American psychologist and author J. McVicker Hunt called "...the problem of the match—finding circumstances that are sufficiently stimulating but not too demanding." Of course, the only sure way to accomplish this is by knowing precisely what each client knows and doesn't know at each stage of the relationship development and delivery process. With this conceptual model of the problem of match, our client whisperers avoided discussing or presenting information that was at too low a level, knowing it would be boring, or at too high a level which would cause frustration. They sought the middle ground—a motivational state—called "disequilibrium" that created a desire in their audience to learn more.

The motivating client whisperer creates the conditions that influence the client's motivation to do what the whisperer believes they can accomplish together. This humanistic view of motivation focuses on the client as a whole person. A trusting client-client whisperer relationship is essential to the development of the client's motivation to accept new challenges. This high-trust relationship allows the client whisperer to help educate the client about the software implementation process, which lessens any fear of failure that might be impeding the client's natural drive toward self-actualization. It's all about helping people feel good about themselves and building their self-confidence to take on a new experience and believe they will be successful. The more they interact and solve problems together, the more they are freed to enjoy the synergistic harmony of their relationship, which in itself becomes a strong motivating force.

An important aspect of our sales efforts and consulting services was our ability to motivate our prospects and clients to accomplish things that previously they considered too complex, too political, too costly—or all three. It was always gratifying just to know that we helped make these things happen, and even more gratifying when the client expressed their appreciation for our high-value services. This was common as our client whisperers "performed their magic" during a software implementation; on occasion, this even occurred during the buying process.

As we were concluding our final sales presentation for a large research university, one of the key stakeholders stood up and said, "Before today, I was not sure we could actually pull off this implementation. However, after hearing about your human-centric approach, I am fired-up to get started." Not surprisingly, we were awarded the contract. Their twenty-month project was completed on time and within budget. Shortly after the conclusion of that gratifying project, the client above met with one of our big prospects, who had been talking about replacing their very old software. This was a large, complex research university that had experienced several failed attempts to upgrade their software due primarily to the decentralized nature of their institution. After that meeting, our prospect asked to talk with some of our consultants who were involved with the previously mentioned project. After a few more detailed discussions, we were able to persuade the prospect that they could successfully implement new software. They reached this difficult decision based on their recently acquired understanding of how our company had helped similar institutions complete similar projects. Their comfort with our experienced consultants was a motivating factor in taking on such a big challenge. This project was also completed on time and under budget. Our client whisperers were very skilled at making people feel that together we could accomplish great things for their institution. This could not have been accomplished simply by telling people how great we were. And it could not have been accomplished prior to establishing a trusting relationship—job one for a client whisperer.

> "We faced the challenge of an aggressive timeline with limited resources to complete implementation of the Campus Solutions software. CedarCrestone consultants helped us in formulating creative strategies to overcome this challenge so that we were able to achieve an on-time, within-budget implementation. CedarCrestone's adaptation of a Collaborative Model fit our unique situation and helped us to generate user buy-in and accelerate knowledge transfer."
>
> Campus Solutions Project Manager
> Public Master's University

Our Wizards of Whispering

Universal Whisperer

A few of our best client whisperers did their work so naturally that their effectiveness transcended whispering domains. One such person on our team used her Iron Butterfly qualities and alchemy of whispering every day of both her personal and professional life. Essentially, she dedicated her life to helping others no matter what their problems and needs might be. Using her interpersonal skills, empathetic listening, intuition, openness, and genuine concern for others, she easily put her clients at ease. A pleaser and facilitator extraordinaire, she quickly engendered strong relationships, many of which continued long after completion of the project. She exemplifies the importance of listening, inclusion, and respect for the individual. Her contributions to the success of our business were both varied and significant. This whisperer possessed an incredible level of intellectual curiosity—she was interested in nearly everything. Almost without exception, her professional relationships went far beyond our business needs. People just felt comfortable sharing with her things about both their professional and personal lives, knowing that the listener was sincerely interested in them and that any information they shared with her would be treated appropriately. In fact, it was not uncommon for people to share information that was in the category of "more than she needed to know."

Our universal whisperer's broad skill set, intellectual curiosity, and willingness to do whatever was needed made her the logical person to take the lead on most new endeavors that we undertook. Her assignments included change management, organizational realignment, business process reengineering, readiness assessments, strategy development, and just about every other type of management consulting for the higher education community. Albert Einstein said "Imagination is more important than knowledge."[156] This client whisperer had plenty of both, and she was always willing to venture beyond the edge of her professional comfort zone.

Our universal whisperer was a practitioner of Genshai, which is a Hindu word that means never treating yourself or another person in a manner that makes one feel small. This is what enabled her to whisper with class. Her uncanny ability to quickly establish relationships as she listened empathetically to each client reflects her instinctive talent. Her finely tuned sensitivities allowed her to empathize with how the client felt and respond in kind. Thus, the combination of her cognitive knowledge, conative instincts and affective sensitivity helped make her a highly effective universal whisperer. She definitely lived what Carl Rogers called "the good life," with a focus on helping the rest of us move closer to self-actualization.

"Thank you for your always positive and encouraging attitude – and not without some humor too. This is a 'hard to accomplish' project, and you did a great job of keeping all of us on track in a kind and considerate manner. We have all felt encouraged to try what we think might be impossible through your guidance. If things get rough down the road, we'll just remember your soft tone of voice and smile."

Enrollment Services Project Team Member
Public Masters University

Tried and True Whisperer

The foundation for most of our client whisperers was their experience working in and their commitment to higher education. This inculcation into the culture of higher education was the essence of our differentiation strategy. Paul was one of these tried and true whisperers. He was a former senior student service administrator at two large public universities. During his more than thirteen years as a PeopleSoft consultant, he had provided professional services to many colleges and universities in a variety of consulting and project management roles. In addition to his industry expertise, his whispering qualities were a combination of an easy personality, solid interpersonal skills, empathetic listening skills, problem solving skills, and attention to detail. He also was not afraid to show his vulnerability and expressed genuine caring for other human beings.

By his quiet nature, this client whisperer had a tendency to be deferential to his more flamboyant colleagues. We observed that once this client whisperer began speaking, there was a noticeable difference in the selection committee's body language. They leaned forward, listened intently, and asked thoughtful questions of him. One could observe that even at this stage he was beginning the process of developing a trusting relationship, based on his understanding of and concern for the client's needs, issues and concerns. His extraordinary client whispering is reflected in the following quote from one of his clients.

"In our first meetings, the CedarCrestone team impressed us with their knowledge of community colleges. How refreshing to have someone understand our pain points and then offer up new ideas. Better yet, they took those ideas and, along with our team, helped design processes and systems that fit our needs. In a culture adverse to change, the CedarCrestone team helped us work through the roadblocks and kept projects on schedule. As the project lead, I have watched our team reach goals that many thought unattainable. Yes, our team worked hard, but our success could not have been realized without the exceptional talent and expertise of the CedarCrestone team. "

Senior Executive Director
Community College

NURTURING AND KNOWLEDGEABLE WHISPERER

Equally effective with her clients, Jill was a former senior student service administrator for three public universities prior to joining our team. She had provided PeopleSoft consulting services to more than ten colleges and universities in a variety of consulting roles. As an exemplary Iron Butterfly, her approach to client relations was to adopt her clients as if they were family, and most of her clients responded in kind.

Jill showed her commitment to client success in a very personal way. For our highly important CSU project in the early stages of our growth, she actually moved across the country with her family to be closer to the client site. She said that she would prefer to spend her time with the client rather than traveling across the country. Now that's commitment! Her genuine care and concern for her clients resulted in numerous creative solutions that, in turn, resulted in many strong client testimonials. In addition to her devotion to her clients, Jill also was consistently responsive to her colleagues internally. I knew that we could count on her if we needed her assistance with a proposal, a client success story, and/or a sales call. I did wonder when this mom and exceptional client whisperer squeezed sleep into her twenty-four-hour schedule.

"I attribute our success to strong internal project management, a cooperative partnership with CedarCrestone, excellent consultants, and a dedicated project team. Without any one of those, the project could have faltered. CedarCrestone's consultants have become like "family," and they are as committed to our success as we are."

Vice President
Public, Masters University

Pragmatic and Productive Whisperer

Todd could always see the "forest through the trees," but knew what trees grew within the forest and where he could chop and still preserve the environment. He had industry experience in both technical and functional roles. Because of his quick study capabilities, he easily and quickly grasped an understanding of and expertise in the software.

In an orals situation, he could establish immediate rapport with the audience. When faced with unusual challenges, he had an uncanny ability to figure out solutions and with whom to figure them out. As the first project manager in the country to complete a full implementation of the first general release of the PeopleSoft student information system, Todd ultimately became one of the most accomplished PeopleSoft implementation services professionals in the world. His easy, likable personality combined with his many capabilities, made him one of our most highly effective client whisperers. At professional conferences, he was like the Pied Piper: he always had a following of former clients, current clients, and prospects all wanting to talk to him. Not only did they want to pick his brain, but they also just enjoyed being with him. Yes, client whisperers can be lots of fun too.

"Our strategic partnership allowed us to complete our technology transformation far ahead of schedule and for a fraction of the projected cost. This partnership will extend into the future as CedarCrestone manages our new production systems and keeps us current with information technology, allowing us to focus on fulfilling the vision of an outstanding education for students of our university."

Chief Information Officer
Public Research University

ANALYTICAL AND INSIGHTFUL WHISPERER

Despite her somewhat deferential style, Lynne was a very talented client whisperer who was both analytical and insightful. She was driven to find better solutions for her clients and was always willing to share her great knowledge and insights with her colleagues. Each time that we were faced with a "mystery" during the implementation process, we could count on her to use her "lateral thinking" capabilities to provide both insight into the mystery itself and stunning thoughts on alternative ways to solve the mystery for the client. Lynne's ability to approach client issues with a "beginner's mind" helped her establish high-trust relationships that provided value to her clients long after the successful conclusion of an initial implementation project.

One of our clients engaged us in a management consulting project to plan their transformation of student services. The scope of the project entailed evaluating their current business processes that were most in need of improvement. This was a particularly important management consulting engagement because the potential existed for follow-on business to upgrade their PeopleSoft student information system. We brought in Lynne. We discussed with her some of the key background information regarding the client, and explained that at this stage of the project we still lacked the level of trust that we desired, and there was some resistance to change. She was to meet with a group of about seven subject matter experts to map their current business processes and begin the process of redesigning the processes.

Drawing upon her natural client whisperer instincts, Lynne asked if she could try a somewhat different approach than we had planned. Because we had a high level of trust in her, we responded that she should proceed in a way that she felt would be best (although we held our breath a little, given the sensitive stage we were at with this client).

In a small conference room, Lynne started off the session in her gentle, smiling way, introducing herself and asking others to introduce themselves. She moved over to her computer and projected the first slide. It was a picture of a monkey—now, we were nervous! Everyone had a strange expression on their face. Lynne looked kindly at them, and then proceeded to show the rest of the "monkey slide show" that conveyed the subtle, underlying message of change. They started to grin after the second slide, and by the end they were laughing out loud—they got it! They then proceeded with a highly positive interactive session of mapping and redesigning their business processes. Her insightfulness enabled her to determine which strategies would work best with this client. She could deal with highly complex situations and figure out how to make the client successful, all without taking any of the credit. Our clients respected and loved Lynne!

> "The experienced higher education consultants from CedarCrestone quickly understood our stateside business processes. They helped our team to roll out these processes and supporting technology to our overseas divisions in Europe and Asia over a twelve-month period. With CedarCrestone's assistance, we now have a single integrated student system across all academic divisions and geographically dispersed locations. This solution enables us to better serve our students, integrate our business processes, and streamline our operations."
>
> Assistant Vice President of PeopleSoft Initiatives
> Public Research University with International Locations

INTELLIGENT AND IMAGINATIVE WHISPERER

During my forty-year career, I was fortunate to have known a handful of these client whisperers. Their superior intellects allowed them to quickly understand needs and issues more thoroughly than either their clients or co-workers. They could create a vision of a solution that typically exceeded the client's expectations. Even more remarkable was their ability to design and develop a faster, cheaper, better solution while others were still talking about the feasibility of such a solution. That was Shawn!

Shawn was accepted into an information technology program of study by a respected research university when he was about fourteen and earned his MBA in a year while working full-time with a heavy travel schedule. In spite of his relative youth, he used his "creative visualization," "critical thinking," and technical acumen to assume a leadership role at the beginning of our journey. As he developed both his whispering skills and his business acumen, he became one of the most accomplished PeopleSoft technical designers and developers in the world and the master of innovative faster, cheaper, better solutions. In the internal company newsletter, in which consultants can submit "kudos" regarding exemplary work by their colleagues, the following kudo was given to Shawn: "Hooray, Hooray for Shawn, our resident Superman who makes the impossible seem like nothing!" And, as Collins suggests, we assigned Shawn to some of our biggest opportunities.

"We presented the CedarCrestone consultants with many unique challenges; but what we saw as problems and challenges, they saw as opportunities. The talent and wealth of experience of our consultants enabled us to overcome a situation in which we had a ridiculously short implementation period and very limited resources. The ability of each of the CedarCrestone consultants to work effectively and efficiently with all of the modules was most impressive....and much appreciated. There is no doubt in any of our minds that we would not have had on-time and successful go-lives with all modules without the assistance of CedarCrestone."

Associate Vice President for Academic Programs
Public Masters University

The examples described above are just some of the many individuals who contributed to our success through their client whispering skills. Without them, we would never have had the audacity to proclaim as part of our hedgehog concept that we had the potential to become the best in the world at ERP systems implementation in higher education. Of course, not everyone was a world class whisperer on day one. Experienced client whisperers, like the ones described above, filled in the low spots and mentored less developed whisperers up to a higher level of client service. Client whispering is a continuum: they begin with being an "aspiring" client whisperer, they progress to an "effective" client whisperer, and they diligently strive to achieve the ultimate goal of being a "universal" client whisperer as illustrated in **Figure R** below. From my sports frame of reference, I think of the universal whisperer as the gold medalist of client service.

Figure R: The Client Whispering Continuum

Whispering Medalists- Value to the Client

		Universal Client Whisperer
	Effective Client Whisperer	
Aspiring Client Whisperer		Responsibility for Outcomes
		Highly Effective Habits
		High Wisdom IQ
	Principle-centered	Transcendent Purpose
	Relevant Experience	10,000 Hours of Experience
	Observant	Shosin
Shares Credit	Respectful	Synergistic
Disciplined Talk	Disciplined Thought	Disciplined Actions
Active Listening	Attentive Listening	Empathetic Listener
Ego-centric	Relationship-centric	Client-centric
Self-Trust	Team Trust	Extends Trust
Enthusiasm	Intrinsically Motivated	Passionate
Curiosity	Asks Good Questions	Asks Great Questions
Intent	Commitment	Courageous
Intelligent	Creative Visualization	Cultured Critical Thinker
Integrity	Trustworthy & Caring	Genshai

CAN CLIENTS BE WHISPERERS?

Yes, indeed. And our projects went much more smoothly when there were whisperers on the client side. In the world of whispering and client success, there is nothing more exciting than to witness two-sided whispering. Great problem solving dialog occurs between a whisperer who is a client and a whisperer who is a vendor because they generally share similar whispering capabilities and a common set of client success objectives. With our continuous knowledge transfer and mentoring approach, it was possible to further develop the whispering talents and capabilities of our clients' staff. Because whisperers are always eager to learn, we too learned much from those whisperers who were our clients.

PROOF OF PERFORMANCE

> "I place the CedarCrestone consultants in the top one percent of professionals I have worked with over the past thirty years. They have been highly effective in working with people throughout the university – from business managers and payroll preparers to senior officers."
>
> President
> Public Research University

LESSONS LEARNED

- The chemistry of whispering changes the matter of relationships.

- The best client whispering results in positive chemical reactions for all.

- There are multiple types of whisperers. They all have equal, but different, value.

- One of the benefits that you can give to a client is to foster whispering attributes among their staff.

- Don't miss a "golden opportunity" by ignoring the "alchemy of whispering."

PART IV: THE CLIENT WHISPERERS' LEGACY

18. What's A Whispering Leader?

Borrowed Wisdom

> "Anytime you're trying to influence the thinking, beliefs, or development of someone else, you're engaging in leadership."[157]
>
> Ken Blanchard,
> Leadership Expert and Author

Guiding Principle

> Seek out the path-finders. The really good ones use a moral compass.

We were unwavering in our pursuit of a market leadership position while also knowing that the probability of short-term success for an underfunded, unknown PeopleSoft consulting business was extremely low. We never established a deadline for achieving our goal. There were many times during our journey when we commented privately to each other about the many challenges that we had to overcome to reach our goal. There also were a few times when it was difficult to be optimistic as we experienced the difficulty of "confronting the brutal facts." One of those brutal facts was that our stretch vision of becoming the trusted advisor for higher education was a very long way off. We knew early on that we had to have the necessary leadership skills to achieve this stretch vision; but first, we had to confirm that our foundation for leadership was well grounded.

What Was First and Foremost?

Stephen R. Covey says, "Principle-centered leadership is the personal empowerment that creates empowerment in the organization. It's not blaming or accusing; it's acting with integrity to create the environment in which we and others can develop character and competence and synergy[158]…At the heart of empowerment is trustworthiness—which is a function of character and competence. Character is what we are; competence is what we can do. And both are necessary to create trustworthiness."[159]

We studied Collins work on the differences in leadership between good and great companies. He observes that all of the good-to-great companies he studied had what he calls Level 5 leaders, who are a "paradoxical blend of personal humility and professional will."[160] American Renaissance woman, Maya Angelou, says this about the importance of humility. "I don't think modesty is a very good virtue, if it is a virtue at all. A modest person will drop the modesty in a minute. You see, it's a learned affectation. But humility comes from inside out. Humility says there was someone before me, someone found the path, someone made the road for me, and I have the responsibility of making the road for someone who is yet to come."[161] I knew that we had strong professional will and hoped that it was reasonably blended with personal humility. We certainly were humble about our beginnings and continued to be so given the strength of our formidable competitors.

One of Stephen R. Covey's principles is to "Always treat your employees exactly the way you want them to treat your best customers."[162] Covey also provides a clear and concise definition of leadership: "Simply put—at its most elemental and practical level—leadership is communicating to people their worth and potential so clearly that they come to see it in themselves."[163]

During my evolution as a business executive, I had to overcome a fixation on the quantifiable aspects of leadership. I wanted to measure everything to demonstrate that we were achieving the desired results in everything we did: more sales, revenue, and profit. As I became more secure in both my leadership capabilities and my business acumen, I began to focus more on the principles of leadership and organizational success. During our twelve-year journey, I strived for the optimal balance between promotion of short-term quantifiable performance and doing the right things for the long-term good of our clients, our people and our business. These right things manifested themselves as principles of leadership. In the parlance of Abraham Lincoln, "Important principles may, and must, be inflexible."[164] Upon my retirement, I felt gratified when I received an email from one of our corporate executives regarding our principled approach to leadership.

> "…you acted as you always do …with an unwavering commitment to your principles. Indeed, from what I've gleaned from your career this is how you met adversity, never straying from what you believe to be the right actions and behaviors for your clients and your people. For this example you provided, I am indebted to you …for showing me what a principled leader looks like."
>
> Executive
> CedarCrestone, Inc.

CAN ANYONE LEAD?

Blanchard says that when he asks people about the influential leaders in their lives, they seldom mention leaders of organizations. The most influential people in my life were people who took a genuine interest in me and helped me understand my potential and how to grow as an individual while being an effective member of a team. As a teenager, I was reluctant to assume a leadership role in any activity outside of the sports domain. Retrospectively, I now understand that my lack of passion for anything not a team sport was the source of my leadership reluctance. As I began to make the transition from amateur athlete to bread winner, I slowly began to understand that a significant part of my passion for team sports was actually a passion for leadership, especially team leadership.

During our twelve-year success story, responsibility for executive leadership of our business venture evolved from the eight original ISEDU partners to a highly effective team of three: Chris, John, and Elizabeth. They were the right people for our bus because they were thought leaders and great mentors for our less experienced people.

All of our client whisperers were leaders in some way. They manifest their leadership abilities through their work with planning teams, sales teams, proposal development teams, functional project teams, technical project teams, and ad hoc internal committees. They all possessed one or more leadership strengths and manifested leadership with their unique style. Sometimes we called these people role players who are positioned to do what they do best and complement the people around them. At times, we had so much leadership occurring in our group that

Lyon's Pride

Sometimes role players have to step out of their comfort zone to ensure team success. One of my high school teammates was not a particularly good shooter, but he was the consummate role player. As our undersized power forward, he specialized in rebounding and defense. At the beginning of our last post season tournament game, the opposing team decided not to guard him and focus all five of their defenders on the rest of us. We quickly passed the ball to Allan and trusted that he would do the right thing. He did not hesitate to take the open shots in an attempt to relieve the defensive pressure on his four teammates. After he made three consecutive midrange jump shots to give us an early lead, the opposing team abandoned their strategy in favor of a more conventional defense. We won that championship game 68 to 54 and completed our undefeated season.

it was hard to know whether I was leading or following. I could relate to the words of Mahatma Gandhi: "There go my people: I have to go and run and catch up because I am their leader."[165]

WHO'S A PATHFINDER?

Angelou said, "I have great respect for the past. If you don't know where you've come from, you don't know where you are going."[166] I share the following personal stories from my family history to illustrate some of the pathfinders in my life. Undoubtedly, they were influential in some way as I found my leadership path. John Alden and Priscilla Mullins (my eighth great-grandparents) found their way to America on the Mayflower in 1620. Their daughter Betty, my seventh great-grandmother, was the first white woman born in New England.

In 1789, when many of my ancestors were migrating from Rhode Island and Connecticut, the adventurous Seth Lyon (my fifth great-grandfather) and his restless son, Walter Lyon (my fourth great-grandfather), set out with twenty other men from Fairfield County, Connecticut to find a suitable place to relocate to the head waters of the Susquehanna and Delaware rivers in Upstate New York. "The Lyons were the mighty hunters of the party. Whether they had acquired this art in their native state, or not, we cannot say, but it is certain that it came very easy for them."[167] Is it possible that I might have inherited some of the path finder qualities of my Lyon ancestors? Although undereducated by today's standards, my mom and dad were self-disciplined, hard-working, entrepreneurial, frugal, trustworthy, dependable, and prideful. Together they gave me both roots (values) and wings (freedom with responsibility).

Tony Dungy said, "Stubbornness is a virtue if you are right."[168] My dad's nickname was "Stub," and although the origin of this nickname was never discussed, I am certain it was short for "stubborn." During my early years, my father worked two jobs—by day he ran a house painting and carpentry business and at night he was a projectionist for the local movie theatre. He was a sixth generation carpenter and could build almost anything without a written plan. He was a great thinker and always seemed to have a well thought out plan in his head. As his helper from time-to-time, I learned how difficult it can be to make useful contributions when you have no vision of the solution and little insight into the master builder's strategies and tactics. As the family trait of stubbornness was passed down to my generation, my brother Tom and I preferred to characterize this trait in the parlance of Collins, as "strong willed."

"There is nothing stronger than gentleness,"[169] said Abraham Lincoln. My mother was a very gentle person but when discussing matters of principle, she was very emphatic and articulate. You always knew her position on such matters. When she graduated from high school in 1935, her father sent her to Mildred Elley Secretarial School in Albany. However, she eventually found her passion as a business woman. For many years, she did all of the bookkeeping for our family business that was comprised of a variety of personal services, including house painting in the summer months, wallpapering in the winter, and operation of a full service retail paint and wallpaper store. After I entered elementary school, she accepted the position of business officer for our local college.

My parents were two very different people who shared a common set of values. From a simplistic perspective, I probably have my dad's mind and my mom's heart, which creates some internal conflict. Any wisdom that I now possess is most likely associated with a learned ability to know when to think through a problem with my mind, which was one of my dad's strengths, and when to use my intuition and trust my gut like my mom always did so well.

As a parent, I saw some of these same family traits in my children. My daughter, Vanessa, was born in late October, which meant that she was about ten months older than most of her classmates. When she was in seventh grade at her school in the Atlanta area, Vanessa made the junior high school basketball team that was dominated by older and more physically mature eighth graders. Vanessa's primary skill was her defensive abilities, which she and I had worked on together during her previous youth basketball seasons, albeit not yet ten thousand hours of preparation.

After a successful regular season, her junior high team had the opportunity to play in the county championship game that was played before a large crowd in the spacious Civic Center gymnasium. Prior to that game, as she was leaving the house, I wished her, "Good luck," to which she replied, "I won't get to play much." Sure enough, she did not play at all during the first quarter as her team fell behind their highly favored opponent. The opposing team was led by a physically mature athlete who scored double figures in that initial quarter of this championship game. No one on Vanessa's team could stop this star player. Then, opportunity came knocking for Vanessa. Her wise coach inserted her into the game with the sole objective of stopping the opponent's star player.

The strongest aspect of Vanessa's defensive skill set was denial defense, which is based on the concept that if the other player doesn't have the ball, she can't score. For the next three quarters of the game, Vanessa played extraordinary denial defense and held her opponent to zero points until very late in the fourth quarter when Vanessa's team had the game in hand. At the end of the game, Vanessa was totally exhausted—but she was a champion! The star player on the other team was visibly frustrated by Vanessa's defensive effort; however, she did go on to earn a full basketball scholarship to the University of Georgia. Vanessa had the gratification that she had actually met the challenge of stopping a formidable player…at least for three-fourths of a game. As a mother of four, active community volunteer, and competitive tennis player, Vanessa's Iron Butterfly qualities continue to serve her well.

Like Vanessa, my son Glenn is also strong willed, but his birthday is in May, which meant that he was about five months younger than his classmates. When he was nine-years-old, he was not chosen to play on the select youth soccer team, so we formed our own team of boys whom the other coaches considered to be "second tier" players. I agreed to be their coach. We managed to win a few games prior to playing the undefeated select team that previously had not invited Glenn to play on their team. For most of the first half of our game against them, they dominated, but failed to score. Late in the first half, our most talented player scored a breakaway goal, and we took an unexpected 1-0 lead. At that point, we turned our entire focus to defense, and I moved Glenn into the role of goalie. For the rest of the game, the select team was in an unrelenting attack mode. The ball was in our end of the field virtually the entire rest of the game, and they fired shots at our goal from every possible angle. Somehow, Glenn found the strength to stop or deflect every one of those shots. We won the game! After the game, the coach of the "formerly" undefeated team (who did not know that Glenn was my son), did not shake my hand. However, he did holler across the field, "Your goalie played one hell of game, coach." Many years later, Glenn used his strong professional will when he founded the Atlanta law firm of MacGregor Lyon, LLC.

As we completed our twelve-year journey, I was able to make a favorable report to my Personal Board of Directors. Using the strong will passed down to me from my parents, I was able to stay true to their values and principles while attempting to balance my passion for our business with my affection for my family and friends. Of course there was always room for improvement in both domains, but in the words of Huntsman, "Everything we need for today's marketplace we learned as kids."[170] I am certain that the will to win that I learned playing basketball had much to do with whatever success I had in the business world.

How Do You Know Your Strengths?

I just described a family leadership trait that I seem to have directly or indirectly inherited: strong will. For a more analytical view of my leadership style, I include the results of my 'Kolbe Conative Index" (copyright © 1987 by Kathy Kolbe) in **Figure S** below. It reveals that I am a natural "Quick Start," a characteristic that was needed to create what became an unlikely, successful business story. On the www.kolbe.com website, I completed the self-test. Based on what you have read thus far, you probably aren't surprised with the result that the largest percentage of my mental energy was in the Action Mode of "Quick Start." My primary strengths were: explaining, adapting, improvising, and imagining. Given the path we had taken, these strengths definitely were needed. In terms of unproductive, stressful tactics that I should avoid, I was not surprised by the recommendations that I should avoid conformity, sticking with the script, and working toward known outcomes. Believe me, I did avoid them — to the extent possible, that is.

Figure S: Kolbe Strengths for Jim Lyon

My Kolbe A™ Index Report (copyright © 2011 Kathy Kolbe and Kolbe Corp. All rights reserved. Used herein with permission) also included the following observations and suggestions:

- "You prevent getting boxed in by staying open to alternatives.

- Your ability to adapt your plans helps you take advantage of opportunities.

- You are likely to criticize another person's idea, book, movie or play if you find it moves too slowly or doesn't get right to the point, is predictable, or is just plain boring or the information isn't new.

- You are likely to procrastinate if you have to follow a highly structured format or system.

- When you need to be persuasive in an unfamiliar situation, wing it. Trust your guts to pull out the right examples and call it as you see it. You'll be right on target."[171]

Rath and Conchie state that, "The path to great leadership starts with a deep understanding of the strengths you bring to the table,"[172] Taking this to heart, I sought out information about my leadership strengths by taking their leadership self-test which is available on their website, strengths.gallup.com.

My report provided many suggestions regarding how to prevent my strengths from becoming my weaknesses, which happens to all of us from time to time. I received many suggestions, including the following:

- "You are instinctively aware that Individuals will be most productive when their environments are suited to their talents. Wherever appropriate, implement organizational policies that allow your associates to work in their own style.

- Stand behind your tendency to treat each person individually according to need, strength, and style. Be prepared to defend your individualization from a performance-excellence standpoint.

- Share responsibility by encouraging others to do the same. Be their champion, and proactively guide them through the opportunity to experience the challenges of ownership. In doing so, you will contribute to their growth and development.

- Help people see the big view. Point out their achievements and patterns of success. Show them in as many ways as you can that their life has made a difference.

- Running a tight ship may not be so important to you, but running a steady ship is. Many people need that kind of leadership to feel secure, and you provide it.

- Your passion equips you to fight. In these battles, strive to be seen as a leader who is fighting for something rather than fighting against something."

It was interesting to read these results in light of how they complemented the strengths of the other executive team members and were aligned with the culture in which our client whisperers thrived. In particular, it appears that these findings were consistent with Rath and Conchie's observations that the most effective leaders are always investing in strengths—and we had many leadership strengths among our client whisperers in which to invest. I was fortunate to have experienced Rath and Conchie's finding that the most effective leaders surround themselves with the right people and then maximize their team. We surely had the right people, and together we maximized our teams and our results. I can validate that Rath and Conchie's finding was applicable to us: "While the best leaders are not well-rounded, the best teams are."[173]

PROOF OF PERFORMANCE

Upon my retirement from CedarCrestone, I received many wonderful personal notes from my co-workers that made me feel I had exhibited some of the important fundamentals of leadership in our championship game.

"I have learned so much about this business from you. I truly respect the leader and the person you are. I will always appreciate your greeting me with a hug and a smile and asking about my family. I know that CedarCrestone is a better place and it's the company I love because of you."

Senior Manager
CedarCrestone, Inc.

LESSONS LEARNED

- You may not recognize a great leader; they come in many forms.

- Principles perpetuate; make sure you commit to good ones.

- With a little talent, some luck, and a strong will you can overcome many adversities.

- Having personal humility does not mean that you "eat humble pie," although sometimes you do have to eat a bite or two.

- Have the courage to ask your employees what they need. You shouldn't be surprised by their response.

19. Can Whisperers Beget Whisperers?

Borrowed Wisdom

> "We are the average of the five people we spend the most time with."[174]
>
> Jim Rohn,
> Entrepreneur and Renown Speaker

Guiding Principle

> Be as good as your dog thinks you are.

What would you most like to leave as your legacy -- when that time comes, of course? Who were your role models and mentors...or have you found any yet? Do you think that others regard you as a role model? I pondered these questions as I considered the impact that role models had on my life, both personally and professionally. I wondered what it was about them that helped me through life's challenges. I then considered what legacy our Client Whisperers would derive from our journey and would perpetuate to those whom they mentored.

Given these reflective questions, I invite you to envision joining me in our lodge-like mountain home, comfortably seated in rocking chairs on the deck taking in the beauty of the surrounding Ponderosa Pine trees, refreshed by a natural spring and small lake while munching on some freshly baked, chocolate chip cookies. I first share words of wisdom that gave me special insights and then describe those impressionable experiences that have been part of my development – all of which might inspire you, regardless of your circumstances, to inculcate and perpetuate those qualities that you most admired about our Client Whisperers. Let's rock...

TRIAL AND ERROR

Between the ages of twelve and twenty-two, I had sixteen different jobs, including full-time summer jobs and part-time jobs during high school and college. Some of these were great learning experiences, but none of them provided much insight into what I wanted to do for the rest of my life. However, they did provide much insight into what I did not want to do for the long haul.

The worst jobs were operating a jackhammer inside the kiln (110 degrees) at the local cement factory and cleaning out chicken coops on weekends during college. Another unpleasant job was when I worked during the summer as a grocery store clerk for The Great Atlantic & Pacific Tea Company (A&P) in the mid-1960s. I participated in monthly store inspections conducted by a senior manager from the regional office. He was a "seagull manager," a term originated by Blanchard to describe managers who, "fly in, make a lot of noise, dump on everyone, then fly out."[175] He would make hasty decisions regarding things about which he had little understanding. He would leave others to deal with the mess he left behind. Experiencing his impact on the morale of the grocery store workers and having to help them deal with the residue of his visits convinced me that "seagull managers" were not worthy of emulation. Perhaps this "seagull culture" was one of the reasons that A&P lost its position as the country's top food retailer and began operating at a loss in the early 1970s.

I was fortunate, though, that during those early employment years most of my supervisors were "salt of the earth" people whose occupations included farmer, house painter, farm manager, youth sports manager, newspaper delivery person, county fair manager, cement plant manager, grocery store manager, paint store manager, food service manager, football program salesman, athletic trainer, and statistician.

VALUES OF THE GAME

Although making money was essential during my teenage years, my priority was basketball, which I played whenever I had time. I was born in June, which meant that I was about six months younger than most of my teammates and opponents. However, my brother Tom was four years older, and a well-respected scholar-athlete. He took me everywhere— well almost everywhere. Although I was just a short, skinny kid, I was allowed to play with the older boys when others my age could not. I recall the way Tom convinced his contemporaries to let me play running back during our pick-up football games in the town park and play point guard (although it was not called point guard in those days) during ad hoc basketball games behind our elementary school. I quickly learned how to overcome my inferior physical maturity that came with a June birthday, and I got my ten thousand hours of practice in at an early age.

After college, I spent four years as an athletic director, basketball coach and mathematics teacher. Although I didn't reach ten thousand hours of coaching, my lessons learned included those characterized by Coach Wooden, "young people need models, not critics"[176] and "a coach is someone who can give correction without causing resentment."[177] (My Personal Best, copyright 2004. By permission of Mc-Graw Hill.)

According to psychologist Norman Le, who studies relationships, "a good sense of humor can help you professionally."[178] My coaching experience helped me learn how to use humor to change negative energy into positive energy and relieve the tension sometimes caused by "tough love." I also used humor in situations when I would stray from my preferred approach of being tough on critical issues (i.e., fundamentals) but easy on people. My time as a coach and teacher was the beginning of my understanding of the role of trust for any successful team or business. I also gained a renewed appreciation for the importance of focusing on the fundamentals of the game. Essential to the success of our business was the constant reinforcement of the following fundamentals: seek first to understand, relationships and results, good-to-great concepts, and team trust.

Additionally, I discovered that each player is different, and that what worked for me as a player did not necessarily work for them. According to Wooden, "Before casually discounting the potential of any individual or team, give them a chance to succeed—give them your sincere belief and full support."[179] In my experience with both basketball and software implementation, it was essential to highlight the strengths of each individual player or employee while avoiding situations that would expose their weaknesses.

Basketball star, Bill Russell, said, "Successful teams of any kind are benevolent dictatorships. If you lead wisely, you'll be followed cheerfully."[180] (Russell Rules by Bill Russell and David Falkner, copyright

2001 by William F. Russell. Used by permission of Dutton, a division of Penguin Group USA Inc.) Others have said that a coach is "someone who carries a valued person from where they are to where they want to be."[181] I guess it is not surprising that the person responsible for the success of a basketball team is called a coach and the person responsible for the success of a baseball team is called a manager. The pundits say that great basketball players have good instincts, make good decisions, trust their teammates, and make their teammates better. Great baseball players are determined by their batting, fielding, and earned run averages.

Leading wisely for me turned out to be a matter of principles, but my leadership approach has always been more like that of a coach than that of a big company executive. My aspiration to be an effective coach was recently reinforced by the following kind note I received from a long-time business colleague: "Thanks for over twenty years of personal leadership, mentoring, and friendship. Your coaching style has proven to be just as successful in business as in basketball."

GAME TIME!

FIRST QUARTER

Transitioning my passion from basketball to business was not easy, although I quickly concluded that many of the lessons learned in my basketball career were transferable to the business world, especially work ethic, team building, and leadership. As I gained experience, I also learned that the "roots" provided by my parents were a strong foundation for the development of a principled approach to leadership. My initial leadership opportunities and my introduction to software implementation occurred during my seven years as an administrator at Cornell University.

My colleagues and supervisors at Cornell were quality people from whom I learned much about almost everything. As I progressed from managerial to leadership positions in Admissions and Financial Aid, I began to understand that my real strength was leadership, not management. So, I decided to apply for the position of university bursar. In preparation for my job interviews, I talked with many of the people who worked in that office and quickly determined that they had a leadership problem. During my interviews, I learned that the senior vice president, to whom the bursar reported, shared this concern. I was well prepared to share my vision of a solution to this problem. Of course, my solution included giving me the responsibility for achieving the desired results for the senior vice president. Even though there were two other well qualified candidates, I was selected for the job.

One of the critical needs of the bursar's office was the selection and implementation of a new student accounts and credit card processing software system. During the first few months in my new position, I created and executed a software selection process and quickly identified two qualified vendors, each with very different approaches to the development and delivery of their product. During this process, I developed a close working relationship with a very bright systems analyst in our Office of Computing Services. In a collaborative effort, we selected our vendor of choice based on a positive reference from Harvard and a strong preference for the energy and professionalism of the people from the software vendor, IA. When I presented the business case for acquiring the IA software to my senior vice president, and pressed him for a decision, his risk aversion began to surface. He finally told me that he would approve the project, but also told me that if the implementation failed, it would cost me my job, I quickly responded "No problem." It was a risk I was willing to take.

Once our software selection was approved, we had to figure out how to get the new software implemented to service the needs of the bursar's office, the financial aid office, the Cornell credit card office, the university cashiers, the dining office, the housing office and a variety of other student service and financial management offices. Cornell was a highly decentralized university with sixteen thousand students and thousands of employees all in one location—clearly in violation of the Rule of 150. Based on their Harvard experience, the IA team recommended a nine-month implementation timeline. Lacking any relevant experience, I deferred to the recommendation of the IA team. To accomplish the implementation within nine months, we created a small leadership team consisting of four people—two from IA, my systems analyst, and me. My primary role as team leader was to interview all of the key stakeholders to gain an understanding of their needs and concerns and reach agreement on how the new system could improve the business processes for which each stakeholder was responsible. In this process, I gained very useful insight into not only the needs of my internal clients, but also the root cause of the leadership problem in the bursar's office. I felt very good about this informal need-development process, but now we had to deliver the solutions that I had discussed with the stakeholders.

As I reviewed my findings with our very talented project leadership team, we reached agreement on the customizations that would be required and on the division of labor among the team members. My teammates astutely understood stakeholder needs. They seemed to easily understand the design of the required functionality. The result: we were able to put the new software in live production within four months—five months ahead of schedule. Although it was a very hectic four months, I enjoyed it immensely. In hind sight, it was clear that the two primary success factors for this project were a small team of the right people and early stakeholder buy-in. These success factors became the underlying principles for our process-centric software implementation implementation approach years later.

Shortly after completing this highly successful project, the IA executives asked me to present an anatomy of our project at a large higher education conference, College and University Machine Records Conference (CUMREC). At first, I was a bit reluctant because I was not confident that the topic would be of great interest to the conference attendees. I was wrong! I had a standing room only crowd for my presentation. Many people stood in line after the presentation to ask questions, some of which were in the category of "How did you do it so fast?" I began to understand and appreciate the value of faster and cheaper.

SECOND QUARTER

Not long after my CUMREC presentation, IA recruited me to join their team on an exciting and professionally expanding career path as the company went on to become the leading provider of administrative software solutions for higher education. At the time I joined IA, it was a company of young and very talented technical people. As their ninety-sixth employee and being almost completely devoid of technical skills, it was not clear to me what role I would play in such a company. However, I trusted my gut and accepted their offer, primarily because of the great people who were already on the IA bus. This professional decision clearly meant that I was choosing to take the road less traveled;

for in 1977, it was rare for a university administrator to leave the secure nest of academe and join a small, for-profit technology company.

Five months into my IA tenure, the vice president to whom I reported unexpectedly resigned, and I was asked to take his place. Very ill prepared for such a responsibility, I told the chairman that if he were foolish enough to offer me that job, I would be foolish not to accept.

Shortly after this unexpected promotion, I participated in an important dinner meeting with some of the University of Colorado executives. Dave, my San Diego branch manager was also in that meeting. He was much more experienced than I was, and I am certain he was not pleased when he learned that he would be reporting to the new guy in the company. My higher education credentials helped get me through introductions and the first few minutes of the dinner meeting, but then the senior member of the Colorado team asked me how our implementation methodology would address some of their multi-institution challenges. I didn't have a clue how to respond because I lacked the requisite experience. So, I deferred to Dave, who must have received some satisfaction from my ineptitude. However, he graciously bailed me out without a hint of any internal conflict. That was just how things were done at team IA.

During my thirteen years with IA, I learned much about the value of getting the right people on the bus and of having a clear sense of purpose. Additionally, the chairman and the president of this special company were two unique role models for an aspiring entrepreneur.

John was the chairman of IA. He understood the wisdom of getting the right people on the IA bus. He also understood that more right people would come to work for IA because of the people who were already on our bus. John was relentless in his pursuit of great people and great client partnerships. Much of IA's success can be credited to John's commitment to what Collins called "First who .. then what."

As the president of IA, Dave was all about designing and building the best software in the industry. He was a hedgehog extraordinaire! His focus on execution of the fundamentals of our business, development of quality products, and doing the right things was instrumental to our emergence as a software innovator and market leader.

Like most of Collins's good-to-great success stories, the IA success story required a focused twenty-year ride on a high-energy bus driven by leaders who had "a paradoxical blend of personal humility and professional will." Kolbe says, "People who are called strong-willed often have a mode of strong insistence."[182] She goes on to say, "Insistence means that given free rein, this is how you will proceed, as naturally and intensely as a cat chasing a mouse. This is where you need to be most of the time. This is where you will soar."[183] And the IA'ers, at least for a time, soared like eagles.

IA was a big success due primarily to the abundance of talent, energy, integrity, client focus, and team trust. We grew steadily by opening small regional offices to get closer to our market and avoid the trust taxes associated with redundancy and bureaucracy. Then, in my tenth year at IA, we experienced growth pains, which surfaced about the same time that the headcount in our corporate office reached 150. That was when our company culture began to change and our business went flat.

During my relatively rapid ascent up the corporate ladder at IA, I made many mistakes. However, in the words of Will Rogers, "Good judgment comes from experience and a lot of that comes from bad judgment."[184] The success story described in this book reflects some of the lessons that I learned during my time with IA. One of those lessons was that it is not enough to be a good employee and provide valuable services to clients. My mentors at IA helped me to understand that to get from good to great you must actually care about the success and well being of your fellow employees, colleagues and clients. Making this adjustment required me to think differently about my professional family.

HALF TIME

Pursuant to the sale of IA to a multi-billion dollar company, I experienced what I hoped would be only a brief intermission, or half time. The manager of our division within that large company was an example of what Collins calls a "tyrant." Shortly after the acquisition, I heard through the grapevine that I was going to be demoted due to my living in Dallas, which lacked proximity to our home office in Rochester, New York. Recognizing the rationale for that point of view, I accepted the inevitable demotion. Upon my next visit to the home office, the manager called me into his office, presumably to discuss my change in assignment. In anticipation of my reaction to the demotion, he began the meeting by saying that he knew that I did not buy into the new organization, and that I was going be a disruptive factor. Without giving me a chance to say anything, he told me to "Get on board and don't be a trouble-maker!" At that point, I was very upset—although I still had not said a word, which was probably very fortunate. I quickly ended the meeting by saying that I would not be a problem for him in the future. This was an obvious example of why Covey advocated that people "seek first to understand, then to be understood." A few years later, we bought back our company sans the tyrannical executive.

With my same skill set and experience, I worked outside of higher education for two years as the CEO of a small hospitality software firm located near both my home and children's high school. Although that job allowed me to spend more time with my family, and I was able to attend all of my children's ball games, my work was not much fun. I never felt the same passion for that market that I felt for higher education. Same skill set, same experience, same executive role; but much less fun and passion.

THIRD QUARTER

About ten years ago, I participated in a December team building adventure in the cold, remote mountains of Northern England. Our company's new British investor hired two highly skilled professional facilitators to conduct a week long gathering that was a combination of team building, mountain climbing, psycho analysis, sleep deprivation, stressful interrogation, group therapy, and personal epiphany. The apropos theme of this exercise was "It's

Lyon's Pride

By the time I was a sophomore in high school, I had made great progress with mastery of the fundamentals of the game of basketball. As a result, I was selected to play on the varsity team. However, I was not ready to be a starter primarily because I had not yet mastered the art of winning. Sometime during my junior year when I became a starter, I found a nice blend of the science and art of basketball, which significantly enhanced my performance and our team outcomes. During my senior year I learned much about the art of leadership after being chosen as team captain by my teammates. I was also elected captain of my soccer team, but due primarily to my lack of mastery of the fundamentals and low level of passion for that game, neither I nor my team achieved the same level of success as we did in basketball.

a nightmare, and it's going to get worse." Most of the group sessions were candidly captured on video. It became very obvious that what we were saying and how we were thinking/acting were very different. None of us was "walking our talk," and our actions—as clearly displayed in the candid videos—were definitely speaking louder than our words. In fact, the video revealed that when the CEO was speaking, I was not listening. Clearly, I was not giving him my full attention. During this grueling week, the two big discoveries for me were: although I was verbalizing my support for our new CEO, to whom I reported, I was actually ignoring almost everything he said during our team exercises; and I realized that being a member of a caring organization was an important factor in my personal performance. These insights helped me understand the differences among disciplined talk, disciplined thought, and disciplined actions. I also gained a much greater understanding of the importance of blending both science and art into the game to sustain a team intent on winning.

FOURTH QUARTER

Most games are won in the Fourth Quarter. Gladwell says, "The Tipping Point is that magic moment when an idea, trend, or social behavior crosses a threshold, tips, and spreads like wildfire."[185] He also explains his "Power of Context" theory. "Human beings are a lot more sensitive to their environment than they may seem[186]...Psychologists tell us that when people are asked to consider evidence or make decisions in a group, they come to very different conclusions than when they are asked the same questions by themselves. Once we're part of a group, we're all susceptible to peer pressure and social norms and any number of other kinds of influence that can play a critical role in sweeping us up in the beginnings of an epidemic."[187] These social dynamics are especially true in higher education where people are always curious about what their peer institutions are doing. This peer interest helps explain why our "promote the success of our clients" strategy was a primary contributor to our flywheel effect. Some of our most successful sales accelerators were getting our prospects and clients together at conferences so that the "Technology Follower" institutions could ask questions about the "Early Adopter" success stories.

In the context of his book, *Tipping Point*, Gladwell's version of Collins's breakthrough concept is an "epidemic curve," which he characterizes as "starting slowly, tipping just as the Early Adopters start using the seed [services], then rising sharply as the majority catches on."[188] He uses the term epidemic because, "Ideas and products [and services] and messages and behaviors spread like viruses do."[189] He then makes a case for his "Law of the Few," stating that special types of people are responsible for his "epidemics." Gladwell calls these people "Connectors, Mavens, and Salesmen."[190] We called these special people "client references"—people who enthusiastically shared their success stories with others and provided us with many supportive, cheering fans.

The Winners

Gladwell explains his thoughts about personal success. "People don't rise from nothing. We do owe something to parentage and patronage. The people who stand before kings may look like they did it all themselves. But in fact they are invariably the beneficiaries of hidden advantages and extraordinary opportunities and cultural legacies that allow them to learn and work hard and make sense of the world in ways others cannot. It makes a difference where and when we grew up. The culture we belong to and the legacies passed down by our forebears shape the patterns of our achievement in ways we cannot begin to imagine. It's not enough to ask what successful people are like, in other words. It is only by asking where they are from that we can unravel the logic behind who succeeds and who doesn't."[191]

A personal example of success is my life-time friend, Tom. As a teenager, he made his pocket money as the shoe shine boy on Main Street. After earning two college degrees, working in the corporate world, and teaching in a small college, he decided to start his own asset management business in our home town in Upstate New York. At the time, I thought his chances of success were extremely low; not because of any lack of talent on his part, but because whoever starts an investment management company in a small town in rural America? Most of his competitors were located in large cities. Tom is a strong willed person and probably the most patient and trustworthy person I know. Most of his initial clients were people like me who already trusted him explicitly. As expected, his "Buffet-like" approach to evaluating potential investments produced impressive results for his early clients. As word spread about this refreshing small town alternative to the large financial services companies, Tom appeared on TV talk shows and his client success stories started to mount. Today, Fenimore Asset Management, still located in our small home town, is a wonderful success story and a great example of how client success can be accelerated by hard work and trusting relationships.

During my college days at Cornell University, I had the privilege of knowing a true war hero, although I never knew much about his background until he was awarded the Distinguished Flying Cross medal in 2003. Tom McGory was the head trainer at Cornell University and was with our team for every practice and game, both home and away. During my senior year, I worked for Tom as a part-time student trainer. The official Air Force account of his World War II heroics reads as follows:

"Staff Sergeant Thomas J. McGory distinguished himself by heroism while participating in aerial flight as Flight Maintenance Gunner, 847th Bomb Squadron, 489th Bomb Group, Hamburg, Germany on August 6, 1944. On that date, his airplane having lost an engine to enemy fire, the left wing on fire and the abandon ship command given; Sergeant McGory, recognizing that the pilot was trapped in his armored bucket seat, returned to help the pilot free himself at great risk to his own life. Sergeant McGory's action was an example of the highest devotion to personal loyalty and duty to his crew and nation which he served. The outstanding heroism and selfless devotion to duty displayed by Sergeant McGory reflect great credit upon himself and the United States Army Air Corps."[192]

Tom was a prisoner of war for nine months during which time he lost almost seventy pounds. When I last met with him in 2003, he described the beatings he endured and his resolve to provide only his name, rank and serial number. His rescue came after an eighty-three-hour march during which only two thousand of the ten thousand prisoners survived. Tom found creative ways to avoid death, including melting the contents of discarded Red Cross cans of shoe polish and then dipped his boots in it. The polish created a thick coating on his boots that kept his feet from freezing and blistering. Without his strong will, self-trust, and ingenuity, he surely would not have survived this unfathomable ordeal.

As a role model and friend during my college years, Tom McGory was one to emulate. He was always there for us to share his wisdom and console us after difficult losses. I was constantly impressed by his insight into the things that matter most in life, and his sensitivity to the needs of young men who were preparing to go off into the real world.

FINAL SCORE

Always feeling accountable to my Personal Board of Directors, I now wonder how each of those Board members will, or would have, reacted to our success story. I feel certain most of them would be pleased with our attempts at principled leadership and client focus. However, given the opportunity for more input, I am sure some would have preferred a little less "quick start" and a little more thoughtful deliberation prior to some of my decision-making, especially those decisions that impacted the lives of the people on my various teams. And there is little doubt that I should have asked more good questions. On the other hand, I am also certain I would get unanimous approval for my choices of the people with whom I spent the most time.

Based on how I played the game of life, there is much truth in the adage "We are the average of the five people we spent the most time with." This seems to be true whether it's a basketball team, a project team, a family, or a social group. Important factors to consider when deciding with whom to spend time include associating with people who have qualities you admire, have complementary skills sets, who trust and have confidence in you, who challenge you, and who are enjoyable to be with. My five most influential people groups changed dramatically during each of the four quarters of the first sixty-seven years of my life. Thus, no less than twenty people were instrumental in shaping who I am today and what I have accomplished, or not accomplished. As with any average calculation, the extremes tend to define the mean. Examples of this phenomenon include Bill Bradley taking his underdog Princeton basketball team to the Final Four in 1965 and Steve Jobs' charismatic leadership at Apple.

In the 1980's during my days at IA, our quest was to dominate the higher education software market. We never quite accomplished that goal prior to my departure in 1989. However, since then former IA people have held high level positions in almost every higher education software and software services company in the country. More than twenty of these companies, including PeopleSoft, were founded or co-founded by former IAers. In the end, we did indeed accomplish our goal of dominating the software and services market–not as one company, but as a community of like-minded people who shared an extraordinary professional experience during a pivotal point-in-time for information technology within higher education.

Three of our founding ISEDU partners and many of our CedarCrestone employees had been employees of IA. Why were IA and CedarCrestone people in the category of what Gladwell calls Outliers? Princeton professor Marvin Bressler says, "You want to know what separates those who make the biggest impact from all the others who are just as smart? They're hedgehogs."[193] Collins says of hedgehogs they "simplify a complex world into a single organizing idea, a basic principle or concept that unifies and guides everything."[194] The unifying concept at the heart of our story was client whispering. To that end, we were all hedgehogs. And according to Collins, "the hedgehog always wins."[195]

ABOUT THE AUTHORS

Jim Lyon enjoyed forty years of providing administrative software and software services to the higher education market. He earned a B.S. degree from Cornell University in economics. Prior to joining IBM as a systems engineer, he spent four years as a high school basketball coach and mathematics teacher. During his business career, he held senior leadership positions with Cornell University, Information Associates, Westinghouse Learning Corporation, Management Science America, Dun & Bradstreet Software, Fisher Business Systems, USA Group, The Hunter Group, Cedar Group, and CedarCrestone. He also was co-founder and CEO of ISEDU, a start-up company that became a market share leader in the PeopleSoft ERP services business. Eventually known as CedarCrestone, a Platinum Level Oracle partner, his business achieved twelve consecutive years of double-digit revenue growth. He also was a member of the CedarCrestone Board of Directors. Jim can be reached at jim.lyon@lyonoffice.com.

After earning her B.S. and M.Ed. degrees from the University of Utah, Judith Lyon became a faculty member and senior planning analyst at the Pennsylvania State University where she earned her Ph.D. She served as Director of Computer Services, Assistant Dean for Budget Planning, Executive Assistant to the President, and Vice President for Planning and Development in the community college sector. Dr. Lyon was President of the Board of EDUCAUSE, [CAUSE] the non-profit Professional Association for the Intelligent Use of Information Technology in Higher Education. She held leadership positions such as Vice President for Professional Services for Information Associates, co-founder and Senior Partner for Marketing at The Robinson Group, and Managing Associate for Coopers & Lybrand. Dr. Lyon was a co-founder and Managing Principle for InfoSolutions.edu, a professional services company, which subsequently became CedarCrestone. Dr. Lyon can be reached at judie.lyon@lyonoffice.com.

NOTES AND REFERENCES

CHAPTER 1. INTRODUCTION

1   **The masters in the art** James Michener, http://thinkexist.com/quotation/the_master_in_the_art_Of_living_,makes_little/ 295791.html (July 2011)

CHAPTER 2. WHY WAS IT A WILD RIDE?

2   **Sweet are the uses of:** http://brainyquote.com/quotes/quotes/w/williamsha155070.html (May 2011)

3   **Too many people think:** "Startups take extra effort; making millions is tough," The Arizona Republic, March 13, 2011, Section CL, P. 1

4   **No one can make:** Eleanor Roosevelt, http://www.brainyquote.com /quotes/authors/e / eleanor_roosevelt_2.html (November 2010)

5   **Opportunities multiply as:** Sun Tzu, http://thinkexist.com/quotation/opportunities_ multiply_ as_they_are_seized/149705.html

CHAPTER 3. WHERE IN THE WORLD ARE WHISPERERS?

6   **Get the right people:** Jim Collins, *Good to Great* (Collins Business, 2001), P. 44

7   **the right people:** Jim Collins, *Good to Great* (Collins Business, 2001), P. 44

8   **first who...then:** Jim Collins, *Good to Great* (Collins Business, 2001), P. 41

9   **Knowledge workers and service workers:** *Peter Drucker: On the Profession of Management* (Harvard Business School Publishing, 2003), P. 164

10   **There are basically:** Jon Huntsman, *Winners Never Cheat* (Wharton School Publishing, 2009) Kindle location 544

11   **the right people don't:** Jim Collins, *Good to Great* (Collins Business, 2001), P. 42

12   **Once you have the right:** Tom Rath and Barry Conchie, *Strengths-Based Leadership* (Gallup Press, 2008), P. 71

13   **Wolf and Bruhn had:** Malcolm Gladwell, *Outliers: The Story of Success* (Little, Brown & Company, 2008), P. 10

CHAPTER 4. WHAT'S THE WHAT?

14   **The main thing is:** Stephen R. Covey, *First Things First* (Free Press, 2003), P. 75

15   **They took a complex:** Jim Collins, *Good to Great* (Collins Business, 2001), P. 91

16   **The essential strategic:** Jim Collins, *Good to Great* (Collins Business, 2001), P. 95

17   **among other practices:** The Seed of Apple's Innovation, *Business Week*, October 12, 2004

18   **The only way to do great:** Steve Jobs, http://en.wikiquote.org/wiki/Steve_Jobs (September 2010)

19   **The good-to-great companies:** Jim Collins, *Good to Great* (Collins Business, 2001), P. 100

20   **set their goals and:** Jim Collins, *Good to Great* (Collins Business, 2001), P. 111

21   **We did notice one:** Jim Collins, *Good to Great* (Collins Business, 2001), P. 104

22   **What enables the:** Sun Tzu, *That Art of War* (Dell Publishing, 1988), P. 77

CHAPTER 5. WHO'S IN THE WHISPERING FIEFDOM?

23   **If you know your:** Sun Tzu, *That Art of War* (Dell Publishing, 1988), P. 18

24   **In business, I look:** http://37signals.com/svn/posts/333-warren-buffet-on-castles-and-moats (September 2011)

25   **a scientific term to describe:** Malcolm Gladwell, http://www.gladwell.com/outliers/index.html (August 2010)

26   **If January 1975 was the:** Malcolm Gladwell, *Outliers: The Story of Success* (Little, Brown & Company, 2008), P. 64

27   **Barnsley argues that:** Malcolm Gladwell, *Outliers: The Story of Success* (Little, Brown & Company, 2008), P. 25

28   **The emerging picture from:** Daniel Levitin, "Tertiary Education," http://teritiary=education. blogspot.com/2007/01/10000-hours.html (May 2011)

29   **definitive inside story:** Ron Zemke and Dick Schaaf, *The Service Edge* (Penguin Books, 1989), Inside Cover

30   **The obvious conclusion:** Ron Zemke and Dick Schaaf, *The Service Edge* (Penguin Books, 1989), P. 9

31   **To manage Service effectively:** Ron Zemke and Dick Schaaf, *The Service Edge* (Penguin Books, 1989), P. 13

32   **Through the 1970s:** Ron Zemke and Dick Schaaf, *The Service Edge* (Penguin Books, 1 989), P. 415

33   **five carefully targeted industries:** Ron Zemke and Dick Schaaf, *The Service Edge* (Penguin Books, 1989), P. 415

CHAPTER 6. WAS IT TIME TO ATTACK?

34   **Good ideas are more:** Bill Russell, *Russell Rules* (New American Library, 2002), P. 180

35   **Our approach is based on:** http://www.greatplacetowork.com/what_we_believe/trust.php (November 2010)

36   **breaking out of established:** Edward de Bono, http://thinkexist.com/quotation/crativity_ involves_ breaking_ out_ of_established/205058.html (November 2010)

37   **If you want to:** Steven R. Covey, *The 7 Habits of Highly Effective People* (Fireside, 2990), P. 238

38   **The real Key to your:** Steven R. Covey, *The 7 Habits of Highly Effective People* (Fireside, 2990), P. 238

39   **33% of all ERP implementations:** EDUCAUSE Center for Applied Research Symposium, (November 2002)

40   **clients sometimes cite:** Gartner, Inc. *Magic Quadrant for Oracle ERP Implementation Services, North America,* November 2010

41   **Think of credit as a coin:** Peter de Jager, *Credit Legerdemain for Managers,* http://www. technobillity. com/docs/article087.htm (February 2011)

42   **The Art of War Teaches:** Sun Tzu, *The Art of War* (Dell Publishing, 1988), P. 39

CHAPTER 7. HOW DO WHISPERERS COMPETE?

43   **Everyone has the will:** Bob Knight, http://www.therxforum.com/archive/index. php/t-166854.html (January 2011)

44   **Shifting Buyer Concerns:** Michael Bosworth, *Solution Selling* (McGraw-Hill, 1995), P. 87

45   **All chickens and lizards:** Scott Belsky, *Making Ideas Happen* (Penguin Group, 2003) P. 83

46   **The lizard brain interferes:** Scott Belsky, *Making Ideas Happen* (Penguin Group, 2003) P. 83

47   **Before the first quarter-hour:** John Medina *Brain Rules,* (Pear Press, 2008), P. 74

48   **This is the general:** John Medina, *Brain Rules* (Pear Press, 2008), P. 79

49   **It is key that the instructor:** John Medina, *Brain Rules* (Pear Press, 2008), P. 90

50   **Emotionally arousing events:** John Medina, *Brain Rules* (Pear Press, 2008), P. 79

51   **Multitasking, when it comes:** John Medina, *Brain Rules* (Pear Press, 2008), P. 84

52   **Studies show that emotional:** John Medina, *Brain Rules* (Pear Press, 2008), P. 83

53   **The most common communication:** John Medina, *Brain Rules* (Pear Press, 2008), P. 88

54   **I decided that every lecture:** John Medina, *Brain Rules* (Pear Press, 2008), P. 89

CHAPTER 8. WHISPERING WAVES OF TRUST?

55   **trust is a pragmatic:** Stephen M. R. Covey, *The Speed of Trust* (Free Press, 2006), P. 2

56   **There is one thing:** Stephen M. R. Covey, *The Speed of Trust* (Free Press, 2006), P. 1

57   **Jerry Kramer did not:** Vince Lombardi, http://bleacherreport.com/articles/86920-nfl-legends-jerry-kramer (April 2011)

58   **about how to establish:** Stephen M. R. Covey, *The Speed of Trust* (Free Press, 2006), P. 34

59   **Cadence of Accountability:** http://www.franklincovey.ro/learning.php?oid=18&otype=1001 001&lang=2&cid=5&ctyp (June 2011)
60   **There is no point in:** Michael Skapinker, "Mastering Employee Engagement," http://www. eusof. com .mastering-employee-engagement-recorded-conference-call/ (April 2011)
61   **As a leader, you can:** Stephen M. R. Covey, *Speed of Trust* (Free Press, 2006), P. 239
62   **Principle of alignment:** Stephen M. R. Covey, *Speed of Trust* (Free Press, 2006), P. 236
63   **All organizations are;** Stephen M. R. Covey, *Speed of Trust* (Free Press, 2006), P. 238
64   **All organizations are:** Stephen M. R. Covey, *Speed of Trust* (Free Press, 2006), P. 238
65   **Rather than focusing on:** Stephen R. Covey, *The 7 Habits of Highly Effective People* (Fireside, 1989), P. 150
66   **If you don't have:** Stephen M. R. Covey, *The Speed of Trust* (Free Press, 2006), P. 250
67   **There are additional:** Stephen M. R. Covey, *The Speed of Trust* (Free Press, 2006), P. 254
68   **Laminins are a family:** http://en.wikipedia.org/wiki/Laminin,(April 2011)
69   **Science is a way of:** Carl Sagan, http://creatingminds.org/quotes/thinking.htm (April 2011)

Chapter 9. Can Whispering Extend Trust?

70   **The single most important:** Peter Drucker, http://www.artsjounal.com.artfulmanager/main/ honoring-peter-f-drucker.php (April 2011)
71   **All about brand:** Stephen M. R. Covey, *The Speed of Trust* (Free Press, 2006), P. 262
72   **The principles underlying:** Jon Kleinberg & David Easley *Networks, Crowds, and Markets*, (Cambridge University Press, 2010), P. 130
73   **Mutual Partners Examples**: Jon Kleinberg & David Easley *Networks, Crowds, and Markets*, (Cambridge University Press, 2010), P. 131
74   **Mutual Competitor Examples**: Jon Kleinberg & David Easley *Networks, Crowds, and Markets*, (Cambridge University Press, 2010), P. 131
75   **Structural Balance in Networks**: Jon Kleinberg & David Easley, *Networks, Crowds, and Markets* (Cambridge University Press, 2010), P. 132
76   **Cores of credibility:** Stephen M. R. Covey, *The Speed of Trust* (Free Press, 2006), P. 43
77   **Principle of behavior:** Stephen M. R. Covey, *The Speed of Trust* (Free Press, 2006), P. 125
78   **contrary to popular belief:** Stephen M. R. Covey, *The Speed of Trust* (Free Press, 2006), P. 2
79   **This book is the manifesto:** Max Anderson & Peter Escher, *The MBA Oath* (Penguin Group, 2010), inside cover
80   **It is the intent to create:** Stephen M. R. Covey, *The Speed of Trust* (Free Press, 2006), P. 275
81   **Extending trust to others:** Stephen M. R. Covey, *The Speed of Trust* (Free Press, 2006), P. 322

Chapter 10. What's a Whispering Win-win?

82   **For when the one great:** John Wooden, *My Personal Best* (McGraw-Hill, 2004), P. 26
83   **under certain circumstances:** Malcolm Gladwell: *What the Dog Saw* (Little, Brown & Co., 2009) P. 288
84   **Why are more pedestrians:** Malcolm Gladwell: *What the Dog Saw* (Little, Brown & Co., 2009) P. 289
85   **help organizations identify:** Bryant Stringham & Jon Stephens, *Finding the Priority Path* (Thomson, 2005), P. 42
86   **The main difficulty:** Edward de Bono, *Six Thinking Hats* (Penguin Books, 1999), Preface
87   **Western thinking is:** Edward de Bono, *Six Thinking Hats* (Penguin Books, 1999), P. 2
88   **can start with seemingly:** Tom Bartlett, "The Gospel of Well-Educated Guessing," *The Chronicle of Higher Education,* May 2, 2010, P. 1
89   **It is as much:** Tom Bartlett, "The Gospel of Well-Educated Guessing," *The Chronicle of Higher Education,* May 2, 2010, P. 2

CHAPTER 11. WHAT'S A WHISPERER'S FCB?

90   **trusted leaders do things:** Nolan Archibald, "Code of Ethics," http://add-marketing.com/codeofethics.html (April 2011)

91   **The Economics of Trust:** Stephen M. R. Covey, *The Speed of Trust* (Free Press, 2006), P. 13

92   **In what they called:** Stephen R. Covey, *The 8th Habit* (Free Press, 2004) P. 115

CHAPTER 12. WHAT'S THE SPEED OF WHISPERING?

93   **The ultimate danger:** Bill Bradley, *Values of the Game* (Artisan, 1998), P. 132

94   **We learned that:** Jim Collins, *Good to Great* (Collins Business, 2001), P. 176

95   **Few successful Start-ups:** Jim Collins, *Good to Great* (Collins Business, 2001), P. 12

96   **the size of a group:** Malcolm Gladwell, *The Tipping Point* (Little, Brown & Co., 2002), P. 182

97   **To go from good to:** Jim Collins, *Good to Great* (Collins Business, 2001), P. 100

98   **good is the enemy:** Jim Collins, *Good to Great* (Collins Business, 2001), P. 1

99   **Leadership is the capacity:** Warren Bennis, http://thinkexist.com/quotation/leadership_is_the_ capacity_to_tranlate_vision/15169.html, (April 2011)

100   **Another term for:** Stephen M. R. Covey, *The Speed of Trust* (Free Press, 2006), P. 266

101   **CedarCrestone has a strategy:** Gartner, Inc. *Magic Quadrant for Oracle ERP Implementation Services, North America*, November 2010

CHAPTER 13. WHAT'S A WHISPERING CULTURE?

102   **I've learned that people:** Maya Angelou, http://thinkexist.com/quotation/i-ve_learned_that_people_will_forget_what_you/341107.html (April 2011)

103   **Every person carries within:** Geert Hofstede, *Cultures and Organizations* (McGraw-Hill, 2010), P. 4

104   **Cultures meet any time:** Edgar Schein, *Corporate Culture Survival Guide* (John Wiley & Sons, 2009), P. 189

105   **The breaking down:** Steven R. Covey, *The 7 Habits of Highly Effective People* (Fireside, 2990), P. 147

106   **Management is a bottom:** Steven R. Covey, *The 7 Habits of Highly Effective People* (Fireside, 2990), P. 101

107   **primarily a high-powered:** Steven R. Covey, *The 7 Habits of Highly Effective People* (Fireside, 2990), P. 147

108   **Management is doing:** Peter Drucker, http://thinkexist.com/quotation/management_is_doing_ things_right-leadership_is/11721.html (May 2011)

109   **The person who:** "Asking 'why' can validate the things we do," The Arizona Republic, November 28, 2011, Page B5

110   **Blending is most likely:** Edgar Schein, *Corporate Culture Survival Guide* (John Wiley & Sons, 009), P. 15

111   **True excellence in:** Linda Elder & Richard Paul, *Critical Thinking* (Pearson Education, 2002), P. 35

112   **Good thinking can be:** Linda Elder & Richard Paul, *Critical Thinking* (Pearson Education, 2002), P. 56

113   **It isn't enough to talk:** Eleanor Roosevelt plague in Glacier National Park (July 2010)

114   **The Good-to-Great Matrix:** Jim Collins, *Good to Great* (Collins Business, 2001), P. 122

115   **The purpose of bureaucracy:** Jim Collins, *Good to Great* (Collins Business, 2001), P. 121

116   **Bureaucratization is a state:** Linda Elder & Richard Paul, *Critical Thinking* (Pearson Education, 2002), P. 234

117   **With good Judgment:** Noel Tichy & Warren Bennis, *Judgment* (Penguin Group, 2007), P. 1

CHAPTER 14. HOW DOES A WHISPERER WHISPER?

118   **We keep moving forward:** Walt Disney, http://barinyquote.com/quotes/quotes/w/waltdisney132637.html (April 2011)

119   **Since the 1980s:** Malcolm Gladwell. *Blink* (Back Bay Books, 2005), P. 20

120   **Thin-slicing refers to:** Malcolm Gladwell. *Blink* (Back Bay Books, 2005), P. 23

121 **if I were to summarize**: Steven R. Covey, *The 7 Habits of Highly Effective People* (Fireside, 2990), P. 237
122 **When I say empathetic**: Steven R. Covey, *The 7 Habits of Highly Effective People* (Fireside, 2990), P. 240
123 **Most people do not**: Steven R. Covey, *The 7 Habits of Highly Effective People* (Fireside, 2990), P. 239
124 **The nine boxes**: Michael Bosworth, *Solution Selling* (McGraw-Hill, 1995), P. 55
125 **Salespeople, consultants**: Michael Bosworth, *Solution Selling* (McGraw-Hill, 1995), P. 60
126 **Refers to having**: http://en.wikipedia.org/wiki/Shoshin,(September 2011)

Chapter 15. Instincts and Habits: Important?

127 **Good instincts usually**: Michael Burke, http://thinkexist.com/quotes/michael_burke/ (March 2011)
128 **Conation is the part**: Kathy Kolbe, "Conation," http://knol.google.com/k/conation (October 2010)
129 **The Three Dimensions of** : Kathy Kolbe, http://www.kolbe.com/knol/keyConceptsOfConation.html (October 2010)
130 **Conation is the mental**: Kathy Kolbe, "Conation," http://knol.google.com/k/conation (October 2010)
131 **Action Modes and Striving Behaviors**: Kathy Kolbe, "Conation," http://knol.google.com/k/conation (October 2010)
132 **Creativity requires use of**: Kathy Kolbe, "Conation," http://knol.google.com/k/ conation (October 2010)
133 **Conative stress results**: Kathy Kolbe, "Conation," http://knol.google.com/k/ conation (October 2010)
134 **Probability of team success**: Kathy Kolbe, "Conation," http://knol.google.com/k/ conation (October 2010)
135 **progressively on a**: Steven R. Covey, *The 7 Habits of Highly Effective People* (Fireside, 2990), P. 49
136 **The Creative process is**: Steven R. Covey, *The 7 Habits of Highly Effective People* (Fireside, 2990), P. 263

Chapter 16. When is a Mystery Puzzling?

137 **Development of the human**: Linda Elder & Richard Paul, *Critical Thinking* (Pearson Education, 2002), P. 57
138 **Creative Visualization is**: Shakti Gawain, *Creative Visualization* (Nataraj Publishing, 2002), P. 3
139 **Country roads mean**: Bill Bradley, *Values of the Game* (Artisan, 1998), P. 17
140 **One of psychology's most**: "Journal's Paper on ESP Expected to Prompt Outrage," http://www. nytimes.com/2011/01/-6/science/06esp.html (January 2011)
141 **Did find that**: "ESP May Be Real," http://www.cbsnews.com/2011/01/18/earlyshow/health/main7257611.shtml (January 2011)
142 **Positive and Negative ESP**: "The roots of Consciousness," http://www.williamsjames.com/Science/ ESP.htm (January 2011)
143 **Tend and befriend**: John Medina, *Brain Rules* (Pear Press, 2008), P.251
144 **Let's do this**: John Medina, *Brain Rules* (Pear Press, 2008), P.255
145 **emotions are useful**: John Medina, *Brain Rules* (Pear Press, 2008), P.256
146 **In the business world**: Birute Regine, *Iron Butterflies* (Prometheus Books, 2010), P. 243
147 **While dealing with**: Regine, *Iron Butterflies* (Prometheus Books, 2010), P. 243
148 **If things go wrong**: Malcolm Gladwell: *What the Dog Saw* (Little, Brown & Co., 2009) P. 154
149 **All require the application**: Malcolm Gladwell: *What the Dog Saw* (Little, Brown & Co., 2009) P. 173
150 **Puzzles are**: Malcolm Gladwell: *What the Dog Saw* (Little, Brown & Co., 2009) P. 172

CHAPTER 17. IS THERE ALCHEMY IN WHISPERING?

151 **When you combine:** Jim Collins, *Good to Great* (Collins Business, 2001), P. 121
152 **effective leaders are:** "Stability in context of change," http://find articles.com /p/articles/ mi_6942/is_5/ai_n31614534/ (November 2010)
153 **The more we trust:** http://en.wikipedia.org/wiki//Paul J. Zak (November 2010)
154 **In his brilliant book:** "Happy Chemicals," http://www.infinite-mind.co.uk/pages/happy-chemicals.html (April 2011)
155 **If you want to:** "Motivation," http://changingminds.org.explanations/ motivation/motivation. htm (February 2011
156 **Imagination is more:** Albert Einstein, http://thinkexist.com/uotation/imagination_is_more_than_knowledge-for/2602.html (April 2011)

CHAPTER 18. WHAT'S A WHISPERING LEADER?

157 **Anytime you're:** Ken Blanchard, http://howwelead.org/2010/05/25/do-you-think-of-yourself-as-a-leader/ (April 2011)
158 **Principled-centered leadership:** Stephen R. Covey, *First Things First* (Free Press, 2003), P. 238
159 **At the heart of:** Stephen R. Covey, *First Things First* (Free Press, 2003), P. 240
160 **paradoxical blend:** Jim Collins, *Good to Great* (Collins Business, 2001), P.13
161 **I don't think modesty:** Maya Angelou, http://www.achievement.org/sutodoc/steps/ int?target=ang0-037 (April 2011)
162 **Always treat your:** Steven R. Covey, *The 7 Habits of Highly Effective People* (Fireside, 2990), P. 58
163 **Simply put—at its:** Stephen R. Covey *The 8th Habit,* (Freedom Press, 2004), P. 98
164 **Important principles:** Abraham Lincoln, http://www.brainyquote.com/quotes/authors/a/ abraham_lincoln_4.html (April 2011)
165 **There go my:** Mahatma Gandhi, http://www.erenkrantz.com/Words/Quotes.shtml (August 2011)
166 **I have great respect:** Maya Angelo, *The Arizona Republic*, March 17, 2011, Section E2
167 **The Lyons were:** Jay Gould, *History of Delaware County* (Keeny & Gould, 1856), P. 202
168 **Stubbornness is a virtue:** Tony Dungy, http://twitter.com/LeadershipQuote/status/ 26786521726 (April 20110
169 **There is nothing stronger:** Abraham Lincoln, http://blogdeli.blogspot.com/ (April 2011)
170 **Everything we need:** Jon Huntsman, *Winners Never Cheat* (Wharton School Publishing, 2009) Kindle location 229
171 **You prevent getting:** Kolbe A™ Index Report (copyright © 2011 Kathy Kolbe and Kolbe Corp. All rights reserved)
172 **The path to great:** Tom Rath and Barry Conchie, http://www.better,management.com/ seminars/seminar.aspx?I=14999
173 **While the best:** Tom Rath and Barry Conchie, *Strengths-Based Leadership* (Gallup Press, 2008), P.2

CHAPTER 19. CAN WHISPERERS BEGET WHISPERERS?

174 **We are the average of:** Jim Rohn, http://www.mediabistro.com/alltwitter/five-people_b3076 (April 2011)
175 **Fly in, make a lot:** Ken Blanchard, *Leadership and the One-Minute Manager* (William Morrow & Co ,1985), P. 38
176 **young people need:** John Wooden, *My Personal Best* (McGraw-Hill 2004), P.50
177 **a coach is someone:** John Wooden, http://brainyquote.com/quotes/quotes/j/ johnwooden130013.html (April 2011)
178 **A good sense of:** "HUMOR" *The Arizona Republic*, August 3, 2003, Section CL
179 **Before casually discounting:** John Wooden, *My Personal Best* (McGraw-Hill 2004), P.98
180 **Successful teams of:** Bill Russell, *Russell Rules* (New American Library, 2002), P. 74
181 **someone who carries:** *Own Your Life*, http://www.livewellownyour life-coach-trainers.html (September 2011)

182 **People who are:** Kathy Kolbe, *Conative Connection* (1997), P.29
183 **Insistence means**: Kathy Kolbe, *Conative Connection* (1997), P. 25
184 **Good judgment comes:** Will Rogers, http://allgreatquotes.com/funny_quotes80.shtml (April 2011)
185 **The Tipping Point is**: Malcolm Gladwell, *The Tipping Point* (Little, Brown & Co., 2002), Back Cover
186 **human beings are**; Malcolm Cladwell, *The Tipping Point* (Little, Brown & Co., 2002), P. 29
187 **Psychologists tell us**: Malcolm Gladwell, *The Tipping Point* (Little, Brown & Co., 2002), P. 171
188 **starting slowly:** Malcolm Gladwell, *The Tipping Point* (Little, Brown & Co., 2002), P. 197
189 **Ideas and products:** Malcolm Gladwell, *The Tipping Point* (Little, Brown & Co., 2002), P. 7
190 **Connectors, Mavens and:** Malcolm Gladwell, *The Tipping Point* (Little, Brown & Co., 2002), P. 34
191 **People don't rise:** Malcolm Gladwell, *Outliers: The Story of Success* (Little, Brown & Company, 2008), P. 19
192 **Staff Sergeant Thomas**: "Local WWII airman receives high honor," *The Ithaca Journal*, July 4, 2003
193 **You want to know:** Jim Collins, *Good to Great* (Collins Business, 2001), P.91
194 **Simplify a complex world:** Jim Collins, *Good to Great* (Collins Business, 2001), P.91
195 **The hedgehog always:** Jim Collins, *Good to Great* (Collins Business, 2001), P.91

CPSIA information can be obtained
at www.ICGtesting.com
Printed in the USA
BVOW06s1414120917
494672BV00016B/200/P